What Reviewers Have Said

"A riveting read from a dedicated professional, that keeps moving forwards despite all his setbacks through no fault of his own, candid words from a caring surgeon."

Eamonn Holmes

"An inspiring journey, beautifully told."

Nazir Afzal OBE, Former Chief Prosecutor

"An honest and fair account from a leading 'very' British Surgeon."

Wajid Khan, Baron Khan of Burnley

"Through Aali Sheen's autobiography one 'feels' what it must have been really like to be a young man of Pakistani heritage, growing up to ultimately become a highly regarded and successful surgeon. Abused by egg-throwers on the way to school, being physically attacked, the sneering racial profiling by immigration officials, and the patronising "Do you speak English?" attitude of some interviewers, Aali Sheen tells it all, but objectively without rancour and in an almost detached way. One also can appreciate the anxieties of medical life behind Covid PPE and similarly the pressures on a young surgeon having to choose between patients requiring urgent surgery. All-in-all a very human and personal story told as it happened over so many years of prejudice."

John Lee, Baron Lee of Trafford

"The very definition of a page-turner."

Fabrice Muamba, Former Professional Footballer

"Telling our stories, our way, in our voice is essential. *The Painted Surgeon* documents the lived experiences of those that arrived upon these shores, faced and overcame challenges and achieved huge success. An honest account, authentically told."

Sayeeda H Warsi, Baroness Warsi

"With honesty and openness, *The Painted Surgeon* shares personal, but incisively relatable, experiences of prejudice, setback and success. It is a reminder of the harsh realities for so many of us who grew up in the 60s and 70s in the UK. As a fellow doctor I can appreciate that the author's successful career and achievements as a surgeon have come with having to toil and work all the harder to overcome discriminatory hurdles along that journey. Holding a mirror up to society, we are left questioning how far have we really come, and how much further we have to go."

Dr Chaand Nagpaul CBE, Chair BMA Council

THE PAINTED SURGEON

Tolerance implies no lack of commitment to one's own beliefs. Rather it condemns the oppression or persecution of others.

John F Kennedy

The Painted Surgeon

Aali J Sheen

SHEENDOC PUBLISHING

British Library Cataloguing in Publication Data
A catalogue record for this book is available from the British Library

ISBN 978-1-7397982-0-8

Typeset by Amolibros, Milverton, Somerset
www.amolibros.co.uk
This book production has been managed by Amolibros
Printed and bound by T J Books Limited, Padstow, Cornwall, UK

Dedicated to my wife Mehreen,
the heart and soul of my life

About the Author

Aali Sheen is a full-time NHS consultant surgeon in the UK. He was born and raised in London by his immigrant parents and fulfilled his childhood ambition by becoming a surgeon. He was appointed in 2005 as a consultant and has gained many awards and accolades within his specialty as well as being invited to operate in Sweden, Turkey, Greece and Holland. Most recently he has also been appointed to a prestigious Professorship. This book chronicles the author's journey from a young boy from Croydon in London to becoming a well-recognised surgeon in his field. The book describes that, despite a journey filled with inequality, adversity and indifference, he firmly believes that any failure in experiencing such disparate treatment in one particular aspect of your life does not necessarily mean that you cannot still achieve and succeed at the highest levels.

Contents

Foreword
by Amir Khan

I have chosen to write a foreword to this book as I know Professor Sheen and his longstanding innovative contributions to his field. I first crossed paths with Aali in a professional capacity and although I am a professional athlete, we found a lot in common. We have both reached the top of our respective professions and have been acclaimed for this, and we both know only too well the dedication, devotion and discipline this has taken. We both use our hands in exercising our skills – hands that are trained, a part of our highly coordinated minds and bodies, whether in the ring or in the operating theatre. Aali is warm, charismatic, down to earth, and always ready to help others. In his professional field, he is renowned for utilising emerging technologies to successfully offer innovative models of care. Growing up in London as the child of immigrants from Pakistan, living between two contrasting cultures, trying to find where you personally fit is not the easiest of paths to navigate. It's made more difficult when coming up against others' prejudices and discrimination, especially when trying to pursue lifelong passions and ambitions. It is a well-trodden path for many and one I personally relate to and have experienced in my own journey.

Professor Sheen's autobiography is a gripping read, it describes his personal journey with searing honesty, charisma and wit. This book will have the reader rooting for the author to overcome the obstacles he faces and cheering for his successes. Aali approaches the difficult situations that confront him in a calm, serene manner, seeking solutions and peace, an approach that has been further honed throughout his highly demanding career, making critical decisions under difficult circumstances. It is a book that reminds you that regardless of the barriers that you may face, you can cut your way through prejudice and achieve what you have set out to do.

I hope you enjoy this read as much as I have and you will also relate to it as I have, irrespective of how you choose to define yourself, whether as an immigrant, a person of colour, or not.

Introduction

1982 – London. School History class
Learning about Britain in Victorian times

Teacher – Yes, that's right. On a Sunday trading was not seen and all the shops were closed, it allowed people to rest at home and more importantly, go to church.
Me – I guess Miss that everyone knew it was a Sunday as it was quiet and still is to this day?
Teacher – Yes, Sheen that's right, although you do see only a few shops open on a Sunday
Rude boy – Yes, only Paki shops!

The class fills with laughter. At least half a dozen boys of South Asian origin in the classroom did not find the comment amusing. 'We' realise that what was said is considered acceptable, not troublesome nor racist, but a mere fact of life that you cannot refute, and if you choose to raise objection it will likely be met with a heavy bruising encounter at break time, as well as making you a likely target practice for weeks on end. Any coroner would label it a misadventure, so no one wants a tell-tale. Despite repeatedly trying to persuade ourselves that these comments were 'probably' OK, after all they are only words, we continued to witness each day a modern form of subjugation based on our perceived difference that was deemed acceptable at the highest levels, given the fact that the teacher also laughed.

★ ★ ★

On May 25th, 2020, I saw that the Minneapolis police had arrested a George Floyd, a forty-six-year-old black man, after a convenience store employee informed the police that he bought some cigarettes with a fake $20 bill[2]. This misdemeanour cost him his life and galvanised the world into thinking about why a man was killed, when he clearly shouldn't have been. Perhaps it was the colour of his skin that was his downfall? This sent out a powerful message to the world and to us as human beings: why are we so fickle at not realising that less than a millimetre of our skin, in terms of differing melanocyte concentrations, can lead to such disparities in life? The Black Lives Matter (BLM) movement forged ahead, gaining much coverage as well as media support and so while watching all of this on the television, I thought it's time I put pen to paper and tell people my own story, a collection of my memoirs from the age of five to fifty. It's not meant to be critical of the country I live in but a reflection of my own life and despite the obstacles I have faced and continue to face, I remain a loyal servant to Queen and country.

When I first sat down in front of my metallic grey laptop to write this book, I wondered how I could put so much into so few pages. I didn't want to compete with J R R Tolkien, yet also didn't want to fill the book with all the intricacies of my memories, as like most, I have too much to share. Instead, I would like to share the key events that changed my life and made me the person I am today. The salient moments that may have ingrained a sensitivity to rough justice, intolerance and discrimination, not only against me, but against any vulnerable person or group.

So I thought I should commence where life itself starts, with my earliest memory, not my birth where I was bit overdue and subsequently fat. The narrative will relate some apt pauses with some inspired as well as diffident moments in my history, and I include some brief encounters with political dialogues. It should be an easy enough script to read, entertaining, hopefully a free-flowing autobiography of life chapters interspersed with pertinent and memorable medical events recalled at different moments in the book. The text 'should' be gripping enough, no cursive staggers, and moments of sudden digression are not the hallmarks of a person with a schizoaffective disorder with a flight of ideas, but an apt moment shall we say, to venture to another part of this memoir. I try to avoid much waffle, but in some situations a degree of elaboration as well as some literary jargon is necessary. The political detours will be pertinent to my ethnicity as well as to a particular moment of the book (or of my life?), but if the language I have used is a little surly or peremptory, then I will say, please read on as the desired effect of the book will have been achieved, but it should not commit you to a life in rehab.

I will explain the medical terminology I use as I go along with the use of definitions as comprehensibly as possible by using layman's terms where I can. Lots of clinical jargon should not overwhelm any reader, but medics will find this book fine and may relate it to some of their past experiences as doctors.

What you read may make you sad with a sympathetic melancholy but hopefully also rejoice at times when you must have imagined there was little or nothing to be triumphant about as an inevitable glib moment again rears its head. So there are some happy occasions, not altogether orgasmic but enough so that you won't end up on anti-depressants with the darker events that I describe. So feel comforted that it is not all melancholic. I did ask myself if I should leave out any controversial moments that may be too upsetting, too inflammatory, and too subjective. However, after much reflection I thought it best to write with an open heart and mind as any honest appraisal of life events are the ones worth reading. I have though been careful not to be too contentious. I was advised many years ago, that if what you write does not spark a hint of some food for thought, then it is not worth writing. I therefore do not intend to upset anyone with the text and tales below but create moments of subconscious recognition in those that have never experienced such treatment, as well as acknowledgement with empathy from those that have.

While typing away, I find myself recording with meticulous precision recollections from life that have shaped my attitudes and perceptions. This book is meant to stir your mind, too. I have called it *The Painted Surgeon.*

I was told many years ago that the way out of poverty is through education. Is this also the way out of prejudice? This is a question this book repeatedly asks. Over the last 1000 years we as Homo sapiens have come a long way. Yet even in the twenty-first century, with globalisation now having crept into our lives and social media able to connect all cultures and creeds at the touch of a button, we still have some way to go before becoming a more pluralistic society.

At the start of each chapter, I relate to a journey I took to the

American Hernia Society (AHS) congress in March 2011. This journey would be set to change my life, particularly in terms of worldly perception. This event altered my global awareness of issues of mankind, having been born and brought up in an overwhelmingly 'white' country as the 'native' population. I am proud of where I was born. I had only experienced overt and ignorant forms of unthinking racism that unfortunately most persons of immigrant stock are very familiar with and often face with indifference. Most minority groups end up having to lead a remarkable double life, often completely beyond their control and based on inherited DNA not 'matching' the context of where one calls home.

I am clearly British, very much part of the furniture, a rational and law-abiding human being, a long-term successful medic, married with children. On paper some may consider me to be a model citizen. Yet when I go to an airport, I am automatically categorised as a different kind of traveller, not an upper-middle class professional, but a potential serious security risk or suspect to be monitored by Interpol or the FBI. This book repeatedly asks why this dual scanner recognition of oneself is so regular. It will reveal a life-changing moment for me where I was subjected to a banal type of mental difficulty purely because of the colour of my skin (Or was it my name? – I am still to this day none the wiser.). I had been invited to speak on interesting research that I was undertaking at the time by my colleagues in the United States. So why was I in difficulty? Was it race or religion, or whether the events would have happened to me even if I were a white Anglo-Saxon – an *Angrezi*?*

Most persons that read this book though, I gather, may well be half-glass full individuals? But again, conversely you may well be of a half-glass empty persuasion and so recognising this very fact that not all persons are the same, I will try to create a good balance.

This book was written between 2019-2021, when the tragic circumstances of the death of George Floyd occurred, which galvanised the #Blacklivesmatter movement. I must say this is true, but I hear you say surely #Alllivesmatter? Yes, they do, but when you see the world today, if you say #Alllivesmatter, then should we ignore that fact that singularly black lives do 'not matter'?

*   a commonly used non-derogatory word in South-Asian languages to describe native English persons.

4

Therefore, it is important to always think about 'your' actions and whether they could be perceived as racially motivated or not?

I have chosen to change names and have not used any actual identities, so any individual implicated is not recognisable. As a clinician, I have not discussed any patient nor patient-related events unless complete confidentiality is adhered to. This requires not disclosing any exact locations, times or presumed diagnoses to ensure absolute secrecy. Similarly, any clinician that I have based a story on has been entirely fictionalised in place and time.

You may find a sense of humour and pleasant sarcasm, as one needs this to experience what I have been through in my conscious life to date. I will also inform you that I may well still, though unfortunately, be experiencing such indifference in life and probably will continue to do so – agonisingly, despite, being at a reasonably dizzy height in my profession.

★★★

So who am I? I should probably try to relate this before the story begins.

My parents were Pakistani immigrants who came in 1964 as part of the great Commonwealth migration work programme in the United Kingdom as part of the generation from former British colonies designed to help rebuild Britain in the post-war era. My late father was a barrister and obtained British citizenship whilst working in Pakistan after passing various tests, including being able to hold a conversation in the English Language. He received a £10 note, a British Passport, and a job in the civil service in London, the Work and Pensions department to be exact, from the British High Commission in Karachi. He had to make his own way to England. With pay for a young advocate being so low in Pakistan, some injection of family money as well as any savings he had were needed to aid his campaign. My father was afraid of flying, but as you can imagine, charting a passage to Great Britain over land and sea needed quite some planning. A journey potentially filled with inordinate pitfalls, rarely attempted, even at this time, across many countries, via negotiations in many foreign languages across uncharted land, crossing two continents. This was an expedition, as the communication may well have been in Klingon. At one stage, he was almost marooned in Czechoslovakia, with just enough funds to get his transport to Calais. This predicament in which he found himself was met with ever-changing terms and conditions of his intended transportation. After some negotiating and less than fluent understanding of Czech customs, he managed it on standard South Asian timings, where 'better late than never' has a different meaning amongst the *'apnas'*, a Punjabi colloquial term for our own. He arrived at Dover, where my father ended his tale in inimitable fashion by describing simply walking into England to his new country and new life, uncontested, unchallenged, and welcomed as a new British citizen about to start the next chapter of his life with a dark-blue passport already in hand.

When I think about my father's refusal to fly, it was very typical of him as a man of great caution and allergic to risk. This made it all the more remarkable that he decided to give up his country and culture for an unknown future halfway around the world. Paradoxically my brothers and I were terrified of him most of the time, as well as adopting the fears that he was afraid of. When we'd go to the 'fun' fair he'd deter us from the Big Wheel on the grounds that it would naturally get stuck when we were at its summit, leaving us stranded for a very long time, so long that we would get cold, freeze and perish. He also would rather we took a ferry to visit my uncle in Holland, and, whilst on this ferry, he demanded we stay indoors at all times, so were never allowed out on the deck. In his mind there was of course a very good reason for this, as little boys fascinated by the sea would undoubtedly fall into the English Channel and drown.

Despite perhaps sounding eccentric, this embedded sense of risk adversity is not an uncommon phenomenon amongst South Asians. Come to think of it, I have now surmised that this probably is a typical *apna* 'thing'. It makes sense, if you look around the world today and ask yourself how many explorers of South Asian background spring to mind that have made it to the North Pole or climbed the steepest mountains? I suppose it could happen, and probably has happened, but we don't generally do exploration for the sake of it, unless there's something significant in it for us. We are in the habit of sending someone else instead. I have witnessed this first-hand whilst visiting relatives abroad, with even the simplest of errands being assigned to the in-house *nokars* (Urdu for servants). Going back to my father's epic road trip to England, many people, for different although not too dissimilar reasons, are still undertaking such perilous journeys from the Middle East, South

Asia and Africa to Europe, with many tragically not even making it to their intended destination. They are travelling at incredible risk for a better life, mostly illegally nowadays, which I suppose my father also did at that time in 1964, albeit legally. Luckily for him the circumstances of his travel and having a British passport in his pocket helped him considerably. His was not in a desperate desire to escape a broken land at any cost, forcing him to stowaway in a lorry in Calais.

If you look at the world today, one could surmise a simple root cause analysis for the exodus of migrants to the West. Poor people often lack access to education, without much welfare protection or any hope of equality in the part of the world they come from, with also a presumed notion in their society that they are either forgotten, or expendable. The need to migrate, therefore becomes a no-brainer, an attempt to escape is forged, yet many then face the realisation that nobody truly wants them in their respective countries, or in their intended destinations either. Life has simply rejected and forgotten them. When your own country doesn't respect you, can't protect you or nurture your family, and when other lands either don't want you or are at best ambivalent to your fate, what do you do? Most humans just want a safe life for themselves and their loved ones, so who is to blame? My mother came over in 1967 after marriage. Unlike my father, she flew, and was and still is more daring an individual. As the daughter of an air force officer, being afraid of planes would be quite an irony. Both my parents were born in Delhi, British India, before Indian independence. India's partition has left me with family on both sides of the border. As a result, I feel very 'English' or *Angrezi* as there is really nowhere else, I can call home. Pakistanis ask me why my parents were born in India, while Indians ask why my grandparents left. The seeds of utter confusion have already been planted.

For generations, dating back at least 500 years or more, my ancestors were from a literary breed; *hakims*, actuaries, and Muslim priests called *maulvis*. While they may well have had conflicts, tax rises, bad marriages, and bad luck, never were they ridiculed, ostracized, or marginalised from their community due to being different. At least I presume not. I sometimes wonder what this is like, as a phenomenon I have never experienced; being a natural piece in a jigsaw.

After arriving in the UK, my father had initially arranged to live with a friend in a small room in his family house. The friend was a childhood acquaintance that came over in the late 1950s and was already settled with a young British-born family. After starting work, my father eventually rented a room in Kilburn, North London, during which time my mother arrived. After two children, they both applied to the local authority for a council flat, which was approved and they eventually moved into a nice three-bedroom flat in Camberwell Green in 1971, with my youngest brother appearing during our time living on this council estate in late 1972. So the three of us were born in London and had little notion of our parents even coming from another country until much later on. We carried on by living a very simple immigrant life.

Having an idea of who the writer is may help you relate to the content in some manner either ethnically, as a person of perceived colour, a fellow medic, or simply as an individual thirsty for more knowledge or a different viewpoint. But I am hoping that you, the reader, may be able to see the funny side of some aspects of my life, as well as chuckle and applaud at a juncture when you thought I was truly stuck! I am actually aiming this book at everyone and anyone, so when you look at our world of nations and their splendid colour with varying exotic looks, you have to think or ask yourself, what it is all the fuss about? Shouldn't we be celebrating our differences rather than stockpiling them to be then used against us.

It is unequivocally clear that you can be wronged in certain situations even if you are a white male. But why are we subjected to constant ethnic stereotypes and racial profiling? Does it make it right? No of course it doesn't, and I wouldn't believe all that you hear from a politician desperate for your vote. Nor would I believe anyone that says that one religion or culture is better than another: try to make up your own mind about life. The gift of your mind and the ability to think for yourself is, in my opinion, the greatest that you have, one that should be used wisely. So wherever you are in the world, and if you consider yourself a minority such as a Tatar living in Crimea, an African American or Latino living in the United States, or if you're a native aboriginal living in Australia (the irony here is that in this context you are not an immigrant), what I want you to do is to emancipate yourself, ignore all the presumptive bigotry, sit comfortably, look forward to turning each page and read on. However, this book is for everyone; so for those that consider themselves as not being from a minority group in their country I hope you may gain some insight into what subconscious discrimination looks or feels like. Why have I written this book now? Because I am sick and tired of the constant discrimination that I have suffered all of my life both overtly and now as an adult, covertly.

More than ever the #BLM movement has galvanised people of colour, so despite repeatedly being called a 'Paki', forty years later, I became a Professor of Surgery by cutting my way through at times a torrid terrain.

Prologue

I began writing this book in October 2019 and completed it during the Covid-19 crisis in July 2021 after several lockdowns (can never recall how many there have been now), millions of worldwide fatalities and on the eve of the largest vaccination program of our generation. I've had time to reflect and review what I had written and have in the meantime read a great deal of literature published during the pandemic, which has dramatically reshaped the medical world. Never in my lifetime has the UK's National Health Service, the NHS, been under so much pressure or felt so central to our lives. So I am beginning with a slight digression from the main themes of this book, which will explore race, medicine, humility, and human perception. As someone from the medical profession, my 'take' on the Covid-19 crisis, a truly unprecedented time for humanity, seems an apt opening.

First, you will no doubt be aware that, like all viruses, Covid-19 doesn't discriminate. Anyone can get it. It isn't pleasant; thousands of people have died and many more may succumb before we see a plateau, a sustained R<0.5, with an eventual downward slope in infective cases. As more people succumb, we will eventually develop herd immunity, as we might for a bacterial infection, and therefore this virus should somehow dissipate to a greater degree – but will it totally disappear? No, it probably won't. But we must strive to learn how to treat it effectively and now thankfully vaccinate against it. However, if we look back at our human history, we see that we have experienced a great number of deadly diseases, including 'plagues', over the past 1000 years, or as far back as records show. We will undoubtedly continue to be afflicted by such outbreaks of new diseases in the future, too.

We have been taken aback by the need for self-isolation, social distancing, and lockdown. It has been important to adopt these measures to beat a virus for which we have no effective treatment at present – and there's unlikely to be such a treatment available in the forthcoming months, maybe even years. Patients are developing antibodies, but deaths secondary to Covid-19 may continue for some time. Experience will help us plan future courses of action, so we must persist with isolation until the vaccines take effect. My concern is how truly effective the vaccines will be against newer variants of the virus that we are discovering and being exposed to. Variants are unfortunately an inevitability, which can mutate, escape recognition, and re-infect a previously vaccinated person. My colleagues and I receive a new vaccine to protect us against influenza each winter. This may also become a reality for Covid-19 virus mutations.

As a consultant in the National Health Service, the virus has had a huge impact on my day-to-day work. My entire schedule has changed. We've been asked to continue with important cancer operations based on a scoring system designed to protect patients – as you can imagine, a patient coming to hospital is technically walking into a petri dish. They are consequently more likely to contract the virus, and are therefore possibly worse off, with a chance of dying from Covid-19, rather than from any risks of surgery. Important surgery, such as emergency operations, continue, but at a different, more protracted pace, due to the increase in necessary precautionary measures. The personal protective equipment (PPE) that surgeons wear has changed – there are new types of face masks, which can be uncomfortable to wear, but which are necessary to protect both patients and medical staff. We've also reduced the number of doctors required daily, so that there is a limit to the number of medical personnel on the wards at any one time. Inevitably some of us will succumb as we will have a higher exposure to the virus than the average person. As senior consultants, we are allowed to continue working in our area or field, however, we initially lost most of our junior doctors from March to May 2020 to areas such as respiratory medicine, intensive care, and general medicine as this is where there is a greater need for their skills, purely due to volume of patients inundating these specialities.

Working in this manner actually takes me back to when I was a very junior doctor, about twenty years ago. I hadn't undertaken any night shifts for a very long time. As consultants we tend to only get called for serious matters, or shall we say, when 'the shit hits the fan!' So now I had once again to get quickly used to undertaking nights, which involved creating my office, which I am very lucky to have, into a makeshift overnight bedroom. A mattress on the floor and a duvet with a pillow sufficed. Needless to say, despite not having a bleep these days but my mobile phone instead, I recall as a junior checking all the patients were safe at night before I turned in, a necessary formality which still remains to this day.

The hospital car parks remain almost full of key NHS workers working tirelessly to treat soaring admissions. It's not only doctors and nurses, but also all the allied medical professionals such as the physiotherapists, dietitians and pharmacists, cleaners, administrative staff, secretaries, and translators. We are still checking scans and blood test results as well as writing letters to our patients. We're trying to make a difference, we're trying to keep the country healthy, but unavoidably it will take some time before we get back to some sort of normality. I do hope life is back to as near to normal as possible when you read this book.

Will the return to normality occur straight away? No. Politicians will have to advise society very carefully, using epidemiological studies in the past, that a staged return is what is required. I know the self-employed are eager to return, but if we manage this properly and in a controlled manner as countries such as South Korea appear to have done, then it will help to reduce any possible detrimental impact that we may suffer from a second surge of the virus, which we certainly do not want.

In this book I will recall some tales as a junior doctor both as a senior house officer covering the first three to four years out of medical school, and as a registrar, the grade before a consultant. While I have not undertaken those roles for the best part of fifteen or more years, all of a sudden, I'm holding all of the bleeps as our junior doctors have been deployed elsewhere. You may think that this would be easy with all the experience in the world, but youth has a serious dollop of energy which I do not have.

I realised that with my experience, I could triage patients away from casualty and their subsequent admission simply by treating them in the accident department. This actually allowed the movement of patients through the hospital to speed up and avoided unnecessary admissions, leading to decisions being made at a senior level with far more expediency than would otherwise have been expected. I undertook similar work as a clinical director, ascertaining how to reduce length of stay, improve patient flow and generally getting patients home more quickly. Any data you analyse in the NHS usually comes to the same conclusion, that it should be predominantly a consultant-led business. One thing I have learned during the Covid crisis is how important it is that consultants spend time continuing to comprehend what happens at the grassroots level, as you can lose touch very easily, especially while sitting in your office or ivory tower.

So what does Covid-19 mean for a clinician? When you have to undertake the ward care of patients, you are now inevitably seeing patients that either are, or presumed, Covid-positive. These patients are isolated or managed in a specialised bay area on secure wards. In my hospital we are all working a specialised 'Covid' rota as senior clinicians. When you walk on to the ward the first thing you must do is wash your hands, don a face mask, then appropriately, gel your hands, followed by what can be described as 'donning and doffing' of personal protective equipment (PPE). We've all been fitted with specialised masks which despite being uncomfortable are better than the normal surgical masks with a far tighter fit and a filter. I've been operating now for the best part of twenty years. While throughout my career I have adhered to the strictest protocols on washing my hands, scrubbing up, putting on personal protective equipment as well as ensuring that the highest level of sterility is maintained whilst operating, this is a different ball game. Now, when I walk onto a Covid ward, there are always staff present to make sure I am gowning the PPE correctly. It is not a simple process. It is one of the most stressful exercises I have had to do in my career in the NHS. It is worse than operating on my first patient where I experienced absolutely little or no fear, because I was counselled all the way through by a more senior surgeon. Now doctors and nurses face the added anxiety that we ourselves may contract the virus, and what that may mean for us and our families. Using the recommended PPE, you must ensure that you are completely covered, you have a visor on which hinders visibility, and only then can you see the patient, assess them, examine them and make a decision on their care. If they cough, you do shit yourself but realise that you have to look after them, so you just crack on. From March to at least July, we employed this level of PPE.

Statistics show that Black and Minority Ethnic (BAME) staff contracting the virus are more likely to die as a result. I am at times keenly aware that this could include me. At the time of writing, BAME staff account for 63% of all deaths amongst NHS workers: 21% of the overall workforce, with 17% doctors, 33% nurses and 26% healthcare support workers (these exact figures may change as time goes on). I can't, and won't pin this one on any form of racial prejudice, but I hope it indicates to British society the sacrifices BAME people have made for the UK, and with their lives, during the pandemic.

Today, sometime in April 2020, at work I asked some colleagues what they thought the percentage of the UK population was of people of South Asian origin. Most said between 20-35%, with only one person close on 6%. It happens to be a lowly 4%. I pointed out that it is all a matter of perception, and that they would need to leave big cities and old industrial towns to see the greater picture.

In the greater picture of the post-pandemic future, with none of us sure how long this is going to go on for, it is likely that society will have experienced a fundamental shift. We may see sick people self-isolating more and those in contact with them being extra vigilant, while we continue to maintain hand-hygiene principles and try to learn from the increased sanitation we are employing today. The fire of London burnt an entire city to the ground, forcing it to be rebuilt for the first time with safety and sanitation in mind, an engineering feat copied by other major European cities. I would hope that the horrors of the pandemic will forever shape our own personal practices and social protocols to become more mindful about our individual roles and responsibilities in wider public health. Throughout history advances in sanitation has helped us to become healthier and live longer, more comfortable lives. It's a no-brainer.

The first lockdown brought about an innate fear as a medic. This feeling at work inevitably seeped into the home environment. Imagine seeing half a dozen symptomatic Covid patients during the day, donning and doffing each time, then going home to shower and change your clothes hoping that you haven't caught the virus and worrying about putting your loved ones at heightened risk. We are naturally exposed to a greater viral load, meaning the likelihood of catching and spreading the virus with its increased severity, are greater.

I have undertaken a number of operations both for cancer and for emergencies during Covid. We are very strict in terms of the care we provide, but also must ensure that our patients after surgery are separated from those we know to be Covid-positive. This has fundamentally changed the way hospitals operate. I am sure many people know what it is like during lockdowns or under social distancing restrictions to find work, and every single thing you do on a day-to-day basis massively changed, while not knowing for how long. Perhaps some of these changes will be permanent. Perhaps in the future homeworking will become the 'new normal', seeing a reduction in traffic and inner city living. We all wait to see what a post-Covid world will look like.

Unfortunately, a second surge occurred. Humans are social. We need to meet other persons for our own sanity's sake. But a virus needs a host and if there are no more hosts to carry the virus from one individual to another, then it should leave our ecosystem. Isolation remains the key, with wearing face masks a simple but necessary priority in everyone's life. September 2020 saw an increase in numbers largely as a result of easing of lockdown restrictions, summer mixing, occasional holidays and with flights resuming. The universities reopened and we were blessed with eighteen-to-twenty-one-year-olds enjoying some post- lockdown freedom with social gatherings, which in essence are the feeding grounds viruses covet most. Students began isolating with the government once again back tracking with a new tier system introduced around the country. By October 2020, the tier system was slowly being abandoned or amalgamated into a one deeply worrying tier, with only those left in rural Britain able to enjoy some freedom in their life-styles.

Despite NHS concerns, a four-day Christmas break led to the surge in January hospital admissions, which condemned many patients with cancer to late cancellations to their surgery as the wards became swamped again with Covid-19 affected patients. Once again new restrictions were brought in to prevent the NHS being affected, with the emergence of closed signs on their front doors. By December 2020, half my consultant colleagues had been affected with Covid-19. Thankfully all survived but some were very poorly.

In June 2020, many working-party groups had started the race to develop a vaccine against covid-19. Vaccines help create antibodies by the immune system to a bacteria or virus by introducing a protein marker into the body for the offending organisms which is recognised by the immune system as a potential threat. By mid-2020 the virus has spread to hundreds of countries and affected millions of people, with the old, infirm, and vulnerable facing a long-term morbid state or even death. So when Pfizer BioNTech, Astrazeneca and Moderna announced in late November the results of their vaccine trials affording 70-95% immunity this was welcome relief for billions around the world. Needless to say, the US President, Donald Trump's idea of injecting detergent into oneself would not work!

On the 8th December 2020, Margaret Keenen became the first person in the UK to receive a vaccine. This was great news and a temporary glimpse for humanity to envision a future free from Covid-19. Time and history will tell whether these vaccines are our salvation from Covid-19, but more so, I think they will put the brakes on a disease that has stunned the world. I must congratulate the immunologist from around the world that are working so hard to fight this virus. Science has come through more than once with illnesses such as smallpox, diphtheria, measles, and tetanus now confined to history.

Yet writing this, having lived and worked during the Covid-19 pandemic, all the lockdowns as well as the vaccination programme, it feels as though humans have come together a little bit more. We need to continue to work more closely together, whether we be scientists, politicians, journalists, teachers, or shopkeepers. It will be as part of a felt collective that we can gain in technology, preserve our societies in peace and seek progress for the benefit of all mankind. Covid-19, a potentially killer virus, may yet succeed where man has failed in a fundamental societal leap forward. Perhaps the pandemic gives us all time to reflect on how we should live together, while showing us how important cooperation is when facing global disasters of this magnitude.

COVID timeline

2020

23rd January – outbreak from Wuhan sparks British government to raise alert

31st January – The first two cases of COVID-19 in the United Kingdom are confirmed.

5th March – The first death from COVID-19 in the UK is confirmed

23rd March – Government announces emergency measures to safeguard and protect public safety

17th April – COVID-19 tests for public service staff such as police officers, firefighters and prison staff, as well increase in restrictions around UK

Suspension of non-cancer and emergency surgery – vast impact on job plans for consultants and junior medical staff in hospital

Consultants' resident on call

Sometime in May — reported death of a consultant colleague

15th June – wearing of face masks on public transport

Late June – slow reintroduction of cancer surgery

July – easing of lockdown, with the resumption of more Cancer surgery

12th October — government restrictions divide country into a tier system ((but how do you control the regions?)

5th November – Second Lockdown – cancer surgery continues

9th November – Pfizer / BioNTech announces vaccine has promising results

8th December – Margaret Keenan aged ninety years is the first person vaccinated in UK

December 2020 – NHS staff begin to be vaccinated as well as elderly and key workers

2021

20th January – very high number of COVID deaths and admissions to hospital surging – further delays in surgery for non-cancer cases

March 2021 – Sadly another colleague passes away from Covid

April 2021 – non-cancer and emergency surgery waiting lists surpasses historic waiting times

13th May – Vaccinations in full flow – but Delta variant warning issued

19th July – Lifting of restrictions in England

13th August – start of non-cancer and other surgery – backlog timetable begins construction

The Future

- Vaccinations will help and some restrictions will remain indefinitely

- Vaccinations will not provide us with herd immunity as the virus can change, but early results show that it will help reduce serious illnesses and may save someone's life

- Self-isolation will become a normality, but its enforcement will be measured by track and trace as well as the rapidity of the spread of newer variants

- Face masks are here to stay and let's work together to save humanity

- All children born in future will receive a vaccine early in life, e.g. like for measles

[REF: Covid timeline https://en.wikipedia.org/wiki/Timeline_of_the_COVID-19_pandemic_in_the_United_Kingdom]

Chapter One

*— The 1970s. How would you like your eggs please?
Scrambled, over easy or boiled?*

In March 2011 the American Hernia Society meeting was in San Francisco, a city that I had always wanted to visit. It's on the West coast, near LA, the home of Hollywood. I couldn't wait to see the iconic Golden Gate Bridge and Alcatraz also on my top ten list of places to visit.

The meeting was an important event for me as I had been a consultant surgeon in the NHS for almost six years. It is a coming-of-age for any young medic to have accrued enough experience to make a mark as the kind of 'surgeon' you are going to be. It is also a time that may determine whether you will stand out as a leader, or not, especially if you are able to innovate a new technique, which I suppose I 'sort of' had. I was presenting my initial data from a UK perspective to the international hernia fraternity. It was a huge box-tick for me. After some travel chaos, which would have been avoided had my wife arranged all aspects of the trip, I managed to get on to a United Airlines flight. I had not flown with them before and had never travelled Business Class, so eagerly anticipated the privilege of getting on first with a welcome glass of bubbly waiting, while basking under the scrutiny of economy passengers walking past, perhaps wondering what the hell you are doing sitting there. I was already checked in, but first had to go through airport security. No problem. I have nothing to hide, so no sweat.

London High School – 1987, 1st team Cricket

So what was it to be this week, bat either 9, 10 or 11? I knew these are the only possible positions that I and my two fellow South Asian origin boys in our First Eleven cricket team would be assigned. The team was composed of boys aged sixteen to eighteen, so from the old fashioned 'fifth form' Lower 6th and Upper 6th (nowadays years numbered 11, 12 & 13). I was in the Lower 6th and despite the fact that there were fifth formers, the captain cheerily ensured that we three brown boys were the ones that always were made to put the boundary markers out before the start of the game. Nobody else was asked. Cricket, after all, is a Gentleman's game.

I managed to get 9 or 10 by alternating with one of my South Asian colleagues, as the other 'apna'* couldn't really bat so would have been 11 anyway, but he was an excellent bowler. So when you're batting 9 or 10 and are never selected to bowl, there is only fielding left. One crucial match after a mighty collapse of the top and middle order, my colleague and I were out batting. We needed about 55 runs to win. There were plenty of overs to go and both of us could bat quite well. The bowling was quick and aggressive, even presumptive, as we were only the tailenders so unable to bat. We both hit countless fours, perhaps as we knew better than most where the boundary markers were. After this great destruction of the opposition's bowling attack, we received adulation and rapturous congratulations, so much so we could have been the focus of a new cult. Our opponents were stunned as true tailenders don't bat like this. I personally didn't even bowl, so what possible purpose did I have in this team? The headmaster called out our names in assembly the next morning. In one earlier game I had actually taken four catches, which indirectly won us the game. Now this was a defining moment in the history of our school, and for us, as two brown boys, with a batting display never to be forgotten, our likely positions in the team would deservedly change for the better. Yet the following week's match came, and we were politely 'asked' to put out the boundary markers again. Our efforts from the week before had already been forgotten.

'Let's get into the right batting order, boys! Sheen you're 9!' My ethnic compadres were of course 10 and 11. The cricket team had its traditions. We were Pakis and we knew our place.

* * *

*   apna – word used by South Asians to describe another South Asian – 'one of our own'

The 1970s were great for music, although arguably less so for fashion. Nevertheless, with the golden era of R&B that excited our ears, living in London was full of colour and large personalities as well as an overt, culturally accepted racism. At times the 'sectarianism' felt so keen that my brothers and I came to take it as an ordinary part of life, as close to apartheid as one could get in Britain, with little cross-race mingling presenting as an accustomed segregation. We had to learn how to stay out of trouble, and when we found ourselves in difficulties, we had to understand quickly how to extricate ourselves so we could live to tell yet another sordid tale to our children.

The key was not to fight back, and definitely not say anything, either. The more I think about this time, the more I imagine playing out those real-life events somewhat differently, especially the fighting part. One often has a sense of justifiable obligation to deal out the same treatment that has been dished out to you by a horrible person. But this attitude, we are taught, is not what life is about. We can be the bigger person I suppose. Yes, all well and good taking this moral and at times overindulged high ground – hmm… . What was needed sometimes was a quick slap across the face and only then you'd expect to be treated differently – an offensive is sometimes a good defence some say? But Pakis don't fight back!

We lived in Camberwell Green which was, and probably still is, as cosmopolitan and colourful a part of South East London as any. A great place to live then, but especially now as an *apna*, with its leafy terraces and smattering of *halal* butchers and Asian grocery stores while being only a stone's throw away from the West End. Our particular block of council flats was called Keswick House. The fourth floor, to be exact, in the far end flat, as near to the emergency or rear staircase as possible, which may have delighted my ever-fearful father, and I think north-facing as on a nice summer's day from our front balcony I could see Big Ben.

I used to love staring at the outline of the Palace of Westminster, naively growing up with the assumption the Prime Minister actually lived there. I also thought maybe one day I could live there, too. The staircase, whenever we decided to use it, smelt of urine, but was less toxic than the actual ad hoc latrine which appeared to be just outside the lift. It is a strange habit to urinate so close to one's home, and I'm not sure whether such places of micturition still exist in modern council estates. Perhaps it was a result of the lifts often breaking down and the sheer volume of stairs being too much for most with a full bladder. The pungent odour of ammonia was a fragrance I fast reacquainted myself with as a young doctor on the wards. Maybe it is the reason why we now don't use carpet in hospitals anymore.

The family that my parents used to associate with the most were a Hindu Gujarati elderly couple that lived on the first floor. They were from East Africa and were called Lala-ji and Ben-ji. There was also a Parsi family from Mumbai that lived in a ground floor flat across the road and another Asian family from Malawi that lived upstairs who mainly spoke Kutchi but also Gujarati as well as Hindi. We all had a common link. We were all genetically from South Asia, and so looked the same. South Asians in the UK have bonded well over the years as an immigrant group, whether Hindu, Muslim, Parsi, Christian or Sikh. We were then, and are still now, one entity in the UK. This is true especially for my generation and something the younger generation should possibly covet. Our school and nursery were only across the road. Crawford Infants and Juniors. It was far from an enclave of immigrant children living in a large poor part of a capital city. Instead, it was a school with a very multicultural mix, but with less than half the children being from an immigrant background. I had White, Black and Asian friends and we all embraced each other's company and played together, oblivious to what racism really was. Rarely do I recall any of us using racial jibes towards one other, although we were children, so inevitably one would crop up (although they were most likely parroting things they had heard in the playground). There were lots of groups of close friends with most having an *Angrezi* child as the centrepiece in any such clique. I guess as I think about it, whilst typing away, I could say that even from my earliest memories, I was under the leadership of a white person, an *Angrezi*.

Racism was of course alive and well, with ever-present decorative language used to describe various ethnicities. The sudden surge of foreigners into parts of the UK, mainly the cities, the hearing of strange languages, the unusual aromas of Indian food and unfamiliar shops and butchers, coupled with a lack of employment and growing poverty, would inescapably bring about a sense of uncertainty and a focussed resentment towards the newcomers. One can only postulate that this is why the younger children that were my friends were morphed to develop a sense of them and us. I guess conceivably from their older siblings and parents, or even society at that time. Division began to seep in, it developed into a crack, this increased, became deeper and eventually lead to verbal insults thus germinating hostility.

When my mother used to drop us off at school, we noticed that every time she spoke to us in her native tongue of Urdu (pronounced Oordoo), other, especially older, children, would come up to us and say – "Hey Paki, what's that language your mum was speaking to you in?" They would then go on to attack what my mum was wearing, usually her *Shalwar Kameez*. We never actually encouraged my mum to wear Western clothes as she often did anyway, especially at her workplace, but we did encourage her not to drop us off at school in such attire and not to speak to us in Urdu (pronounced Oordoo, remember). These were necessary steps in order for us to survive racial ridicule and taunting. Although I remember naively thinking that everyone went home and spoke a different language, including my *Angrezi* friends. I definitely thought this of my Caribbean friends.

Digressing somewhat, have you ever thought about the fact that the P word, this racially descriptive word used by almost everyone I met as a child in an insouciant manner would never have existed if there had been no partition of India. No, I guess not, as it is short for Pakistani, but not technically meant as a term of endearment! No Partition, no god-awful racist word that makes me cringe to this day if heard and no substitute word as far as I can work out. Let me take a moment to think about this word or any other word to describe my South Asian ethnicity. Hey Indie! This would be cool, just imagine being named after a musical genre. Fab! Even the Beatles would have wanted to look like us. Hey darky? Too vague, can mean lots of us, so doesn't narrow it down enough to a select group, i.e. South Asians. Well, you get my drift, I don't wish to dream up other possible racist terms for South Asians, but you have to ask yourself, who helped break up India? Yes sorry, this is a different part of history, not one I wish to dwell on as I was not there at the time, but if you ever have such questions, why not ask anyone still alive, preferably in their late 80s who lived through the breakup, doesn't matter what religion, as they will generally tell you that Muslims, Hindu and Sikhs lived side by side together as a communal family for hundreds of years before the East India company came along. I do not discount that there would have been a few alienated fools that didn't like each other with a pretext of religious intolerance, but not the entire country.

At this time of my life as an innocent very young child, I suffered the most painful racist experiences. While growing up in an environment where some children openly objected to the way you looked or smelt, I often worried that I would become a victim of an assault. As a small child I experienced a light pummelling or two, a quick slap on the head, making me cry. I was never sure whether they beat me up because of the colour of my skin or whether they just didn't like me. As a small boy, I was sensible, polite, respectful of girls and rarely used bad language. Not the sort of child who got into scuffles or arguments.

I was walking to school with my mum and brothers one day when suddenly my younger brother was hit on his back by an egg, followed swiftly by one just missing my head. My mum turned around to notice a group of older children calling us all the P word. The barrage of abuse was swift but full of venom. It was also very loud. They continued by yelling that we smelt, that we needed to go back home, that is we needed to 'f off back to where you came from'. They were intent on delivering a senseless ambush.

My mum shuffled us into school, protecting us as much as she could from this barrage of physical and verbal abuse. Her *Shalwar Kameez* was visibly splattered with eggs, more or less drenched as she used her body to shield us from the assault. The school gates were made of iron and consequently were very large and heavy. So my mum had to push them with a considerable force to gain entry. I cannot recall whether there were other people watching at the time, but I conclude there must have been. My mum wasn't the most punctual person, but I can remember very rarely being late to school. So undoubtedly, there must have been witnesses. But I do not recall a flurry of persons coming to our aid, with cries of "Leave them alone". There was no one to comfort us. No one to ask how we were. No one to say how sorry they were for the abuse we had just suffered, a mother and three small children. Hearing the P word was hardly a life-changing issue for us. We were slowly becoming accustomed to this name at school. Yet often when we heard it, we knew some sort of assault or abuse was shortly coming our way, like a warning siren.

The fact that our mum was also there affected us more as she was an adult. For an adult to be attacked by children is positively obscene, virtually unheard of, but clearly possible. However, these kids were emboldened to throw eggs at a parent. Perhaps they knew no one would catch them or if the police were called, it would be a verbal warning. Or perhaps they were themselves comforted by a sense of social superiority that we, in our fear, allowed to become real. I do not recall my mother saying anything to the teachers. My brothers and I didn't say anything either as we just took it as a part of our everyday life, not realising at that moment in our lives of how wrong this was. However, these kids knew or felt that it was OK to throw eggs at the Ps. I suppose they knew no one would catch them and if they did what would they say?

They knew the police would never be called but if they were, they would never find them. If the police caught them what would they say? 'Don't do that again.' But you're not going to jail, you're not going to be fined and you're not going to have counselling to guide you to understand that what you're doing is a criminal offence. Not only is it a serious misdemeanour in this country but a felony against humanity. It was as almost as if, like Emmett Till[3], our witness statements would be inadmissible, with our fate a predetermined outcome based on our own ethnic liability.

I think this endless cycle of disobedience without punishment I think 'has' finally ended in the United Kingdom although I cannot be absolutely sure as I now live in the suburbs of middle-class Britain. Here I am now virtually sheltered from the inner cities, where I hope life has changed from forty-five years ago. I have to ask though why black footballers are continually subjected to racial abuse on twitter and elsewhere, with hardly a prosecution in sight. But if society hasn't, or is not to change imminently, then we are still struggling as a nation. Did we ever think as young children that my mum has got to go home with her *Shalwar Kameez* drenched with egg yolk? I didn't really consider asking her if she was OK at the time, but you wouldn't if you were four or five years old, I suppose. You don't think to empathise with your mother in that way, or at least I didn't at that time, a moment I clearly regret as I look back. Actually, thinking out loud, I do recall that the schoolteachers must have known that there was an abhorrent form of racism infiltrating the school each day. I expect they possibly even knew who the perpetrators were, as well as the victims, guess school discipline was not the same then or it was too much trouble worrying about counselling, which was a thing only wimps and despots required.

Social media has perhaps provided an unlikely safety net with any adverse event immediately gaining national as well as international exposure at the touch of a button. One can only see how the reporting on social media of a disgraceful action of one person towards a Syrian refugee in Huddersfield galvanised an entire nation to that poor immigrant boy's defence, with condemnation of the perpetrator (from a BBC report).

This is the earliest memory I have of such an attack, orchestrated just because of the colour of our skin. I am unclear if this still happens much in Britain today. I hope and expect not, but there are other forms of human hatred that still thrive. I always think back to this time and wonder whether there was anything that I could have done differently. Would social media have made a difference to the attack with worldly condemnation as well as provide some justice for us? As a small child fear was the only emotion I had. My mother being present made the guilty party seem to me truly untouchable.

When you are five years old, all you can think about now is what will happen to you on your way to and from school. This was my tangible reality at this tender age.

I thought and dreamt, even as a child, that I needed to try and improve my life so much so that it would help improve the outlook for me as well as South Asian people living in the UK. I assumed that we all as immigrants had to face this while living where we were. I think as a diaspora we have succeeded to a degree to improve our social standing; however, you will read on and see that despite my attaining a high level of education, the colour of my skin still affects what happens to me in life to this day, especially when it comes to adverse or indifferent treatment that you would not expect to experience as an *Angrezi*.

I often asked myself whether this would have happened if I was of Caribbean origin, whose community seemed more assertive and streetwise, physically stronger and unlikely to take such nonsense lightly. Yet their community faced their own issues. Not enough youngsters were going into higher education despite many being capable. Police brutality was weighted heavily against them and they struggled to take up well-paid jobs. My father, although very low-paid, had a solid job in the civil service, although his days of practising as a lawyer were disappearing if not gone. Most of my parents' friends were well educated and either accountants or doctors. But one could not help noting that the doctors, who were mainly general practitioners, had a slightly better quality of life. The doctors managed to own their own home, had a car and seemed to have a bit more financial reach. Perhaps it was this that encouraged my dad to guide me to a career in medicine. His younger brother, my uncle, had a top position in Saudi Arabia as a paediatrician and had sent his children abroad for education, buying a house in the UK in 1979 without even needing a mortgage. We had role models and aspirations.

Growing up in SE5 taught me a lot. How to sense danger, how to know whom to trust, how to predict who will beat me up if I talk back, how to fit in and pretend that you're someone you're not. Perhaps being of South Asian origin meant that we could not have *Angrezi* friends, although I had plenty of *Angrezi* friends and attended a decent enough school, but was this really correct with regards to my school? Education seemed to be at a slower pace than I have experienced with my children, although to be fair, I cannot be entirely sure of this. My memory is good but not that good, so I cannot boast enormous familiarity with the school core curriculum in the 1970s. With medics around me, I thought that by educating myself as highly as possible and becoming a doctor, a profession I was genuinely attracted to despite the stereotypical push from my South Asian parents, would help me feel more equal in society and gain respect amongst my peers. Only then would I not have to hide from who I was, or where I came from. To a degree I was correct. But life has taught me that while you can change the way you speak, dress in a suit, even alter your name, you cannot hide the colour of your skin. As Martin Luther King preached and is written on his grave: "Free at last. Free at last. Thank God Almighty. I'm free at last."

Some of you reading this have experienced such outlandish verbal insults and frankly brutal behaviour directed at you through no fault of your own – and if you have, I would like to say how sorry I am and know that I can empathise with you irrespective of the reasons why you faced such prejudice. These lamentable experiences of mine have taught me great empathy and have enabled me to relate to patients from different cultural backgrounds or with a protected characteristic. When you're ill, in hospital, you are generally scared and afraid. I have made great efforts over the years to learn simple words in various languages, such as pain, fever, diarrhoea. I have mainly concentrated on the languages and words based largely on the local population and the kind of diseases I treat, for example Cantonese and Nigerian dialects. The sound of familiar words puts patients at ease, and often raises a smile when my pronunciation is invariably wrong!

This brings me to a moment about two or three years later. It was the Queen's Silver Jubilee, and my brother and I were faced with the task at school of making a craft project to reflect the occasion using household items. My brother had made a little castle from yoghurt pots and I, a rocket, although I think this was just an easy option, as I cannot recall any member of the royal family venturing into space. Proudly clutching our classwork, we came across the same individuals that had thrown eggs years earlier. One of the perpetrators was in my brother's class, only a year above mine at Infant School. I wonder what this regular terroriser of ethnic children became? Perhaps I have come across him as a doctor, as I have worked in South London in three different hospitals. The ringleader always looked out for us and shouted his verbal assaults with impunity, in front of anyone, as no one cared, nor did anything about it. This boy would often punch us if we walked past him, knowing we would not fight back. This ringleader was embroiled in a life of misdemeanours as well as petty improprieties knowing full well that he could get away with it, so why not carry on? I suppose you could actually make a career out of it at some point in your life, but I guess it will be a cash-only job, so you would never pay any tax or national insurance.

As the group of bandits with the all-too-familiar assailant approached, yelling out the P word, he demanded to see what we were carrying and said, "What have you got there, P?" We reluctantly showed them what we had made at school as they were impossible to hide. The ringleader took my rocket and smashed it saying, "Oh dear, look I've broken it, P!" My brother had his castle's main turret destroyed. We were both distraught, scared and bitterly angry all at once. All we could do was go home, throw our once proud projects in the bin and not tell our parents. At least we didn't suffer any black eyes, bruised cheeks or broken bones. Thus was our celebration in 1977 of the Queen's Silver Jubilee. We certainly were not happy that our masterpieces, which we made aged six and seven respectively, were now utterly destroyed. But I feel they probably felt more power by humiliating us, a more cruel and potent use of their sense of superiority. As an adult you can't help think what you could have done differently at the time. We were two very small boys facing much bigger children. Our chances were already zero to none. We did the only thing that we could: tried to keep our chins up, bear it and take the abuse, hoping one day it would stop. Inevitably during such moments, you were fearful that it wouldn't ever halt, at least throughout school anyway.

In late 1977 we moved to suburbia. Thornton Heath in Surrey to be exact. But the ever-present reminder that we were not part of mainstream society followed my brothers and I wherever we went. Walking into the public baths close to where we lived, we were immediately laughed at as three skinny brown kids by some *Angrezis* mocking, "Hey look, the Ps have come to have a wash!" This was met with roars of laughter with even the lifeguards joining in. Despite moving away from the council estate to our first terraced house with our own rooms, we were still an object of ridicule. The public baths episode immediately reminded us with lightning agility, that despite relocating from the council estate into suburbia we unfortunately could not shake away our preordained ethnic disadvantage. It was like a contagion of disgrace spreading like wildfire wherever we went. Or was it that we were the infected individuals, with the *Angrezis* attempting to cure us of this illness with vitriol fit for a condemned man in medieval times, only for their healing power one day to take effect with our forced repatriation to our parents' homeland or by colour assimilation?

It was the 1980s and matters seemed to be slowly improving, although the era of the skinheads was still apparent and the National Front had taken hold of certain areas. I had learned that racism worked both ways. There was a growing mistrust by Asians of people of black origin, something I believe to be rooted in misplaced fear more than anything else. Between the ages of twelve and sixteen I worked for a newsagent. His surname was Patel, as were half of the thirty newsagents in the area. Occasionally I dragged friends along to help. One friend in particular, TJ, a white boy, was not only a good friend but always grateful when I called him, as we were treated to pizza at lunch, and a bit of cash (usually a tenner) at the end of the day. We had to go to a cash-and-carry. On arrival, immediately as Patel walked in, the large chap at the entrance didn't even look at his membership card. I was a little bit behind, so I swiftly followed him in thinking that this was some kind of ethnic right, after all, this was a cash-and-carry! TJ, who was always a bit slow, however was stopped from entering the warehouse by the big white guy at the door. He automatically assumed that TJ could have nothing to do with the cash-and-carry business and as such must be a lowlife coming to steal something. TJ was quite tall, very well built and already had some whiskers, despite us being only thirteen years old at the time. I very gently said, "No, he's with us," before Patel turned around, backed me up, with the security guard ushering TJ in. We had a good laugh about it as a strange role reversal. Knowing that over 90% of the newsagents were of Asian origin in South London, you can see where the doorman jumped to his conclusion. "You'll need to stick with us when you go to a cash-and-carry, mate, or you won't get in," I joked. I lost touch with TJ after the age of about eighteen. I'm confident he's doing well for himself. Although I don't think he owns a cash-and-carry or newsagents.

If I actually think about the seventies and early eighties, people, regardless of skin colour from the poor and presumed social underclass faced prejudice. It was a different form of subjugation and social discrimination created by our society that still flourishes in ways today. The wide social gaps were also responsible for the air of racial hatred. There were not many jobs, a winter of discontent, and a young Secretary of State for Education and Science called Maggie. Despondency was deepening, wages were low and many people struggled to live just above the breadline. It is said that the seventies were perhaps the worst decade for most industrialised nations. It was like going through the Great Depression all over again. Those suffering from hardship because of social circumstance needed a vent for their anger. For me, unfortunately, this meant that as someone who didn't look English, I was an easy target.

Chapter Two

– School battles

Back at Manchester airport, the security officer gave me a strange look at first when I approached his stand. A slow grimace with a Spock-like raised solitary eyebrow. He looked uncomfortable. After momentary eye contact, he asked for my passport which he opened with some urgency and began frantically flicking through its pages only to stop when he noted some Arabic writing.

"Where was this – I see an Egypt stamp?" he asked.

"A family trip to Egypt," I explained – if you must ask, I thought. Arabic writing was a possible sign in his mind of a person who required further questioning. Maybe he now needed to treat me as a contentious passenger. I imagined if this was a court room drama, he would ask his or her honour for permission to treat the witness as hostile. If this was indeed to be akin to a courtroom drama, all I needed was an aggrieved admission that an air of enmity was about to follow. His subtle change in attitude on seeing the Arabic writing with obvious postural exaggeration, for once, didn't really make me feel uncomfortable. I was quietly confident that this conversation would not go any further than it needed to. He paused and stated that I had entered Egypt at Luxor airport.

"I believe Luxor is the place to go for the museum?" he asked. I pondered. Was this a trick question?

University second year pathology assessment, 1990 – an unplanned meeting with a lecturer.

Second year was a topsy turvy year for me at med school. I managed not to get enough marks for the coveted 50% pass for a pathology assessment. I only fell short by three marks, however I was duty bound to go and see one of the lecturers about it. He was a nice chap, slightly overweight, lovely Scottish accent and a balding scalp presenting an overriding intellectual appearance. He looked at me and then looked at my exam answer sheet, then looked at me again, then again looked at my exam sheet once more.

"You've got rather gassy handwriting."

"Yes, I know I've been working on that, I think I write too quickly."

I was hoping he would realise that I had much to write, with most of it correct.

"I think the examiner didn't really know what you were trying to say. Read me this passage, what is this word?" I read him the word "bone osteitis" He just looked at me, he had no other reply. It was clearly a correct answer as part of a question.

"Where were you born? Where were you educated?"

"London."

"Where were you educated?"

"In London."

"So all your schooling was in London." He scratched his chin back and forth, maybe some afternoon stubble or a sign of his thinking mode.

"Well yes."

I was already advised by a fellow medic that he often tells students who are not Angrezi, the reason they failed the exam is because English was their second language.

He stopped caressing his chin, looked at me.

"Do you know about Hamartomas?"

"Yes."

"Do you know about the risks of Atherosclerosis?"

"Yes."

"Have you read about Uterine Fibroids?"

"Yes."

"I'd work on your handwriting a bit – you can go now."

Bizarre conversation. I left. Only three months later, when sitting the final pathology exam, to see the questions were on Hamartomas, risks of atherosclerosis and uterine fibroids. I thankfully passed …

★ ★ ★

Between the ages of twelve and thirteen we all have to go to a dentist for a routine check-up. It was an apt moment for most children this age to have their fillings done as sugar consumption was high. If you think about it, the good dental guide was slowly emerging with any school tuck shop full of sweets. We all receive an appointment; our teachers advise us to let our parents know and I acutely observed that both my mum and dad did know about it. Some gratification at this fact was met with the knowledge that I wasn't really going to go to the dentist with them. They would start speaking to me in Urdu, leaving everyone to take the mick out of me. I didn't want that. I needed to hide some specificities of this appointment as I painfully realised that all those with the surname beginning with R and S would be there too. Best I just go by myself. Croydon Health Authority, I believe the location was Lodge Road.

I turned up by walking probably about twenty minutes from my house as I had a rough idea of where it was. At this age it was perfectly normal that most children my age either walked everywhere or used their bikes. We were, of course, not allowed bikes by our father, as this would have been another means for us to have an accident and be killed in the process. On arrival, I promptly signed in, no one asked me where my mum or dad were, although it didn't really matter. Those were different times and so I sat down. There was a familiar smell of a clinic with the heavy pungent aroma of the sanitation liquid used to clean the floors. In the waiting room on the first floor the furniture looked pleasantly comfortable enough with green leather couches. One of my friends was already there, he was obviously accompanied by his mum, so I sat with them. I was chatting away for quite some time. It was very easy as his mum was a smiley and cordial lady, she always asked how we both were doing on school tests, asking what books we liked; there were absolutely no issues or difficulties in the conversation whatsoever. About half an hour passed and then all of a sudden, my mum walked in. I was shocked to see her, she immediately spoke to me in Urdu and I shuffled her away to sit somewhere distant from all my friends and their parents. They all continued to sit with each other as more came in. They would all talk even though my mum was conversant in English, I knew she would have little or nothing in common with their mums. She did not try to engage in conversation with the other mothers, nor them to speak with her. Unfortunately, rather than embarrass myself, observing her just sitting there amongst them only then to mutter a few words to me in Urdu was not something I was intent on. So I chose to sit away from them all. They were all very polite, they didn't say a single word to us either. So I guess it was not all my mum's cultural nuances that was the problem. I went in to see the dentist.

"Your son has got good teeth."

I still have no fillings even at this grand age now of fifty (as I type away). If I rewind the clock and think back to that time, I guess it was that typical of someone of South Asian origin with their subsequent disposition of keeping to themselves. Most of my South Asians friends, who had their parents pick them up from school, I noticed, walked about six yards ahead of them. It was almost as if they would rather walk with their friends than their mums or dads. This is not unreasonable though as we were all growing up, we liked a little bit of independence, but when it came down to social events and gatherings and parents' evenings I would actually rather my parents stayed at home as I didn't want anyone to hear me speak Urdu with them. I'm not sure what it is, but children can be cruel if they hear some funny words in a language that they don't understand. Immediately it is a moment of ridicule and mockery. There was nothing I could do about it.

To be fair to my parents, my brothers and I never informed them of this problem. I must surmise that they had a feeling that at school everything was not right. My parents would always speak in their native tongue and to be honest, thanks to them, being fluent in two languages has made my speech centre over developed, so learning a third language was not problematic for me.

I already had a physical difference, which to my mind was less important, but the language barrier created another divergence from accepted normality. So I had to resist this as much as possible, break it away from my vernacular, loosen its activity in my tender existence, so my life curve could start heading towards acceptance.

This next particular moment in school at the age of twelve was quite rough. I unfortunately managed to find myself in a precarious position amongst some boys from my year hanging around the corner with their scarves. The scarves were fashioned with a knot on one end. On catching sight of me, I was coaxed into a corner where two of them started hitting me repeatedly with their scarves. It was now obvious as to why there was a subtle re-design with the knot at one end, a worldly weapon indeed. I couldn't say anything other than to duck my head and try and avoid as many blows as I could. When I looked up, I notice those two boys had swiftly multiplied to eight and then I think at last gasp about eleven boys had joined in. That was roughly the final count; although a moment I will never forget, I cannot be sure of the final count, so please forgive me. The pounding was quite severe. I hit my head against a brick wall, didn't cry because this would have been a sign of weakness, but I stayed resilient throughout. At home in the evening, I felt very ill, quite drowsy. My mum asked the GP to come round as house calls were relatively straightforward then. I was diagnosed with a mild concussion. My brother let loose and explained what had happened as word spread throughout the school.

"He was attacked and beaten up by boys in his class."

My brother was only in the year above. My mum was horrified by this and later, the next day made a phone call to the school headmaster. I actually stayed away from school for about three days as I knew that I was going to be in serious trouble especially if the friendly mob found out I had told on anyone. Any reprisal attack would be a much more brutal and painful experience, so I was very worried about this. When I did eventually return to school, I actually didn't get beaten up, no further painful experiences, attacks or surprise ambushes with a reprisal. I was bemused, perhaps even more conciliatory than normal, especially as I was not responsible for the grassing up. But did the perpetrators know this fact? Apparently, the head of year lambasted all the boys that were involved a few days earlier after my worried mother's phone call. He consequently told them that I had a head injury and was being admitted to hospital. This was a slight exaggeration of the truth, but I didn't mind as I actually milked some sympathy from everyone as a result. They say if you're going to break news then make sure it is sensational. Those boys were clearly very mean, horrible, they decided to let loose and beat the poor old P up, why not, he won't fight back. No doubt the school will decide on how to punish these boys. Well caning was still around, or perhaps they were going to get the slipper, maybe a full month's detention. I thought yes any of these will do.

Finally, some deserved justice and penance for cumulative abuse. For years I had been suffering a surreal life at school, which felt like a prison at times. You have to ask yourself why home-time was met with such pleasure, more than just a homely environment, safe and away from danger as well as any retribution. I was always grateful for home, as I could speak Urdu with no fear of anyone overhearing with my brothers providing great entertainment with orchestrated and well-timed childhood battles.

The punishments ensued – from the group, five became prefects the following September and one became head boy.

It was this very year while sitting in the top set of maths, next to this tall, well-built boy who insisted on some blond streaks in his hair, but more so seemed intent on constantly harassing as well as tormenting me. I had no idea what I'd done to him, I hardly knew him, was consigned to sit next to him based on some teacher-fashioned seating algorithm, but the P word came up quite often as well as a brisk pummelling at times when the maths teacher was not looking. I refuted a lot of what he was saying, tried to give some argument against his tone. I audaciously even disagreed with the way he was treating me most of the time, but unfortunately, I ended up being labelled a bit of a talker in class by the teacher. So all of my efforts to appease the situation, defend myself from this torrid treatment ended up being counter-intuitive. Little did the teacher know that actually I was defending myself against a racist bully, who was twice my size with seemingly half the brain.

Once, while this boy was committing another impeachable offence against me, I swiftly told him to get lost. At that moment I felt a huge thud, as the teacher smacked the top of my head with a book.

"You need to keep quiet, Sheen."

There was nothing I could say or do. He got away with it. what did I really expect, a sudden realisation from this teacher that I was actually constantly being derailed by this boy sitting next to me? He knew that he could get away with it, he knew that anything that I would say would be inadmissible in any form. No one would care to listen.

One parents' evening my father vehemently objected to my maths teacher because of a few of the low scores that I obtained in some tests. I knew the reasons why, he didn't, and certainly the teacher was totally unaware. This debacle was further compounded by the fact that after parents' evening, my teacher along with the head of maths, decided I should go down to the lowest set, this was in my best interests. I was easily better at maths than half the kids in my set, but this did not matter as my father had kicked up a fuss, he was unaware of the vitriol I was experiencing from one individual that I had to sit next to in the class and the teacher didn't really seem to care. Some of the other bright boys were stunned by my sudden demotion. They didn't empathise, only decided that obviously I wasn't as clever as they were, and a quiet snigger with some verbal jibes followed suit. One even went on to candidly advise me that any aspirations I had of becoming a doctor were now slowly coming to an end.

"Bad show, Sheen."

The rest of that year and the following year I constantly outperformed most of the boys in the top set. But I had to stay where I was, there was a communication breakdown with the teacher and she thought I was a bit of a talker, created a fuss in class and yet uncannily no other teacher ever said this about me. All I was doing was defending myself against a racist bully. Maybe I should have come clean but if I had then another scarf thrashing incident would notoriously be on the cards, and this time I actually could end up in hospital. This was a risk that I wasn't prepared to take but I didn't have the guts to tell my parents, which haunts me to this day, a moment of regret. If I truly think back, I actually never spoke a word about the daily conflict that was in my mind when at school. It was relentless at times with each day bringing its own nuances mainly designed to test my resolve as well as wondering how I could extricate myself from yet another difficult situation.

School bullying unfortunately has infected classes for probably as long as I can remember. It still goes on with social media having the ability to highlight it more so than ever in this day and age. Like most, I find it abhorrent and appalling. Name calling was bad with physical abuse and violence towards another individual worse with far reaching mental anguish experienced by the victim, which can never be forgotten or forgiven. I am all for punishment and stricter sentencing for those that commit heinous crimes, but when it involves children acting reprehensibly in this way at school, I think understanding, compassion and possibly spending time with your bully's family may actually make a difference.

They can then see that you are a child, a normal innocent human being finding his way around early life, just like them, and you want to enjoy each day as well as share all the good things that happen to you with your friends.

My childhood memories have always led me to ensure I smile when I see someone I recognise, in a corridor at work or just passing them by. It makes a difference and maybe that person needed someone to smile at them that day.

From the ages of eleven to thirteen when I experienced such wretched treatment and ostracism from mainstream acceptance, I bore a constant feeling of inferiority. You cannot help but think when will this end? At this time in my life some of my examination marks were not good, they remained above average, but fell short of what I could have achieved. I felt maybe I was being hindered, with a net negative psychological impact, which had then led to some failures. One important aspect was that I doubted that the circumstances I found myself in would improve for me. However, I never doubted myself with my sheer chutzpah; it's probably why I ended up where I am today. This subtle self-confidence may have been an innate subconscious act. I have never been sure of the subconscious and whether it exists. I have always relied on science to give me an answer. But when there was no rational answer, reliance on another explanation such as subconscious thought is what I often ended up with. I, like most, needed this part of my life to move on.

I always felt from my earliest memories, that if the environment I found myself in gave me confidence, then maybe I could have achieved more, or that what I did achieve would have been achieved more quickly.

Chapter Three

− A lucky place at Medical School − call it Kismet

Back at Manchester Airport, I don't think the security officer was stupid but was evidently alerted by a man with my appearance visiting a country that speaks Arabic, as a Muslim. How was he to know that the man in front of him, despite speaking in a quintessentially English accent isn't in actual fact a fully trained expert in espionage, fluent in eleven languages and able to infiltrate even the Russian ice hockey team albeit I cannot even ice skate? I immediately replied:

"Well, no, you do not go to Luxor for the museum, you go to see the Valley of the Kings and Queens, if you want to see the museum then it's Cairo you need to go to," I said in a very soft, polite tone as if I was talking to Her Majesty herself. He looked at me as if I had lit a fuse. I am still unclear as to why he asked me a question on this and no other country I had been to, maybe it's paranoia on my part, but if you read on, you will hopefully sense where this mulling over why certain patterns of behaviour I encounter keep repeating themselves? Thankfully the security officer moved on to ask me what my business in the United States was:

"I am a surgeon and I have been invited to speak at a meeting in the US by my American colleagues," after which, he gave me a wry smile and let me on my way.

London, School – Autumn 1987

As I wanted to apply to medical school, I had to undergo a compulsory meeting with the most appropriate science teacher to guide us into our chosen career path or profession. This usually involved making sure that our UCCA (university application) form was appropriately completed and that we had a good personal statement, followed by some much-needed interview coaching and discussions about which universities we wished to apply to. When I walked into his office the first thing he said to me was,

"Not another Asian boy that wants to read Medicine?" It was just a glib comment that led to my sudden realisation of what I was up against as I closed the door behind me and entered his office. I felt nothing more as I walked towards him than an indignant resignation. I was meant to meet a teacher that was supposed to provide me with crucial guidance to overcome the hurdles designed to weed out students from the thousands that apply to one of the country's most oversubscribed university courses. He didn't want to know why I was applying, nor to which university. There were quite a few clever boys in the years above but only one person had actually secured a place at medical school in previous years, despite the fact that it was a very good comprehensive, an old grammar school to be exact. But instead of seeing an individual's future, he saw a bright boy, yes, but an apna, no doubt chasing his parents' dream, not his own. There was an inherent judgment in the observation, as if one's aspirations were less valuable if they were made to do it, rather than wanting to do it by choice. Most people chased other dreams such as finance, law and engineering degrees, while a handful of boys always ended up joining the Metropolitan Police. The icing on the cake for my school was that at least two to three boys ended up at Oxbridge. But as a South Asian, I was simply conforming to a stereotype.

One fellow sixth former jokingly said, "You only have few choices in life, work in your dad's shop, taxi driver or a doctor." We both laughed as he was a friend (but having secured eleven O' levels, I was wondering if maybe I was overqualified for those other jobs?).

The conversation with my teacher then took place concluding with a resultant affirmation that he thought I should also apply to a polytechnic to do pharmacy.

* * *

In 1988 through a bizarre combination of the postal strike and a decent set of A-level results, I managed to gain a place at Dundee University Medical School. All the universities that I had applied to had rejected me, bar one, which instead asked me to re-apply the following year, a bizarre request as I was unlikely to change my career choice or grades in a year, especially as I had gained the required grades for med school. Universities are interested in academics with the highest grades these days. But I will categorically inform you that this level of achievement desired for a potential medical student will not necessarily make you a good doctor. You do need a half-decent memory but mostly, great social skills with an ability to show some empathy as well as an unequivocal and innate desire to see sick people in order to try and heal them of their ailments, with no hidden prize disguised as financial gain. I subsequently rejected the offers I had from the polytechnics to study pharmacy as a waste of time for me.

But the hand of fate saw me fortuitously going to a Medical School that I did not even apply to through clearing. Let me confirm that this is more than rare, unheard of and realistically unlikely to happen in this day and age. I remember receiving a telephone call from the university to invite me to attend for an interview. I have to thank my late father for this because he called all the universities alphabetically, and by the time he ended up at D, Dundee said yes, they'll be happy to interview me based on the grades that I had achieved at A level. So the postal strike worked in my favour. All written forms of communication were in disarray, but my father was quite charming on the phone. Importantly, he did actually call Oxford University first as he knew that I more than just toyed with the idea of going there. I had even investigated the collegiate system. I visited at the end of Lower Sixth where I eventually decided not to apply, as I was made to feel uncomfortable whilst there. My O' Levels would have let me down, in addition to which my friends and I were surrounded by privately educated children. They seemed more prepared, confident with an obvious grooming for greater things. It was apparent to us that we perhaps were not as welcome as they were, especially as their engagement with the tutors was almost rehearsed. They knew their schools, they knew they had a chance, they knew it was a possibility. Whereas my friends and I were there to make up numbers.

With an invitation to interview at the University of Dundee, I made my way in late August to Scotland – alone by night train. I boarded the night train at Kings Cross, my dad wished me luck and said goodbye from the side of the platform. It was my chance to deliver on my pre-prescribed destiny. My parents did not come with me. I'm not sure if I ever knew why and furthermore, I don't think they or I expected that they would be taking me – they trusted that I had the audacity to make it count when it mattered. This was though, a massive step in my career, so maybe some parental support was a good idea, n'est ce pas? But if you imagine that dealing with the constant attempts to derail me at school hadn't got the better of me – maybe I was prepared now for this moment. I disembarked on a brisk summer morning after enjoying the culinary delights of a British rail intercity breakfast.

I had decided to walk to the university, which thankfully wasn't far and consequently managed to see a bit of Dundee. 2 Cross Row on campus, the admissions office, was my destination. One matter that I have never really thought about was how my parents paid for my train journey. They didn't ask for anything from me, as I was working in a 24-7 store, so had a little bit of cash saved up as I knew that they both had bank overdrafts. My dad tried a little business venture after leaving the civil service, which failed miserably to the extent that we were in debt. My mum kept her job going as a seamstress, so with her £120 per week and with my father's UB40 card, this was all that kept us going with food and a roof over our heads. But they still had a mortgage to pay, thankfully it wasn't huge by now, so we luckily didn't end up losing our house, although I think it was close. Many of my friends and colleagues that will read this would not have known that during my years at medical school. My father was unemployed and as a family we had to survive on less than £800 per month. From the time I started working after finishing my A levels, I recall never asking my parents for money, and I continued to work most of the holidays.

At the university, I had no problem finding the correct location and the interview lasted about fifteen minutes. I recall looking at the old-style buildings made from granite, heavy Northern stones, the kind we do not see much of (if at all) down South. This was architecture that could only signify to me a building of great learning or some other intellectual propriety. They asked me to wait outside after the interview and called me in about thirty seconds later to offer me a place.

I must at this point thank the university for giving me this chance and in particular, a Clinical Microbiologist and the admissions tutor who both provided the opportunity I had so longed for from my earliest memories. After my interview on the main campus, I knew so long as I didn't screw up, I'd be a doctor. I realised how lucky I was and throughout relished my studies, although perhaps I didn't always show it: seeing patients, learning how the human body works, and, of course, student life. I am eternally grateful to have had the opportunity to study at one of the best medical schools in the UK. I received a great education, so in return I now help with donations to the university for less advantaged undergraduates also to have access to a life-changing higher education.

When I got back home that night my family picked me up from Kings Cross. Thankfully there was no sign of any inebriation when I disembarked the train. My family already knew the good news as I had called them from a telephone box at Dundee railway station. Yes, no mobile phones in those days, no text messaging, no Instagram or WhatsApp groups – life was easier I guess, even less complicated, less stressful. All I needed was a 10p coin to make a call to bring some joy into my parents' lives. Social media, though, does have its benefits, usually when you're in trouble or need to make some noise. My parents gleefully started telling all their friends as this no doubt placed them up a few notches on the parental social ladder in our *apna* community. Most were happy for me, although you will not please everyone with this sort of good news, especially if their offspring didn't get on to a similar course, but you'd unfortunately be trumped by someone who got into Oxbridge.

"Ohhh yes VERY nice, BUT my betta got into Oxford, achaa."

What did disappoint me however was that only a couple of my friends from school were genuinely happy. Those that had also applied to medical school and hadn't succeeded were naturally pissed off; how could I tell, you ask? Well, it's that moment of uncomfortable silence when they hear the news from you over the phone which is relieved only by some disingenuous praise and celebratory remarks. Slowly but surely, I leaked the information and disguised it with a narrative to suit the person, so thumbs up to someone I liked and a forlorn air of my anticipated five-year imprisonment to anyone that was obviously 'unhappy'. Adjusted empathy with your peers is what matters at times like this. I am not going to be sanctimonious here. As human beings we're all not innocent in feeling such occasional and pitiful emotional traits.

As I ventured into the field that I had wanted to enter all of my life, hoping that it would rid me of racial discrimination by demolishing the 'Pakistani' stereotype, I didn't realise that my skin colour would still have a part to play in the road ahead. At the tender age of eighteen, possibly I might seem to have had some pent-up resentment at the way life has treated me. May this inevitably have led me to end up in some form of mental rehabilitation? Then like Amy Winehouse I could sing 'They tried to make me go to rehab, But I said no, no, no?' – well when you read on you will no doubt find out if I do or not.

Medical school is a great place. I was immersed in an environment with other like-minded, highly-motivated school-leavers, all bristling with energy to learn how the body works, what each bone is called, to try to understand how to engineer a remedy for infections and learning how we could one day make a difference to someone's health or even to help save a life. Our excitement was palpable, but it had to be nurtured and maintained for a long five years. Medical school was full of exams while also facing practical assessments by learning how to examine patients.

I remember very well arriving in Dundee in October 1988 ready for my five-year adventure. I'd brought a bicycle with me, having assessed whether the journey between my accommodation and the medical school hospital was a reasonable cycleable distance. It's only after I arrived in Dundee that I realised that my first year and a half would be in the Medical Sciences building, just a five-minute walk from my halls of residence. The bike would have to wait.

I recall the first night there, as this was the only night I felt homesick. I settled in quite quickly otherwise, made good friends, mainly with chaps from my corridor in the halls and fast got to grips with the gruelling timetable. There were two other medics on my corridor and one directly opposite, so I felt a sense of security that I was not alone, as did they. I had managed to purchase all the books I needed, some new but most second-hand and had hit the ground running.

I remember the second or third night was quite harrowing. Some drunk older students were knocking on all the doors at around 2 a.m. They continued this ceaseless woodpecker-style banging for about twenty minutes whilst shouting, "Wake up, fresher, wake up, fresher!" I remember feeling relieved that my door was locked so they couldn't get in, worried that my PJs were not the best nor the trendiest!

The first year of medical school mainly consisted of learning how the body works and what every bone, muscle, artery, vein and nerve is called in a subject called anatomy. There was also basic science in the form of biochemistry and physiology which paves the way towards being able to diagnose and treat patients with various drugs and other pharmacological agents. The medical school programme was very traditional, made up of lectures, cadaveric dissection, white coats and a military-style silence for most of the time. It was quite didactic in its structured approach, piecing together a huge mosaic of the human body in such a manner that at the end of it we would all come out with that total understanding needed to train competent, proficient young doctors. Nowadays many medical schools use what is called self-learning or problem-based learning (PBL) which I personally think leaves no real focus in terms of a systematic approach to training. The result can be quite haphazard, with less guided learning, meaning some students caught up in the novelty of student life easily drift away into an oblivion of fun with inebriated nights lying on strange couches due to the unaccustomed freedoms of student life. If you're going to mould the healers of the future, I feel they need a more prescribed guidance, rather than a collapsible framework. Just imagine an eighteen-year-old, especially a boy, pretty much like a dog on heat, being told he must go away and learn everything for himself. He will come back having learnt a few random facts or at best with some cracks in the foundations. I imagine a slightly more adventurous faction would no doubt know where cheap beer and half-price pizzas are to be found.

In my second year, we were all assigned a personal tutor with whom we had to meet at least two or three times per academic year. My personal tutor was of course a medic, but a healer of the mind, a psychiatrist. As all my friends knew at the time, largely due to the fact that I kept going on about it, I had my bicycle, so would manage to get almost anywhere without the need for public transport. I was naturally much fitter in those days with youth on my side, always counting my pennies, so the more time I spent on my bike the cheaper it was for me. Most students in my era had no cars, no money and no mobile phones. The fact that we had no phones generally was never an issue, as my friends and I always knew which pub we were going to meet up in on a Friday night, so essentially social life was easy. Importantly, we all talked to each other in the pub, with only the most pleasant attractions the cause of our distractions!

So I made an appointment to see my tutor and cycled all the way to his office. It was a nice windy day, normal for Scotland. I managed to get there in one piece. I cannot now remember my tutor's name, but recall subtle nuances in his accent, remember him as probably in his mid to late fifties as he had lost all of his grey hair from his frontal lobe; he never wore a suit, instead a shirt but no tie, and almost looked as if he'd just crawled out of bed. But he was genial. We started off with a very simple discussion about how I was getting along. He asked where I was up to, what topics I found interesting and how I had performed in the exams to date. In terms of the latter, I informed him that I had passed, no merits or prizes yet, which seemed like too much hard work for a boy from South London pleased not to be at home for the first time, as the freedom was just too irresistible. I didn't really want him to know anything else as my marks were not those of an awe-inspiring potential Nobel laureate.

My tutor then went on to ask me if I was managing OK with reading all of the books. I said yes, no problem, there is much to read but that is to be expected I guess, after all this was medical school. But what he said afterwards did come as a surprise.

"Are you not finding all the translating difficult?"

At this point I had no idea what he was talking about and thought he'd gone mad, albeit temporarily, so I asked him, "What do you mean?"

"What language do you speak?"

"I speak English," which I said in my very normal Southern English accent.

"Oh no," he replied, "you misunderstand me, you must speak another language?"

I felt again that this situation was turning quite bizarre, as clearly, I sound very 'English' but he had automatically observed with his eyes that I did not 'look' English. Despite his position and presumed intellectual capacity and the fact that he spends his time psychoanalysing patients with depressive illnesses and anxieties, dishes out hallucinating pharmacological medication, he should also be well versed in offering some psychological support and advice. He ignorantly had managed to alienate a young student sitting in front of him for his counsel. It felt like an earth-moving experience. He wasn't a child, nor the type of person I associated with the sort of naive or wilful racial profiling I had suffered in my early childhood life. It did inordinately appear that he himself did need some advice as I felt that he deserved to know a thing or two about the modern world. For me, unfortunately this was an utterly uncanny as well as shattering experience. I was actually hoping that this sort of stereotyping would come to an end eventually, especially once I had educated myself – or had racism just taken a different form?? A more intellectual form of prejudice is, I think, more harmful so more dangerous! I suppose you can say that the middle-class, educated racist is the one to be really afraid of?

Digressing briefly if you look at right-wing racist organisations, certain newspapers, media outlets and, also unfortunately, even some governments, they are run by educated individuals that prey on the insecurities of the less privileged by creating an aura of fear about what would happen unless there is a pretext of covert racial segregation with the necessary differentiation of all of us into our various enclaves of 'tribes'.

At this point I had to make a quick decision as to what I was going to say in reply.

"Well yes, my parents speak Urdu."

"How do you spell Errdoo?"

"U-r-d-u."

"Ah, I see, Erdoo, so that's your main language?"

"No, it's English, as I cannot actually read or write Urdu, only speak it?"

"Why not?" he asked.

"Because I'm not from Pakistan?" Or I should have said, I am from England and the official and main-spoken language there is 'English'.

"Oh, why not?"

"Well, I guess because I can't help where I was born?" That sort of depends upon where my parents were at the time, you know when conception occurred and all that sort of stuff – 'Phew' glad

I got that off my chest. I didn't have a clue where I was conceived. I didn't really want to think about it, as one doesn't really, does one! But I guess the 'event' happened somewhere in North London as my parents were living in Kilburn at the time.

He eventually accepted the fact that I was actually born in England, that I was sort of English or conceivably even British. Perhaps I should have shown him my birth certificate, something the only 'non-white' President of the United States had to reluctantly release in a press statement! He was actually quite worried because he then went on to remark on how I was reading all these medical textbooks in English and then translating them into Urdu, followed by making notes in 'Errdoo', then revising in English or maybe some weird Anglo-Indian language? I thought 'Oh my GOD' – but I didn't actually say the words because, I thought that the Dean of the Medical School would definitely find out and I of course, not he, would be in a spot of bother.

I think maybe the colour of my skin was affecting his train of thought, did he think he was meeting with the wrong person, perhaps I should have spoken with an Indian accent and asked him if he wanted rice or naan with his main dish? My name was Sheen. Had it messed up his habitual thinking, what happened to Khan, Patel or Singh?

Yet he then went on to remark on how it was incredible that I was reading all these medical textbooks in English, translating them into Urdu followed by making notes in Urdu, then revising these in English, yes he still believed this was true.

"I just read it in English," I said, "I actually understand it in English."

He was surprised at this and truthfully why wouldn't he be, he was totally devoid of any common sense or purposeful knowledge of everything else. I hadn't even approached the subject of the world not being flat or tackling other more common medieval ideas that surface occasionally. But I thought that too much new information may make him implode, so I refrained from this with some light self-reflection and control – otherwise, then I would have no tutor. The university may then find me someone who was probably even more stupid or worse, street wise, so consequently keep tabs on me and my extracurricular activities!

"Ah right, OK, so all your schooling was in England?"

Yes, there were no places left on Mars!

"Well yes," I said, "I've not lived anywhere else."

This was a very strange conversation, one that I was not expecting! At this point I thought that I should perhaps have actually laid him on the couch and began some counselling, fact checks, with a swift introduction to life in modern Britain. This seemed the correct route to pass the time, rather than him asking me any more questions on why 'segregation' was a logical way forward. I would have also given him a great deal with no charge, a 'freebie', just for humanity's sake, God knows he needed it. One could logically conclude that he really did have no idea what was going on in the world, he was living in his little shell, hadn't come out probably for the last thirty to forty years. This whole episode I decided was really rather sad, and to be honest to my reader, it does not sound attractive in the least. That's because it wasn't. This Consultant was now my personal tutor. I dare not complain about him, nor did I wish to tell anyone, as I did not want to get into any bother with the university. I could only imagine if I were to raise an objection, they would think that I was at fault. Medical students had been thrown out in the past for various deeds, actions and misdemeanours that the faculty thought were inappropriate. Here I was, having been born in the UK, being reliably informed by a supposed intellectual that actually I must be a foreigner with a less than adequate command of the English language required of a med student. To add insult to injury, he went on to imply that I spoke mainly a different language and so spent much time translating all my medical textbooks – I wish I were that clever. Now I had to see him twice a year for the remainder of my med school years. I thought about turning up in Punjabi clothing a few times, with a swift change to an Indian accent with a delivery of some poppadoms, as this would have suited his archaic assumptions.

Actually, if I had turned up as this very ethnic version of myself, I reckon he wouldn't have noticed, or perhaps not even recognised me but he would have happily accepted the poppadoms.

Such events unfortunately started to become commonplace at medical school. I often received narrow-minded remarks from patients and automatically forgave them for any stereotyping, but not the doctors. I could never forgive their actions. I recall one lovely Dundonian man in 1990, who gratefully gave me permission to listen to his heart sounds. They made a long swishing noise.

This was a type of murmur indicating a heart valve disease that we had to be aware of. We all had name badges, wore white coats, all the male students had to wear a shirt and tie, with no jeans. In this get-up it was very rare that a patient did not know that you were a medical student. I introduced myself, asked if I could use my stethoscope to listen to his heart sounds. He gladly agreed, willing to have his condition be used as a learning instrument for the students. Afterwards he thanked me, saying that he hoped I learnt something and cheerfully remarked, "You speak English very well for a person from India."

"We have good English-speaking schools there now." He was happy. So was I. No harm done.

But in my final year I remember very well during my four-week medicine attachment how the senior registrar, also from England with both of us largely surrounded by Scots, remarked on meeting an English patient. He commented on how nice it was to hear another English accent as all the students in my group were Scots except me. I bet he didn't even realise that what he had just said indirectly was that, regardless of the way I spoke, the way I looked made me evidently not English in his mind.

During the second year, over the Easter break (I was still only nineteen years old) I had decided to take a trip. At the time the cheapest way to go to Amsterdam from London was by coach and then hovercraft. The hovercraft was a stupendous invention, creating an unforgettable trip that everyone should have taken before it was retired for good. It went from Dover to Calais in forty-five minutes flat. It unerringly bounced off the water whilst making its way to France. I managed to secure a nice seat at the front. No one in my family had ever been on a hovercraft, so this was a first for the Sheens. At passport control before boarding the hovercraft, everyone in front of me in the queue was *Angrezi*. Not a single one of them having their passports checked, they just showed the cover and on they went. Yet when it came to me, *I was stopped*. The border control official took my passport and stared at the photo. I thought that things were changing, but I was still living as a second-class citizen in my own country, so I resigned myself to the label, of the painted medical student! While this smarted, this paled in comparison to the return journey, where the French authorities took me off the coach from Amsterdam to Calais – the only person along with a couple of hippies who appeared visibly stoned. They searched my bags soberly. The fact that I spoke to them in French seemed to help the situation – "J'ai rendu visite ma famille en Amsterdam," I said. He pointed to what was in my bag.

"C'est simplement du fromage" – some cheese I had bought while out there.

Despite feeling singled out, the officials were otherwise pleasant and promptly sent me back to board the coach to Calais to catch the hover special to Dover.

Once on board however, another unexpected turn of events would add more to my growing sense of injustice. Whilst sitting comfortably and looking forward to my whirlwind journey back across the English Channel, an announcement asked all non-UK passport holders to complete a boarding pass and could such persons raise their hands. I did not of course need to raise my hand, so I didn't. However, this made no difference as I was handed a boarding pass anyway.

For once, after nineteen years of existence, I felt that I should clarify the incorrect assumptions behind this action.

"Excuse me," I said, "What is this?"

"You need a boarding pass completed when coming into the UK?" the hovercraft hostess replied.

"I don't need one."

"Why, what passport do you have?"

I showed her my then, and unfortunately soon to be again, dark blue passport.

"OK, well, you don't need one."

But I felt that a subtle challenge was in order.

"What made you think I needed one then?" I pressed. "Is my accent not good enough? Orrrr, was it something else?"

No answer.

Did she realise that she had made a mistake? It was 1990, and we as a nation, and the world too for that matter, were all changing. I mean Sir Trevor McDonald was reading the news on British television.

These experiences live in one's mind for a long time. While it becomes easier the older you are, as you learn to ignore it, as you are growing up they leave a permanent impression on you psychologically. Some may choose to deal with such rejection somewhat differently, more aggressively perhaps, they could also end up clinically depressed or even disenfranchised from mainstream life. This is what radicalisation looks like and perhaps begins from. It has nothing to do with religion, that's just an excuse people use. I think the Home Office should pay particular attention to this sentence as their 'Prevent' training in 2020 is making matters worse! What utter nonsense, where was this training when other terrorists that were white were attacking London in the 80s?

People need to hear words of encouragement, be liked, congratulated. Not made to feel unwanted, ostracised or unseen.

Medical school did have its ups, I'm pleased to say, more of them than the downs. What was good for me was the feeling that there was a sense of community, especially amongst the students. One example of this was that I had a few friends from London, Birmingham and Bradford who were Sikhs. They used to go to the local gurdwara on a Sunday. I quite enjoyed the outings when I went. I recognised many similar religious practices in a gurdwara from a mosque. The respect inside was notably identical. I wore a handkerchief over my head, again very similar and we knelt down and bowed to pray which is identical to how Muslims pray. It was very peaceful, quiet, I was offered some Prasad which is sweet *halva*. Even though as a student I didn't need to offer any gratuity for the gurdwara funds, I did so anyway. Most of all it was a sense of community. The Dundee Sikh community made a point of welcoming Sikh students who were miles away from their homes. Everyone knew I was born and raised a Muslim. This didn't make any difference; you were welcome regardless. Lunch was very nice vegetarian food; I loved the curried chickpeas or *chana* served with *pooris* as well as a smattering of *daal*. I must confess it was quite nice to have some home-cooked food so far away from one's mother. This was a great experience for me, and I learned more about Sikhism on these trips than I did in religious education at school. I think it was about the caring and sharing in the Sikh community I liked so much. So if you're lonely, a bit depressed where you are, away from home and whoever you are regardless of your prescribed ethnicity, I would just pop to your local gurdwara on a Sunday and I am positive you will be welcomed.

This chapter may leave you feeling too low and depressed as it highlights that although the 'egg-throwing' days of my life were over, I still felt like a *'paki'* at medical school. It was just that the constant reminder of my supposed inferiority had taken a different form, with subtle but depressingly too-regular nuances disguised to make you aware of your own colour – which appears to be predestined as a 'bad' genetic choice you were not responsible for. I am sorry if you are melancholic right now, I will try not to upset you too much, but if you read on, I hope to cheer you up. After all, I do end up with the title of Hon Professor of Surgery.

Chapter Four

– The infamous ward round

Back to Manchester airport

Once I passed through security, I was allowed into the lounges, which was not a regular flight experience for me. On my inaugural journey in business class, whilst stepping onto the plane first, I could not help noticing that there was already a person sitting in a business class seat, nonchalantly reading a book. Clearly this was not a passenger, but a man appointed to stop any person from taking down the flight and possibly hijacking it – an air marshal. I thought in my mind that my seat was probably going to be next to his as doubtlessly I was the only Muslim in business class. I soon learned that yes, he was indeed adjacent to me. I was in fact the only *non-Angrezi* in business class. I was of course confident that in 2011, unlike Mahatma Gandhi on his famous train ride in South Africa in first class, I would not be met with a compulsory boot out of my seat because no coloureds were allowed to sit there. I started to wonder about the air marshal's job, and whether he had a bullet-proof vest on? I wondered where his gun was, was it a taser he had or just a pair of handcuffs? Fantastic, I thought, at least I can feel safe as there's nothing more secure than having a man with a gun in his pocket sitting next to you when you fly to the States or frankly anywhere!

My wife had carefully organised a 'Muslim meal' for me so that I wouldn't be offered pork. But when the air hostess proudly announced my Muslim meal it sent me into a paranoid state, feeling everyone's eyes transfixed on me. Perhaps the air marshal was alerted ahead of time to this fact, I thought. After 9-11, the attention by the media afforded to Muslims flying to the US has not been short of controversy to say the least. I had nothing to hide, so decided that I would watch a few films and prepare my talks for the congress, but somehow, I suspected the air marshal and I would have words…

London, Peckham. Routemaster bus 1975

When you hopped on to an old Routemaster bus everything was very convenient. Shopping bags were neatly stowed down a little cubbyhole, but with a pram, life was a little more difficult. I have to admit my mum was not the fittest person, even though she was only in her late twenties at this time. Dragging three children around while going to the halal butchers and Asian grocers, laden with aloo, bindi and sabzi and a tub of Ghee, took its toll on her. My younger brother still required carrying in her arms when he felt especially clingy, along with at least two carrier bags full of shopping. She plonked them down as soon as we boarded the bus and took a seat nearby. My brother and I stood next to her as the bus was packed, but she asked one of us to go and stand next to the shopping bags to stop them falling over and breaking the eggs. But it was too late. The bag fell, the eggs splattered. Tired and frustrated, my mum had stern words with us in Urdu:

"You should have stood there, betta."

You could say as very small children that this was not our fault! The shopping bags were right at the bottom of the stairs, so any sharp turn by the bus would have sent not only the shopping bags out of this lovely open entrance and exit of the Routemaster bus, but any small child standing there would have also been flung out. This was life in the 1970s. There was nothing you could do about it, it all seemed normal, we were survivors.

Thankfully the Caribbean bus conductor said in endearing patois on seeing the fallen carrier bags and smashed eggs at the entrance to his bus a jolly "Oh dear", and helped pick up the shopping bags, placing them somewhere safer. When we arrived home that day, minus a few eggs, the infamous gang occupied their customary corner. As children you were only keen to get home to play with your brothers as well as looking forward to whatever your mum decided to cook that day. Once in, I always recall hearing the whistle of the kettle as my mum brewed up her customary tea, with toys eagerly awaiting our return for an after-school game. Tomorrow was school. There were likely to be more smashed eggs to come.

★ ★ ★

I realised from an early age that caring for the sick and infirm is what I was made for. Receiving an accolade of congratulatory as well as warm remarks from grateful patients still pleases me to this day, with the reassurance that I made the correct decision. Despite coming across some recalcitrant teachers, even friends at school, the overwhelming impulse that I had kept me on track and was by far the biggest reason for me arriving at med school. While there, I led mostly a double life with some nocturnal activities taking serious precedence, especially as I was bit of a night owl. I reluctantly ended up studying mostly after hours with the curtains drawn and a simple lamp shining over my desk. Much later in life I was to discover that the fresh air in the morning after an early rise was better all-round. I was quiet and more reserved during the day, in class or lectures even tutorials, and felt by mid-way through the five years, that I had seemingly struck a balance, having worked out how to get through both a gruelling academic timetable as well as a hectic social life. After all, my friends somehow learned to rely on my company on weekends in the local student hangouts. Girls were ever-present, but mainly in my thoughts rather than by my side as an itemised companion or as more commonly known a girlfriend.

In third year at medical school, we were obliged to attend a morning compulsory clinical session. The skills I learnt at these teaching sessions, which were the introduction to our nascent clinical experiences, are still with me to this day. We all had to wear white coats, a shirt with ties for the boys. Our stethoscopes were brand new, and it was a time when we all received a £90 grant for equipment (a policy sadly dropped for the current intake of aspiring doctors). More importantly, we also had access to a special bar in the hospital open to medical students and doctors only, with pints as cheap as they were in the student union. I diligently turned up to nearly all the teaching sessions. The teaching was structured with a meet on the ward at a certain time with small groups established to practise formal bedside teaching. There is something to be said about the old-style method of teaching and learning. It was as close as you can get to Sir Lancelot Spratt teaching in 'Doctor in the House', a truly great depiction of how we must learn our trade and then use our skills to help diagnose the sick and infirm. The wards were always clean, not cramped, and smelt of disinfectant and chlorinated latrines. I recall this sense of illness in the air, lingering over the beds of poorly patients, many of whom were elderly. Their various ailments were a breeding ground for our learning, with bedside teaching being the most coveted and rich route to schooling in the art of healing. There was one memorable surgeon who, with his own unique but fiercely effective antiquated style, coached us in how to examine the abdomen for the first time, made us all crouch down and observe the tummy of a young man while he just lay there and breathed. All we did was watch and watch, gaze and become mesmerised. The Consultant knelt, folded his arms across the bed with his face in line with the patient's tummy, then he just looked and looked and looked. He said, "Just look at how it moves when you breathe."

I think both the patient as well as the Consultant were probably in some trance and spellbound fascination with human breathing patterns on the abdominal wall.

The hypnotic start to the lesson gave me the impression that this would be the easiest morning session of the year so far. None of us were mature enough to fully fathom what we were being taught. But it trained us to inherently look and connect, to think about the body's mechanics and observe anything untoward, thus plotting back and building the evidence. So what did we learn you ask – when you're in pain, have you noticed that you breathe differently?… Yes, I hear you say, so unless you know how the normal abdomen behaves, then you won't know how the abnormal one does? He was an excellent teacher, although he did also ask the male students to sit in the bath and pass a finger into their bottoms to feel their prostate glands!

Despite refraining from the finger up one's own bottom trick, I realised at this time that I much preferred the practical, rather than the theoretical, side of medicine and I guess that's why I ended up as a surgeon. I found the academic side more tedious. It required a lot of reading and I tended to read in bits, rather than in one long slog. I was always very careful in choosing which books had all the information I needed. I carefully selected the ones that were not as thick nor had small writing and some pictures too, as pictorial representation on what I needed to learn suited my grey matter in absorbing information. I guess as a professor now, I can say that I grew into academia, but at that time it bore little appeal.

One thing you must never do is lie about your findings when examining a patient. One of my colleagues seemed to always be able to hear an odd heart sound when no one else could. They could feel a spleen when no one else could. We were always stunned repeatedly by their incredible clinical acumen. Reading books was a waste of time for that person, there was nothing that they did not already know, they may as well have already been awarded their degree with two years still to go, while the rest of us stumbled along in awe of the maestro. One morning, we were all asked to feel for the pulses in the leg of a patient. There is a particular pulse behind the bony bit of the ankle on the inside of the leg, called the medial malleolus. The pulse and artery you can feel here is called a peripheral pulse from the posterior tibial artery. We could all feel a pulse on one side only, but on the other side it was difficult, possibly non-existent, a sign of disease perhaps. But not for the perfect medical student. You could see that person now with glee on their face, so much so that they are about to be cast in the new Mister Men book called 'Little Perfect Med Student'. This book will be in the stores by Monday or even by the end of the teaching session we reckon! We all were, once again, mentally battered by their brilliance, but then the Consultant raised the trousers of the leg that none of us, bar one, could feel the pulse on, and it was wooden. A prosthetic limb! Our perfect colleague was actually a very good scholar and I am sure is an excellent doctor, too. But we all learned the lesson that day of the necessity of truth, certainty and humility.

There was one surgeon that was known for his fondness for the ladies and knowing this fact fully well, the Senior Registrar who allocated medical students always gave him a group composed mainly of young women while he took on the men. Interestingly, I don't blame the Senior Registrar for arranging the teaching sessions in this way, as he was to be a consultant soon enough and clearly needed to forge good relations in order to secure a good reference. In the early 90s jobs as consultants were scarce. It was apparent that you had to wait for someone to retire or go prematurely six feet under. In retrospect however, it is glaringly obvious how inappropriate this deal was.

I loved the bed-side teaching sessions, so made a real concerted effort to read all of the clinical books. I made good progress, had passed the exams and made it past the halfway mark, having also achieved milestones in downing a yard of ale, losing my trousers at a disco and having met a few girls. I had also made friends who would last for life.

As I alluded to earlier, a resolute fact about my profession is the importance of honesty and forthrightness, without which you could perhaps be a politician, but which are critical in an operating theatre. The same is of course true of medical students. Even when asked a very probing question, as I was about to be.

The usual Senior Registrar was busy, so a more junior registrar one morning assigned us our bed-side teaching sessions. I was put into a random group with the previously mentioned consultant. He took a long look at the group, and then at me, and stared at me for what felt like an inordinate amount of time. Like a coiled viper, he suddenly sprang into action. "Who are you?" he asked. "And where have you been for the last three months?"

A sudden brownish -red glow came over me and I was about to 'crap' myself knowing that a man of his seniority could technically ensure that I did not finish medical school. I took a deep swallow and said in a whispering schoolboy's voice,

"I have been here every morning the past three months, sir."

He then asked the other students the same question. But not where they had been the past three months, but where had I been. What an arse! I thought.

He decided to lay into me. He was clearly pissed off that there were not enough girls in this group and who was I? A skinny 'dark' cockney whose presence was nothing but an invasion onto his utopian like ward? I thought that he would move on, but there was no respite. We then moved onto the ward where we encountered the matron.

"Have you ever seen this boy?"

"No," she replied.

Finally, he took his focus off me and asked a few questions to the group, mainly concentrating on the only girl. It was one of the few times that she had turned up to the teaching sessions, but she was not subjected to the ridicule and interrogation that I had received at the hands of this eminent surgeon. It was clear that her spectral presence the past year had evaded any challenge merely by her looks and gender. Guess she was prettier than me, so 'got away with it'. She got away with not technically being in our group, not turning up for three months, not attending a ward round for even longer but she had great legs, so get over it, shit happens!

The morning went on and I was wondering when it would end, desperately in need of some reprieve. The Consultant was intent on badgering me. The ward round went from one patient to the next, but he had rattled me so much that I tended to stand at the back to avoid being noticed. I did not want him to screw me over any more than I could take. I guess I could take a lot, but there's a limit with everyone and he had already surpassed mine!

"You, AWOL boy!" He asked me to look at a lady with varicose veins. I had very recently read about varicose veins in a textbook, and more importantly knew how to examine them, so despite the Consultant's demeanour, reddened face, portly presence and intimidating persona, I proceeded. I could tell he didn't like my proficiency. He bitterly remarked about how AWOL boy wasn't so bad after all, despite not turning up for three months. I resigned myself to the fact that he was going to make my life miserable regardless of my good intent.

Each morning session was between one and a half, to two hours long. I was unsure how much more of this I could take, but I could not leave, could not complain, just had to suck it up and see. All of a sudden, I saw a solution to my problem approaching. It was the Senior Registrar that normally divided us into ugly male and pleasant female groups, to appease his senior. I was desperate for him to approach and rescue me, but he wandered off after a brief wave of ironic recognition. He eventually returned looking drawn and stubbled, suggesting he had been on call the night before, or possibly three or four nights in a row. Good old days, 80-100 hours per week, no rest but plenty of action as well as play with actually, a better morale in many ways – of course the department of health had to interfere and change it all.

The Consultant spoke to him and asked about the night on call, then looked over to me. I had no idea of what was going to come but suspected it could go either of two ways.

He could either send me to Iraq where there was a war on in 1990 and no doubt a medical student with some skill would be of some use. This was akin to a past story I was told by my mother's old neighbour who qualified from medical school, King's College London, in 1947. He remarked that if you failed an exam or a year, you were out on the front line, as a medical student had some use in those days on the battlefield – a place that would not have scared me but only my mum, of that I am sure. The other clear choice he had was to recommend me for a knighthood and insist that her majesty was to appoint me to the Privy Council for my outstanding honesty and good character. In truth I was hoping for somewhere in between, which to me was merely staying on and finishing medical school.

The Senior Registrar turned to me, then said to the Consultant that he knew me quite well.

"Yes I know him quite well, he comes every week," he remarked. The Consultant said nothing, didn't even look at me, just walked off, the teaching session was over, *'khallas'* – The Senior Registrar just saved my *halal* bacon – he actually rescued my medical career. I'm not sure if you feel that this was an example of just being in the wrong place at the wrong time, or maybe my mere DNA and gender prevented me from presenting an affable image. Was it a case of a systematic bias which we perhaps all see in everyday life in some form or another, although this could have been a career ending mistaken perception that the mighty Consultant had forged of me, or to be honest, anyone like me?

Was it a coincidence that there was no one like me on his ward in any position of influence?

Once the ward round was over, I forgot about this episode very quickly and made haste to the pool table in the medical club bar. But in essence and many years later, an honest and true self-reflection would possibly be a feeling of overt discrimination, but was it gender or colour you could ask? Such behaviour is witnessed by many all over the world, poor by the rich, low caste by high caste, commoners by the aristocrats. Women in banks and the finance sector are underrepresented as well as sometimes being maltreated at work with sexual innuendo as well as misogyny and unequal pay. Sadly, skin colour with its various shades still matters in many countries around the world.

Chapter Five

– Finally finishing after a long five years

Once I had finished my Muslim meal, which was actually a very nice lamb curry with basmati rice, I washed it down with a few cans of America's finest to then settle down to have that dessert that I've been wanting to eat for some time. The air hostesses cleared my tray and asked me,

"Did you enjoy your meal, sir?"

"Yes, it was fab, a nice rice and curry."

"Yes, we are always very grateful when we have such delicious special meals as we invariably have a few spares, so we get to tuck into a nicer meal too."

The business class menu wasn't bad at all, you were afforded your little salt and pepper, a nice napkin, and you had a free bar. So what more could one ask for? I could feel a nap coming. I thought if I had some shut-eye, I could wake up a little bit fresher. I was a young consultant now, still full of energy, in my very, very early forties, actually bang on forty, with three small children at home. I could operate and managed to even see some private patients. Life was ticking along nicely. On this particular journey I had managed to procure a seat in the front section of the plane. The pilot emerged from the cockpit with his nicely pressed shirt, golden look, surrounded with an aura of 'Yes I can fly this plane'. He promptly said, "Hello how are you all doing?" to all of the business class passengers. This degree of cordiality was more than just a perk of our seat. I felt privileged. He looked at me but did a double take. I looked back at him. I trust he didn't think about re-routing the plane to Guantanamo, just to drop me off. But he obviously wasn't thinking this. I guess it was pleasant and above all for me a congenial bonus sitting where I was, as God knows I did not exactly have a silver spoon up-bringing. But he appeared pleased enough to see me in the light as all the passengers whom he afforded more than just an air of civility. He then went over to speak with the air marshal.

London, local high street. Summer 1990

One of my friends from medical school decided to visit me at home, as he was from London too. We spent the day together and then he and I decided to walk up my local high street. The street was heaving. He, too, is an apna. As we were walking down one side, we noted two approaching skinheads, green bomber jackets on, beautifully shined Doc Marten boots and Fred Perry shirts. One of them was quite tall, and both had very skinny Levi jeans on. My friend looked at me as if he had just wet himself. He quickly manoeuvred to cross the road and encouraged me with his body movements to join him. I looked at the two and thought, just keep walking, but my companion was clearly uneasy. He dared not look at me, then at them, as he didn't want to give away that he was afraid. By this point, I felt confident with my fighting skills. I had white belts in three martial art disciplines and also watched reruns of Hong Kong Phooey, so really with this resume, I was an eager and proficient fighter. As soon as we met the skinheads on our inevitable collision path, I decided to say hello, as one of them was staring at us.

"Hi dude, how's it going?" I said to one. (It was TJ who was now twenty.)

"Yeah, Whatcha mate, you've finally grown, ain't ya?"

"Yeah, see you're out and about then?"

"Just loafing mate, catch you sometime soon, laters."

"Laters."

And off they went. I turned to my friend, his eyes wide as though he'd just seen Jesus walk on water.

* * *

In final year medical school, I had the fortune of going to the middle of Scotland to undertake my final year psychiatry attachment. Psychiatry is an interesting field. I learned about various mental disorders, such as depression, anxiety, schizophrenia and so on, but unlike my prior experiences, no individual patient had a typical pattern of presentation, which was difficult for me to comprehend. I often find I am a black and white person. If you have a chest infection you prescribe the correct antibiotic, and the patient is better. There is a lot of 'grey' in psychiatry and this is probably why I didn't fancy it as a full-time career, with the potential risk of constant treatment with no conclusion. In surgery, it's more cut and dried. You see something, you decide if you can remove it or not. If you can, so long as it is safe to do so, crack on.

Once I arrived at the hospital, I was under a very interesting psychiatrist. A short chap with a round face full of bristles. He noticed that I was very quiet and shy most of the time. Generally speaking, I only became louder when in pubs. He observed that my quietness was always when we were in clinics and on ward rounds but not when I was speaking to patients. In the final year, you were paired up. My partner liked to ask lots of questions. I would let them carry on, she was a friend, and I was quite happy to just chug along, not say anything, and learn as much as I could. When I eventually did ask the psychiatrist a question he actually used to frown and look at me as if I was a complete idiot. I thought why are you looking at me like that, I'm just asking a simple question?

The first patient I was asked to take a history from in psychiatry was a young lady. I spoke to her for about an hour. She asked me if I wanted a cigarette, and I said yes and obliged. Why not? I thought. I'd been shown how to smoke in my first year at med school and consequently would spend time with tobacco in my earlier life. So we both sat in this interview room and I took notes for an hour. At the end of the hour, having smoked about five cigarettes with her, I think she knew more about me than I knew about her. It was an important lesson. When I relayed this back to the Consultant, he said, "I had a feeling that she would do that to you. She's a very intelligent young lady." He went on to say, "I bet you found out little or no reason as to why she's here?"

I said no, but I knew who her boyfriend was, as he was one of the other patients. So I guess I remained in the Consultant's bad books for some time.

★ ★ ★

A week or so into the six-week attachment, the Consultant approached me and said "I've got to go to prison so why don't you join me? I have to interview an inmate for a psychiatric assessment."

I was strangely thrilled at the prospect of going to prison. I had my jacket and tie ready to go, got into his car, an old estate Cortina, and off we went. During the journey he was quite pleasant to talk to. We had conversations on many topics and as we travelled, he offered a packet of crisps to eat on the way. When I'd finished the crisps, I noted that he was almost finished too, but I was wondering what to do with the empty packet. I thought about scrunching it up or folding into a fourfold arrangement to neatly put it into my pocket, so later, I could throw it into a bin. I noticed when he finished his, he just threw the packet between his legs under the steering wheel where it lay on the floor of the car. When I looked around the car it was like a litter bin, so I surreptitiously pretended to stretch my arms, and casually dropped the packet on the floor, too.

Despite the apparent untidiness, he was very well suited to his post as a psychiatrist. He was a very good listener. He dealt with the more difficult psychiatric patients very well and used to focus quite intensely on the more aggressive ones. He tackled them by informing them that they were there voluntarily, that he couldn't keep them detained unless they really wanted to help him to help them. He wanted them to take the medication that was prescribed, but also encouraged them to engage with his colleagues. He was keen to take them forward by helping them to develop a certain composure and measure of self-reflection. I admired this about him and wanted him also to have a favourable opinion of me. Driving to the prison was quite scenic. There were lots of beautiful hills, valleys, streams, and rivers. I commented on how serene it looked, what a lovely place it would be to live, in the middle of nowhere. He then looked at me and said, "I had you down as a typical Asian boy who likes to live in inner cities like London!"

I was shell-shocked. I hoped that he had no idea what he had just said. I did not think he was a racist or prone to extreme views. Perhaps he just lacked exposure to my kind? At this point possibly his slightly reticent behaviour towards me and clockwork indifferent looks were becoming clearer? I reckon he didn't really understand my phenotype at all. I had, at first, momentarily, no idea to what to say or do. Should I just gobble up this information, accept it? He had just stereotyped me into a little box, put me there so tightly that I would have to fight Genghis Khan and his mighty army to get out. I'm strapped in, chained, I also actually have no apparent exit strategy. By now I was almost twenty-three years old, I was going to become a doctor in less than six months, but I had another bigoted consultant to deal with! I thought for a little while, then I very quietly replied:

"As you know most Asians in this country are economic migrants. I think 60% of them to be exact, have had little or no formal education. They came to work in the mills and factories, undertook jobs the average British person wouldn't do, or there were too many jobs with not enough people to undertake them. Therefore, the majority of Asian immigrants are from the lower social and economic denominations who had to live in the inner cities of London, Bradford, Birmingham, Glasgow and so on, as that's where their jobs were. There would be no point living in the country especially if you can't afford the bus journey to the factory where you work. I guess that's why the immigrant population is concentrated in these areas."

I thought about saying some more, about not stereotyping all Asian people, and reasonably educated professionals should know better. There was a momentary silence in the car. I'm not sure how he took my reply, but I think he thought about it and reflected that what he initially said was quite wrong. He never said anything after that conversation with the rest of the journey mostly filled with an uncomfortable silence.

We saw the prisoner and I got to learn first-hand about his psychological landscape and psychiatric support. The whole episode was a good experience. I thought I'd made a positive impression on the Consultant. I had earlier shared with him some of my own life experiences especially the fact that I'd grown up on a council estate for part of my life and knew what it was like to have very little or close to nothing.

"I think that you have something to offer the world," he said. He then took a long sigh, looked down at his feet and brushed the hair off his face before saying, "But I do not think you are the keenest medical student I have ever had."

"Well, I do not ask lots of questions, and I'm mindful about not asking questions, especially if I already know the answers. I know I could have asked lots more questions, but if I came across anything I didn't understand, I would ask."

A simple and honest reply I thought to a man that had a pre-determined idea of the person I was based largely on my lineage and immigrant background.

I actually only ever asked him one question. And his reply to me was you need to read some more; he actually never answered the question. He clasped his hands together and looked down at them, and then looked up at me with a profound look on his face as if he was regarding a total idiot.

Two weeks later I was called into the Head of Psychiatry's office at the university. He said I didn't do well enough in my final psychiatry attachment. I promptly was given a borderline fail. The psychiatrist seemed impervious to the fact that he was basing his analysis on someone in my opinion without just cause, as he was only interested in one side of 'any' story. I guess he was in such a position in life. So for anyone effectively challenging him or with an inkling that he may have missed something through his own lack of insight, that person would be routinely misjudged in his own mind. They were wrong and he was right.

I would even boldly contemplate a suit against medical malpractice as a resounding injustice had been served. I had done everything that was asked of me. I felt betrayed. I was disappointed, but there was nothing more I could say or do, I just had to put up with it as any grievance I formulated would have been taken as career suicide. I thought at that moment that the car journey showed what I was up against – did I once again fall short because of preconceived ideas mapped out by another *Angrezi* on people like me? In my, at the time, self-deprecating and almost gentrified manner, I said nothing to anyone including my friends.

★ ★ ★

Medical school was peppered with happy memories and wonderful teaching, leaving me with anecdotes to last a lifetime. As a trainee doctor, the number of eye opening first goes, comical mistakes in addition to stomach-churning surprises keep you on your toes as you learn your way around the human body. I will share with you some of the lighter moments at med school, which helped me achieve the ambition I had harboured from about seven years of age.

I was asked on a teaching ward round what I would do for a patient I had correctly diagnosed with renal colic (a stone in the kidney). I said I would give the patient a drug. The surgeon teaching us at the time looked at me inquisitively, raising his eyebrows, and asked, "Drug?"

I said, "Yes. A drug."

"What drug?" he then asked.

I said I'm not quite sure of the name, to which he remarked that when I found out, I was to let him know so we could make lots of money. Despite prescribing a fictional treatment, the humour and graciousness of this incident has stayed with me as a happy memory.

On another day, I was asked to test a young man's leg reflexes. I bent his knees and looped my arms underneath and tested them by gently hitting the tendon hammer just below the knee cap. His reflexes were so brisk that the sudden jolt from the response knocked me far away from the bed and onto the floor for at least a couple of metres. I do not think I have ever been able to elicit such a knee jerk reflex again.

As a third-year medical student I was asked to listen to a person's chest with my stethoscope while standing behind him. As I did this, the doctor teaching us asked me what I had heard. I admitted nothing much.

"OK," he said, gently, "this time, why don't you put the other end of the stethoscope into your ears?"

When I delivered, I recall, the third of the five babies we had to deliver as part of our obstetric attachment in the final year, the expecting parents were very young and elated, crying with joy once their baby had arrived safely. They asked me what my name was so they could name their baby after me. It was an incredibly moving moment, although I think in the end they opted for 'Ali' – short for Alistair. I would imagine he'll be about twenty-eight years old by now.

University was great fun, hard work, truly well worth it in the end. I made every effort but didn't always show it at the time – as you've probably found out – but I did feel the experience of medical school was like a huge pole vault into the profession. You go from being a medical student to a student of medicine on leaving university, to quote one of my colleagues. This is a vocation with the ability to diagnose and heal, a profession that has been practised for thousands of years. An ever-evolving story of human progress. We are all still learning. I felt part of a large family during my time at medical school, something I think most people in the medical profession share. A family that despite some unfortunate events, I feel very much part of. This is why I wanted to share with you my experiences with the ever-present bigotry that you may not have been aware of, which was apparent during my training years at that time, and which I hope has virtually disappeared by now. Whilst at medical school, however, you may ask yourself if these incidences were ever likely to be investigated? Was I exposed to a slightly harsher environment than my *Angrezi* colleagues, or was the pain and anguish that I had suffered as a child making me more sensitive to the treatment I experienced? This could be a correct analogy, but one thing is surely I can relate far more easily to any individual or patient who knows what it is to be disadvantaged. I am pleased to say that there were enough minority students being awarded prizes and distinctions during the five years I was at medical school to give me confidence that any prejudice was not universally systemic or wilful. I will always say with pride and conviction if asked that I went to one of the best medical schools in the country. So thank you, Dundee.

Wherever you are in the world, gaining a place at medical school is a coveted prize indeed. It often affords a little bit of respect in society. According to WHO statistics, becoming a doctor is a profession coveted by so many, yet open to few. It costs to become a doctor. You really do need good grades at school, but if your parents have no money, your schooling won't be as good with the all-important prize of an offer of a place at university hindered from the off. Being poor, you may not achieve the academic success you may wish otherwise.

Therefore, knowing that my parents, despite being middle class, were immigrants and poor, I am always aware that if it wasn't for the overall good schooling that I had, I would not have been able to be what I am today. This feat is still possible today, but with tuition fees now sky-high, I'm not sure how long the next generation can continue down this path before a distinct two-tier class system evolves.

I did slowly but surely overcome my inner struggles with the legacy of my early childhood still following me at med school. I sensed that some life experiences give you a sense of self-reflection as well as maturity, but only if this is the path afforded by your character. For some persons, being badgered can send them into a spiral of melancholy. I'm very grateful to my country for providing me with this privilege and will endeavour to help fund less financially advantaged people around the world to attend medical school and become the healers of the future by using some of the proceeds from this book.

Chapter Six

– A Doctor. At last.

United Airlines flight

I had managed to work out all the settings on the enormous seat. It reclined enough for me to sleep. I was eventually flying on to the West Coast via Atlanta so it should be fairly late when I arrived; time for me to crash out. One air hostess noticed I was from the medical profession, and I was relieved when she uttered it within earshot of the air marshal, with whom I felt locked in a psychological battle as the plane traversed the Atlantic. She was from Carolina if I recall and had suffered from breast cancer having undergone surgery followed by chemotherapy. It was nice to listen to her and the journey of her healing. But in the back of my mind, constant anxiety about what the air marshal was thinking of me haunted my subconscious, an ever-present figure looming in the adjacent seat. Maybe it would have been easier if he had just cuffed me to my seat. Then we both could have relaxed. I was paranoid about sending the wrong signals, worried whether or not if I went to the bathroom too many times it may look suspicious. I was also aware that my prostate gland was now forty and so making me feel a greater desire to relieve my bladder of all its urine more often than was the case merely ten years ago.

I went to use the toilet, making sure I only looked straight ahead, and avoided any route close to the air marshal. While there I could not help thinking that I had better be quiet. Certainly, no extra noise or shuffling which may alert the air marshal to believe that I was constructing a makeshift device to stun the pilot into a stupor, so I could then take over the flight with a sudden diversion to the Middle East, as I was out of apple-flavoured sheesha tobacco at home. The toilet was of course filled with the lavishness that you would expect further up the plane, toothbrush if you needed, small, individualised towels with a mild and cordial soap-like aroma designed to allow pleasant defecation. I reckon I needed a good uninterrupted sit down, so I did. As I stepped out after washing my hands, the air marshal was standing in front of me. "Sir, please – stop right there."

February 16th, 1999, London

As my brothers and I lowered my father's body to rest in his grave on a crisp but bright morning, I can recall in the Muslim cemetery hundreds of people, all men, paying their final respects to one of the elders in the community, with the customary duty of all present to place soil over the body as the Islamic prayers bellowed out to give solace to the passed soul. Most of the attendees we knew, but there were some that my brothers and I did not. A young man approached after we completed the final Islamic prayers and said that he knew my father well.

"I used to talk to him regularly about all of my girlfriends." He then went on to say, "He always told me to use a condom, stay safe and make sure I married the right person." I knew my father was liberal and open-minded, and always encouraged us to emancipate ourselves from certain cultural rituals and medieval misogyny, but it still took me aback that he had bestowed his wisdom in conversations with many young persons about their personal lives that they were likely afraid to have with their own parents.

By contrast, my brothers and I never discussed any such matters with my father. We felt they were too embarrassing. So we laid to rest the first-generation immigrant of our UK family, who came all those years ago from Pakistan, now committed to British soil, leaving behind his children to continue in his adopted country. It was apparent that his second new land had superseded both the old ones in moulding our lives, as none of us wore a white kurta pajama at the funeral, but instead, well-groomed Western attire. My father was a proud Brit. He never looked back, tolerated all verbal, and at times physical, abuse he received for being a foreigner in a country that he considered home. The only thing that actually mattered to him was Pakistan beating India at cricket, although he did have family on both sides of the border the British Empire had left. As we laid him to rest, I realised that his fears for my brothers and I suffering poverty and exclusion had been banished. He could be certain we had made our way in life. But as grown men, with children of our own, the psychological scars of racial injustice stretched beyond his life and into our own.

That night I looked at old photos of us with our parents when we were children, the old council estate where we lived, the sky always radiant with its blue colour as the camera mostly came out on a clear sunny day. Thankfully there were some photos with him on my graduation day from med school. He was overjoyed with happiness, but sadly would never see me get married or any of my children. The only saving grace here is that he met the woman whom I had chosen to spend the rest of my life with and was there at our engagement.

★ ★ ★

Once the elation of finally finishing med school is over, your life is for ever transformed. It is not just a job, but a vocation with no clocking in or out. Donning that white coat each morning provided me with a great sense of purpose, it was a privilege, not a moment to be ignored, with a responsibility that I have to this day of my duty-of-care. The first years of work are called the House Officer years, although this nomenclature is changing all the time. I sometimes wonder if there is someone out there that has this regular name-changing job or has been given this perfect posting to alter names and titles at such pace, that it will continue to provide their job with some credibility to then justify their salary in the following year's budget. The repercussion of this constantly evolving terminology is followed by the necessary alteration of all the paperwork, thereby spending more money in a service already stretched.

I was working in the Midlands, having managed to secure a job in an area covering a population where at least one in three people attending hospital was of South Asian origin. The hospital that I was working in went further and was in a suburb that was composed of almost 90% South Asian immigrants. So my bi-lingual expertise would finally come in quite handy. It was a medical job, so most patients that came in under my care had either heart disease, diabetic issues or pneumonia. The cardiology ward was one of the friendliest places to go and meet patients. The nurses were excellent and nearly every single patient was of Pakistani origin. I think at one point there were no fewer than fifteen Mrs Begums on the ward. Begum actually just means 'lady' or 'Mrs' so you can imagine why it makes such frequent appearances.

I was actually quite ignorant of my own cultural norms and practices at this time, so when their husbands came to visit, I used to call them Mr Begum. My father politely informed me that it is not traditional in Pakistani or Indian culture to take your husband's surname as people do in the West. So I had been inadvertently calling their husbands 'Mr Mrs'.

Talking to the patients was easy for me; they mostly spoke a Punjabi dialect as they were mainly from the Kashmiri province, so I could just about understand what they were saying, but they could perfectly understand me. They were always very grateful to see that 'one of their own', an *Apna*, would be the doctor looking after them. They felt comforted I could speak a language, albeit a different dialect, that they could understand. Yet these patients would read my name badge and fall into utter confusion with my surname, 'Sheen'. My first name was obvious, a Muslim name, so I had to be either Bangladeshi or Pakistani, or possibly Indian. I then had to convince them that I was nothing other than a British-born Asian. This usually led to even more confusion, so I found myself at times reverting to a slight Indian style head-wobble by pretending that I was a first-generation Pakistani depending on the nature of the patient that I was dealing with. This proved easy enough, except with the Bangladeshis as I couldn't understand Bengali, but possessing a rough idea of what the language sounded like, I learnt to converse with them in a very pigeon version, which basically consisted of 'hello', 'goodbye', and 'do you have pain?' Most assumed, though, that my surname was a misspelling on my name badge. Naturally on finding out I was an *Apna* doctor I received a number of marriage proposals via elderly relatives keen to marry off daughters over their hospital *halal* lunch. Coincidentally the niece or granddaughter would turn up, dressed in their finest, ready to act the role to demonstrate that they should be the person that I should spend the rest of my life with. I had spent five years at med school both playing hockey and attempting to chase women (badly, I confess). But now, I was the one being chased. I felt a little bit like a Bollywood actor,

B list of course, OK C list even, but I'm not going down to 'Z'. I was still only twenty-three years old and quite immature in some ways. I think most men are to be fair, as we can often giggle at anything including a change in wind direction moments after we break some undesired flatus, which would of course numb most people's olfactory nerve.

The hospital at the time made a great effort to provide *halal* meals for patients and also had vegetarian food options. Importantly, the actual supplier of the food concentrated on making them healthy. Ghee is often used to cook Asian foods, a rich clarified butter that's extremely high in cholesterol. My mum still likes to use Ghee in her cooking. If I eat it, I can almost systematically feel the cholesterol building up in my coronary arteries. Trying to fix the culinary norms of a South Asian population thousands of miles away from home is difficult. Not only had they left their homes, but they were also trying to carry on with as many traditional aspects of their life as feasibly possible while being thousands of miles away. This was apparent by the way they dressed, the main language they spoke, the way they lived, usually in tight family networks with many people in one house, as well as the food they ate.

South Asians are extremely susceptible to heart attacks, coupled with diabetes and usually a poor understanding of healthy food options. So we are left with this never-ending cycle of an unhealthy population, with the highest incidence of heart disease, on repeat, with a lower than average life expectancy. As someone who was clearly of South Asian origin, I thought I'd try to help, especially now that I was a doctor. I persisted with my patients trying to instil in them good food and exercise habits. Some of the conversations centred around trying to encourage the women especially, who had been in the country for thirty or forty years yet were not able to speak a word of English, to actually try to learn some of the language. I tried to explain to them very politely that it may save their life one day, that they perhaps have an obligation not just to others, but also to themselves, to learn the language of the country that they live in. I think the messages were slowly getting through, but I also think for them these were just conversations that they had with me to pass the time whilst in hospital, so they could get back home, carry on eating all the food, rest, watch some TV, ignore the exercise, as going up and down the stairs twice per day was enough. Then finally cook for their husband and family, followed by more Ghee-saturated food. I actually couldn't begrudge this lifestyle as it seemed less complicated, really easier than other social nuances involving healthy eating with regular exercise, gym classes and so on, but unfortunately led to sickness, premature illness as well as inevitable hospitalisation.

Most of the women when they became sick were accompanied to hospital by their husbands. Usually, they used their kin as interpreters.

"How long have you been in pain?"

The female patient looked at her husband, who looked at me and said, "Yes pain for two days."

"Any problems with your bowels, such as constipation?"

The female patient looked at her husband, who replied, "Yes toilet good, too much toilet sometimes and very smelly!"

"Oh, OK, can she go for a wee OK?" The husband paused and replied, "Yes, period fine!"

"Oh, OK, but I didn't ask about her periods."

"Yes, period very good, but no baby."

"Oh, OK, so everything else good, vomiting, eating?" The patient again gives no answer and again looks at her husband.

"Yes, period fine, no baby!!"

Back to that again, I thought. Perhaps I should ask Gynaecology to come down, I expected that a sexual history was coming fast.

Once you're married, cultural norms dictate that an *apna* needs to start reproducing pretty damn quick. A couple of years without a child is probably OK, but any longer than that and it is going to be the talk of all the family as well as all of the extended friends. Most blame will lie with the wives, no doubt 'who may be suspected of ovarian malfunction'. So if there's no progress, this leads to a visit to the hospital with fake pains to seek a potential medical solution. This isn't as uncommon as you may think. In these situations, I generally try to keep the husband away from their wives. I had a subtle advantage in being able to speak their language, therefore I should be able to get to the bottom of why they were suffering abdominal pain. Most of the husbands were only interested in when their wives were on their period so they could go out drinking with their mates, all-male social occasions often interspersed with conversations about sexual potency once they had offspring of their own. I have always found, and still do, that most South Asian men try to control their wives to a degree. I suspect this display of traditionally unquestioned male dominance will hopefully change over time. I'm not sure why it still exists but is likely to have done so for a long time. Of course, this cultural trait is not exclusive to South Asians, but this traditionally misogynistic culture is, I hope, beginning to dissolve slowly, heading towards the correct direction of extinction. However, in some social circles, it rears its ugly head more than one would like. There are many successful British women of South Asian origin, with proud, intelligent voices and good positions in society, even members of parliament and cabinet. It is these women as role models who need to guide younger women into getting on with their lives, earning a degree, getting a job and making their own plans for their future.

Once I remember being on an on-call shift in general medicine. I was in the accident and emergency department, often all day, where some of the doctors were from overseas. It was probably the first time I had actually encountered people of my age, from the Indian subcontinent or Pakistan, working together. Most were a little older than me as I was fresh out of med school, and were born and raised abroad, leading to some recognisable differences between us. Often, the hairstyle was a great giveaway. Sometimes a difference in fashion sense, such as brown trousers with orange shirts, as well as an obvious South Asian accent. From these colleagues I learned to ask various clinical questions in Urdu far better than I had been doing at the time. My main vernacular as well as vocabulary in Urdu largely consisted of asking my parents what was for dinner, telling them what time I'd be home, what the names of my friends were, what the name of the girl was someone reportedly saw me with last weekend and whether we were going to watch BBC or ITV that night. While I could hold a reasonable conversation with my parents and their friends, mainly to inform them repeatedly that I had no interest in getting married, I hadn't acquired technical or clinical vocabulary. The trouble when speaking to South Asian patients in Urdu is that it is easier to throw in English words, such as 'digestion', 'severe pain', 'heart attack', 'diabetes', 'bowel movements', 'diarrhoea' and so on. Diabetes was an easy word I learnt. It's just 'sugar' said with an Indian accent – 'Shugarr'.

One of the general medical SHOs was a good friend of mine,

called Ashok. One day he emerged from behind the curtains having just seen a patient, remarking, "Can you go and see that Pakistani family in there?"

I asked, "Why do I need to go in there, you can speak Hindi and they'll understand you?" but he then went on to say that they refused to see him because he was an Indian doctor. They were from Kashmir, a disputed territory between Pakistan and India. I had for the first-time experienced racism not from white to non-white, but actually between people whose ethnicity was identical. This really hacked me off.

I decided to go behind the curtain to confront the patient with her family.

In the bed lay an older lady in pain with her two sons either side of her and a daughter-in-law. None of them could speak much English. I don't think they really understood why asking the Indian doctor to go away was not really permissible in modern UK society. I managed to communicate, with the help of her family, a diagnosis of pneumonia. She required antibiotics given through her veins which would require being admitted for at least a few days. We would give her all the care that she needed. Yet I was in my first year of work, I couldn't finalise any decisions without a slightly more senior doctor signing them off. I needed Ashok back. I spoke to them very candidly and explained that whilst I knew what the problem was, and could treat the condition, I needed to get the diagnosis signed off so that the treatment could continue ASAP. I scrambled to track him down before they could say anything else. This time they received him with warm smiles. I haven't resolved the India / Pakistan issue, or even got close to Kashmir, but I guess I'll leave that to those guys over there but, a life was made better by a South Asian born in England and an Indian doctor to a Kashmiri family that were from the Pakistan side of the border.

The Kashmir issue cannot be summarised here. Everyone has an opinion, but truthfully only those living there can really know what's wrong and what needs fixing. My guess is there are usually a handful of individuals that are making life difficult for everyone else, which is pretty much what is going on everywhere else in the world today. This process of the strong controlling the weak is a natural phenomenon, which will continue unless we get ourselves together. We must use our time to help people that are less advantaged than us, ensure the world is safe and clean, curtail violence as well as nonsensical killing, stop wars and global warming This may sound like sanctimonious bullshit that no one's really going to pay attention to so why don't I just get back to the book?

Working as a junior house officer was great fun. I had friends from all over the world, met many doctors, saw a plethora of patients, and learned exponentially feeling part of a multi-talented team. We all worked seventy to a hundred hours per week, which although tiring at times was relieved by the good camaraderie. We looked out for each other with the registrars buying everyone dinner when on call. This consisted of us congregating in the doctors' mess at about 7:00 pm so long as there was no desperate emergency. The general takeaway order was from a local curry place. Most people ordered a CTM (Chicken Tikka Masala) with naan plus or minus rice. I remember working all the time, over many hours, with many patients, most of whom got better, but learning to face the unfortunate fatalities which become a normality for hospital medics. The most important part of working was continuity of care, something which we lost after the EU Working Time Directive. This directive reduced junior doctors working hours from one extreme to such ridiculously reduced hours that intelligent, bright individuals that have entered a caring profession, but need to learn and develop through the experience of seeing patients more than sitting in a classroom or lecture theatre, are limited in their ability to do so.

To plug staff shortages, enable thorough training and guarantee continuity of care, I believe it would be far better to pay junior doctors a little more, allowing them to work longer hours to improve their experience, which would then have a positive knock-on effect with the expected uplift in care giving rise to much preferred outcomes. With this routine we may indeed reduce the length of stay in hospitals, clearing our wards, to ensure that the very sick are guaranteed a hospital bed.

This chapter describes something that I hadn't experienced before: Asian on Asian racism, Indian and Pakistani racism, something that exists still unfortunately to this day and will continue to do so unless people can sit round a table and discuss their differences, talk to each other candidly, be tolerant of their various political views as well as religious beliefs in a civilised manner. Very recently World War Two saw Europeans fighting for various reasons, they all look the same but now they sit down discuss and talk things through, it's called the EU*. I am wondering if the South Asian population needs to take a hard look at this moment in European history and try to discourage dominant religious uprising, indifference towards each other with a movement towards more humane tolerance. South Asians are all actually genetically the same people, or as close as they can be, we all look the same, eat the same food, have the same regional languages with varying dialects. Also, indisputably we have the same cultural practices dating back thousands of years. So what if someone amongst your forefathers decided to follow a particular God, religion or path? It doesn't make them any different a person, you can still be their friends and companions.

Amongst us doctors there was never any differing treatment; we all worked as a team, didn't care what or where you were from as long as you did your job properly. Unfortunately, though, there are possibly some still out there who may choose to look upon certain persons uncharitably or judge them based on where they are from, where they went to medical school, which country they qualified in and how well they spoke English. Thankfully, I'm not one of those persons nor will ever be, but I have been treated in such a manner.

* War against Ukraine started and progressed after the bulk of this book was written. Again the same principle applies, anger is wasted energy.

Chapter Seven

— The early surgical years. What, do you want to be a surgeon, mate?

The air marshal stared at me for only a split second. This was suddenly followed by a grab on my rather non-muscular arm, then all of a sudden, two other men from economy with badges on their lapels appeared with what appeared like stun guns in their hands. There was a momentary panic in business class as some of my fellow passengers looked on aghast. I was immediately thrown face down on the floor as well as cuffed with my hands behind my back. I had never had handcuffs on before, so realised for a surreal moment their purpose in design was not only to detain but also bring pain. One of them swept the bathroom that I had just used with a handheld instrument designed to detect explosive materials. The other checked my seat. Once handcuffed, I was sat down beyond the curtains and informed that the rest of my journey would be in economy, so as not to upset the privileged passengers.

Just imagine the homeland security chief or even the NSA coming on air in the next hour in the US media explaining, "I have some NEWS, we have caught a terrorist on a United Airline flight, he used the bathroom, may have even watched a movie, which did depict subtle female anatomy with bare legs as well as cleavage. We have reason to believe he was about commit a heinous crime by drinking alcohol and eating a ham sandwich. We have now advised his mother about what a *'harami'* he is. We also believe he is working for an enemy of the United States called

UK Surgeons, with the mighty Lord Cornwallis resurrected to take the helm. We are clear that they are intent on attacking our freedoms, *Alhamdulillah!*"

This is perhaps one news outlet's take on the event, with another claiming a grave injustice of mistaken identity. I was not sure what to expect next – perhaps I did need that visit to the loo, again.

What now you ask…?

London, 1984

As my dad and I walked back from the supermarket with our shopping bags, all of a sudden a small old Angrezi lady fell. My dad quickly rushed to help her and I followed. I put our bags down, so I could help her up, slowly. We helped her to her feet, she was able to walk, which was a relief. My dad asked if she was OK, to which she replied yes and thanked us. I managed to grab her trolley and we watched her walk slowly away to make sure she was not in need of further assistance. She was very grateful, and we were pleased we were there to help her at the time. At that point I was thirteen years old and already started thinking to myself, I wonder if she twisted her ankle or had broken her hip – bechari (poor thing in Urdu / Hindi)? I could just about name about twenty to thirty bones in the body and I knew some of the organs as I'd already learnt about them at school. I was naturally taking note of people's ailments, possible injuries and underlying conditions. I guess, for me I ended up in the right profession.

★ ★ ★

I had graduated to the level of 'SHO', a title given to a position at the part of your career after your internship or house officer years and before the registrar years. I had worked as a demonstrator in London, teaching first-year medical students anatomy, passed the first part of the Fellowship exam, and was looking for a two-to-three-year hospital post to complete my junior surgical training. In the New Year of 1996, I saw an advert for a SHO rotation in London, at a largish hospital that would allow me to achieve what I wanted to, so I applied. The job ad was very specific about the primary fellowship exam being desirable, which I had already achieved, so that was one criterion fulfilled. A newspaper investigation a few years ago reported that candidates with foreign names did not get shortlisted as readily as their white counterparts.

I subtly took note of this and never actually used my first two names on my CV, only my initials. This I continued for the first five years of my junior doctor life.

A month later I received an invitation for an interview. So far in my career I had a hundred per cent success rate in job applications, so didn't see any reason why this would be any different, although statistics dictate that this was going to come to an end eventually. The interview was held by three consultant surgeons. I recognised one of them from when he was a senior registrar. I guess that is the trouble in all careers, you can spend years not knowing whether your boss likes you or not, then spend minutes in another job and he/she does think you're not bad or even OK? Feedback is important, with this coveted aid lacking in the medical profession when I was a trainee. Rarely, consultants patted you on the back to praise your achievements with, "That operation you did was great!" or perhaps, "We should see what we can do to help you some more?" Most consultants merely cared that you knew their patients, did not bother them and of course did not do any serious damage, otherwise they would have to sort it out, thereby conferring more work on them, more time in the NHS, with less time at home.

As you went up through the ranks the onus was generally passed down to the person below, so the top of the pile just carried on with their general life, which included dealing with managers, complaints, much craved private practice as well as any family idiosyncrasies – one of my old bosses went home to an empty house on three occasions, wife and kids left, gone – not even a note – guess operating all day then coming home, talking about how your operations went isn't everyone's cup of tea! To be honest he was a bit too scrupulous at work, as well as the fact that he had his favourites, but most people do so you can't really judge him for this particular nuance. Interestingly, I was actually one of his favourites! I managed OK with him, better than most, learned to operate as he was an exquisite and brilliant surgeon with great finesse, an aspect of his work that I aspired to. The difference between him operating on someone and another consultant, although they were good in their own right, was notable for the trainees. He really did demonstrate with his own little elaborations on how one should 'operate'. But unfortunately, this meticulous and at times pedantic nature did tend to rub people up the wrong way at times. As a result, I don't think he had many friends outside of work, and his marital life was clearly affected in the same way.

Medics, though, do talk too much shop when at home or out – whenever we socialise outside of work, we discuss work, but usually the funny or disparaging side of seeing sick people more so than the joy we may have brought to someone's life by removing a cancer or fixing a fracture after a bad accident. Actually, I tell a lie, as, just before I applied for this job, I undertook an orthopaedic post, and this was definitely a job for boys with their toys. All the registrars were egotistical maniacs, they used to compete on how fast they could fix a hip compared to one another. Guess this was a comparison that they could make without getting undressed, as none of them wanted to risk losing especially in cold weather! I would imagine more self-appraisal in the medical profession is still warranted. It is, though, slowly coming through with time.

For this job, there were eight candidates and three jobs, but none of us saw each other until the end of the interviews when they called us all back to wait for a decision with bated breath. My interview went well. They asked me about what I had done so far, if I had undertaken any operations by myself, where I was up to in terms of college examinations and courses as well as what I had managed to complete. Luckily this was a training centre and they had much to offer, making it a job that I was very keen on. I also hadn't actually applied for another post. They asked about the primary part of the fellowship exam, which I admitted I found difficult, but managed to pass. One of them asked whether I passed the first time. Most surgeons struggle with exams, which are rigorous given the critical precision required of the field. I hadn't passed the first time and had no hesitation in letting them know.

I actually realised why I had failed at the time…well it's because I wasn't prepared! Get it…a bit silly really, damned anatomy. My so called friends that generally always crop up and provide sound advice, well the kind of advice that you really need to hear: "You'll be OK", "The exam is easy", "I have no idea why or how I passed as I did no work", "I just read the night before"…"Guess I'm just a blinkin' genius!" Well, anyway, following on from this great advice, I sat the exam, having read as well as assiduously revised the human anatomy from head to knee! Yes, it's as far I had managed to cover, but considering the stupendous as well as the resoundingly sound advice I was offered, I decided to sit the exam and part with about £400 of my hard-earned cash. So, at the anatomy viva, which was a key part of the exam, as I followed my examiners to a model of the human skeleton, the first question I was asked was, "Where is the spring ligament?" It's in the foot of course, where else, as I have not read that bit!! Ehhhhhh, blank face, raised eyebrows, blank look again...

I do recall having this hot and cold feeling going through my body as I felt clear anxiety. If I were a white-skinned person, I would have gone red, so here for once the colour of my skin protected my utter embarrassment by not knowing what the blinking 'spring ligament' was. I thought, I thought, I thought maybe I should actually say something or maybe I could just pretend not to have heard the question, start talking about a completely different part of the anatomy, point to a part of the bony skeleton I knew, a part I knew really well. It should ideally be as close to the part of the anatomy that I've just been asked about, which clearly I knew nothing of? This is a trick that I was advised to do when stuck. I didn't actually want to use this trick as in the examiner's mind I would be even more of an idiot, as I didn't listen to the question. The other trick that I momentarily thought about using was repeating the question back to them slowly..."The spring ligament???!!" "Well it springs," I should have said...this actual moment of genius should have helped me as you 'spring' from your foot! Oh bollocks! I wasn't that clever to ingeniously dream up the notion that I had any idea of what I was going to talk about, or even attempt to point to the correct part of this skeleton's foot..."Shall we move onto something else?" the examiner then said to me. I then merely gave a shy and reserved 'nod' yes. I fared much better in the rest of the viva so all the subsequent questions I nailed. But, alas, it was too late, you cannot pass with that start and why should you?

The second time I learnt everything super well that I had failed on first time, then failed again! So immediately I decided I had better knuckle down, work harder. Furthermore, I had better remove any distractions that I had. There were a few young women knocking on my door, albeit very occasionally, and I decided to despatch them, as like most men, I'm easily distracted. I really needed to pass this exam, I couldn't fail again, it was costing me too much. My parents were already wondering what I was going to be doing as a career and obviously the marriage question always cropped up as it does in most Asian families. So third time lucky – yes, but it was close! Too close!

Tough exams with increased pressure as each time it costs! It was a tough journey and it was an exam I had needed to pass. There are high hurdles to be traversed to get into surgery. About six-hundred would-be surgeons sit the test, and only three-hundred pass the MCQs, after which they face an oral examination. From those remaining, fewer than half pass.

When I informed them that I had to do a resit, my interviewees laughed and acknowledged most surgeons fail the exam, with one joking 'only the best ones'. At 4 pm all the candidates were invited back for the results. Everyone was eyeing each other up wondering which three would get the posts. There were three women and five men, all about the same age, in their mid-twenties and I was the only ethnic minority person there. A name was called out, and one of the men went into the room briefly before coming out and leaving. One gone. Another name was called out – mine. I went in, nervously, but they quickly congratulated me and offered me one of the posts. They asked which speciality I would like to do first. When I left, I could sense that everyone was looking at me.

About a year later while working away, I visited another, more senior, trainee's apartment, where he showed me a letter, dated a year earlier. It was handwritten. I knew the person that wrote it, an excellent surgeon who was always good to me. It read "Dear X, I have vetted the CVs for the SHO rotational posts, then placed them in order as discussed – UK/Irish at the top, other EU second and African/Asian at the bottom." I asked him where he got that from, and he said he had seen it lying on a desk. Just in case? I looked at it again and couldn't believe what I was reading. I realised it was for one of the jobs that I had held. Perhaps putting Dr A J Sheen on my CV was working.

As well as having much sought-after employment for a reasonable period, there were many courses available to me, such as basic surgical skills and advanced-trauma life support. I felt as any reasonable young budding surgeon would. To repay this good will and my appointment I worked hard. I learnt to operate quickly, as I guessed this would set me aside from the other appointees. By mid-1997, I could undertake a lot of straightforward surgical emergencies, such as a wound washout, abscess drainage and of course the benchmark operation of appendicectomies (UK spelling). Removing an inflamed appendix defines you as a junior surgeon. In addition, the ability to carry it out with little or no help, with proficiency, makes you a marked person. Someone good, someone able, someone that's going places. In one year of junior surgical training, I undertook just over fifty by myself. I rarely needed the registrars to help. This operation is taught by registrars to the more junior doctors like me. And I was taught by three different, very able registrars. They all had slight nuances to their respective methods for the same operation. I too developed my own technique with certain idiosyncrasies, which was generally an amalgamation of the three registrars' methods. This fact remains true to this day. Many surgeons learn bits of operating techniques from their seniors as they progress. No one is right, no one is wrong, everyone has their own way. Remember there's more than one way to skin a cat. The truly great surgeons and ones that remain in my mind are the ones that throughout their careers are always eager to learn and continue to do so. They will learn from their colleagues just as much as junior medical staff. This job is a vocation, and to become excellent requires continued learning. I have met many surgeons along the way that have been blinded by their own ego and ambitions, so confident in the knowledge that what they do is so right that you end up wondering how they ended up in this profession. I recall when I undertook my first appendicectomy that I had a very senior nurse assisting, which was the normal practice at this time. She was from the North of England, and always called me love or chuck, and was probably in her early sixties. At each stage of the procedure, she gently reminded me exactly what to do, which instrument to use and how to find the appendix if I got stuck. Consequently, my first solo appendectomy went very well. It's interesting who you can learn from, and experience counts more than anything. Such senior experienced scrub nurses are not allowed to help the trainees today by assisting in simple operations. There are some things in your professional life that are best left untouched especially if they're working, for as they say, "If it ain't broke don't fix it?"

There was one memorable case that you would probably like to hear about as it wasn't so much the inflamed appendix but the patient who imprinted some of their characteristics to memory. Of course, I can say no more about any patient specific details, but I'll describe to you what happened so that you can decide.

One day I was called down to the emergency theatres as, out of the Junior SHOs, I was perhaps the most able to undertake an appendicectomy competently. It was also appreciated that I would naturally call for help if needed. The registrar had been called away, so the patient was already in the anaesthetic room. I said that I would help as much as I could. But I first needed to see and speak to the patient awake, as this was good practice, if only to confirm it was the correct patient, having the appropriate operation for the right reason.

I rushed down to theatres, excited as I enjoyed operating, got into my theatre blues, went to the anaesthetic room where the patient and anaesthetist were waiting. The patient was awake and had signed his consent form. He was young, otherwise fit, perhaps a little overweight which can pose a challenge in surgery, but happy to see me. I introduced myself after which I instantly felt that he was comforted, even though I was about to undertake an emergency operation. I chatted to him, checked the consent form, asked him if he knew why he was here, then informed him of what was about to happen to him. I felt his tummy and could detect appendicitis. He did though have a large tattoo on his chest, which I couldn't make out fully, but this was not relevant to his care, just a moot observation by me.

When my anaesthetic colleague wheeled him into the theatre, fully asleep, he was not entirely happy. In all seriousness, he looked more disgusted than unhappy. The patient had intravenous fluids running and his oxygen saturations were good, his heart ECG trace was normal. He was in an excellent anaesthetic condition and ready for surgery. I asked what was up. He explained that the patient had a large tattoo of a Nazi swastika on his back. He then asked me to look at his knuckles where he had white power tattooed. I just laughed it off and went about what I was there to do. I took out his gangrenous appendix, patched him up and put lots of local anaesthetic into the wound so he would not feel much pain when he woke up. I wrote up the operation note impartially, as one would expect from a professional person.

After the operation the patient was managing very well in the recovery suite. I memorably felt that I'd done a great duty, not as a surgeon, but to people of my ethnicity because the patient may now regard his prejudices under a different light. The next morning, I reviewed him, and he was very grateful and doing well. Later in the day, I saw that all his mates were visiting, they seemed like normal everyday people, roughly his age, yes, all *Angrezi* & interestingly male, but I guessed that they may be old friends or probably aligned with him from an Aryan brotherhood perspective? So I decided to interrupt, say hello again...! "Hi, remember me, your surgeon – *the P word I should have said*?" "Yes," he said. Again, he was pleased to see me. All his acquaintances acknowledged my presence, they also seemed kind enough, even nice about the fact that I had fixed their comrade. I reviewed him again before I went home that day.

The next day or so before discharge, I saw him more often than not and even while just casually walking past his bed politely offered my humble altruistic services. It wasn't that I was singling him out, as I do like to think that I keep an eye on patients that closely anyway, but I wanted him to perhaps understand that we are all human beings, so should not be discriminated against or treated differently because our ancestors were from another part of the world or that we merely looked 'foreign'. I thought maybe I should even take him home make sure he gets in OK, has his tea, coffee and is eating well etc. I did wonder if I drove him home, then dropped him off, would there would be a nice gathering of the tall men all dressed in white sheets, waving a Confederate flag to greet me? They may even burn a crucifix in my honour on his front lawn with a note of thanks from the Grand Wizard himself. Surreal, unimaginable, and very unlikely to happen.

I feel from my perspective I was probably about twenty-six years old, but I hope you will see that this is a great moment to share with you all as it showed how, when you as an individual are at your most vulnerable, sick, infirm, in pain, and clearly need help, it doesn't really matter who helps you. You're very grateful for the aid that you receive. This is why I think that the last fifty to sixty years of immigration into our country has sort of calmed the real right-wing issues down a bit. Don't get me wrong, we still have a long way to go with only a mere spark needed to ignite another catalogue of racial tensions. We are, though, in a much better place now than we were when I was growing up as a child in South East London, which was a bad time, where most native Brits were not aware of what the immigrants were about, what we stood for, why we smelt a bit different and clearly our parents spoke English with a funny accent or not at all. For being singled out like this I don't in all honesty, entirely blame society, but I think *Angrezi* that see people like me need to know that what we have experienced in life perhaps makes us a little bit more sensitive. It will also be important to realise that we are more emotionally susceptible when we are accused or attacked in ways that we ordinarily would not expect a human being to be, as this is when we are at our most vulnerable – growing up in an unfriendly environment has made us this way. So we need more room and when this room or space has finally disappeared, then so will have discrimination at all levels. Other than in my childhood at this time, I had not actually suffered any direct racial taunting and/or been subjected to overt vulgar ridicule because my parents were immigrants. The indirect discrimination I experienced at med school, I put down to sheer ignorance. I had secured a job coveted by many, was treated like an equal and more at times by my peers as well as colleagues. I also commanded respect for my professional role in society. So were those days growing up in London a distant memory, and was a life free from discrimination all that remained? Well so I thought!

One day the junior house officer was off work and there were two locums (doctors temping) filling in. I remember one distinctly, who sounded posher than posh. He never saw the patients, was always found asleep on the couch in the doctors' mess, thought he was rather an Adonis, flirting continuously with the female staff. All I wanted him to do was keep up with ward work, see the patients, prescribe the drugs that were needed, fit any IV cannulas that were required and call me if there was a problem. Instead, all I got was call after call from the nurses saying he hadn't done this or he hadn't done that. I remember him to this day. He wasn't bad at pool though he did work out a lot so always insisted on wearing uncomfortably tight shirts thereby enabling most people to make out that he actually did have a six pack. It's important for you to know that I never did complain about this chap, I knew he was only there for a week. So I tolerated him well, beat him at pool, which was important for me just to put him in his place. I also ensured that he didn't just slip away and made sure he undertook his job. Once he had completed his week, I was terribly relieved, so we procured another chap.

The new locum doctor was a British Asian man with a rather rotund hairy abdomen trying to force its way through the bottom two buttons of his shirt. He was very good at what he did. All the ward work was undertaken in a timely and proficient manner. He sorted all the sick patients when I was in theatre; I very rarely had to go to help him with a prescription. He'd come down to theatre when required. He was an excellent doctor. He told me he was between jobs and wanted to do some charity work somewhere around the world, so was locuming for three months for cash.

Then his plan was to come back from his charity work and carry on working on some sort of rotation to become a GP. I think he's probably a good GP somewhere in the South of England managing well, he may have settled down with someone, I doubt he's lost weight and those buttons have probably since left his shirt.

When our house officer returned from sickness, I remember operating with my boss and registrar. They both spoke randomly about the two locums we had had. They thought the first locum was a super bloke and excellent doctor and would make a fine surgeon but had very little or no opinion of the other, remarking on his weight and laughing that perhaps he should consider an alternative career. I was astonished, Hell! They have got this completely wrong. I was actually very, very disappointed in their analysis, it was totally incorrect, the wrong way around, perfectly topsy-turvy. Then I got to thinking about what they thought of me. If they've made this decision based on those doctors' ethnicity, then I'm screwed!

I felt I really had to work hard in that unit to try to make them feel that, despite any preconceptions, I was as good as any other doctor. I was wondering what the future held for me at that point in my life. I guess I thought that I may become unstuck at some point. Over the years so-called friends had told me I would never become a consultant or even make it into a surgical job. All of that was untrue so far but then slight occurrences such as this conversation I heard while operating with my two senior surgical colleagues was a little bit distressing to say the least. Life had to go on, I couldn't let one episode like this affect me. They say you shouldn't let one event in your life decide your entire future. I think this is true and if you have such an experience in your life, just think about it, brush it aside, swiftly move on as there are more important things to worry about.

Chapter Eight

– Fellows of the Royal College – We salute you – Doctor to Mister!

Whilst sitting on the loo on the plane in a slightly more salubrious latrine than I was used to, there was much turmoil in my mind, paranoia, a long flight, surreptitious looks with some inebriation at a high altitude can have a surreal hallucinogenic effect on you, I suppose…I finished using the bathroom, came out the door with no sudden surprises as envisaged and made it back to my seat to await a smooth landing. I was excited about landing, as my fondness for eating the hot dogs in the US (made with beef, so happy days for me) was getting closer. I was so looking forward to tucking into one with the normal trimmings of ketchup and mustard. I had at least three hours before my connecting flight to San Francisco, leaving me with ample time to have a nice sit-down meal, and pick up something from the airport duty-free shops for my three children as they expected presents!

I surreptitiously made sure I disembarked after the air marshal in case he was planning to follow me, which was again another paranoid delusional thought I was infected with.

When I reached the line for passport control, the queues were enormous. The waiting masses were kept company by American customs officers patrolling up and down the aisles, some with guns. I waited patiently. No one could approach a desk without being invited. I scoped the immigration officers being careful not to make eye contact with any one of them. As I had boarded the plane first, I was consequentially afforded a quicker exit. This resulted in a speedier arrival to the long immigration queue. There were only one or two flights ahead of us, so I managed to stealthily approach the end at a reasonably swift pace. In front of me were a few US citizens that I noted on my flight. They joked and had a bit of a giggle with the immigration officers and were waved through very easily. One of them couldn't even find his passport. So he went on to have a few more discussions with the immigration officer. Actually, it would be the immigration officer that I was about to see but I didn't know it at the time. Whatever ID card he showed, maybe it was his driving licence, it worked, and he went on his way. I was called over to the vacated space at the American nationals' queue to help speed up the process as another flight had just landed.

I remember his face to this day. If there were a line-up now, almost ten years later, I guarantee that despite him being at least ten years older, I would spot him. He was a big chap with grey curly hair.

"Hello, how are you?"

London, Summer 1980

– There was nothing more exciting during the summer holidays than when TJ and a few other friends, all Angrezi, came to my house. On one such day we decided that we were going to go under a bridge to experiment with fire. There were five of us. We managed to construct a small, rather modest inferno, but it was enough to alarm an onlooker sufficiently to call the fire service. We slowly watched as the large fire engine roared on to my road, blue lights flashing, with delight. The firemen, twice our size, crawled underneath the bridge to extinguish the fire. They then hosed off all the dirt on their fireproof overalls and started chatting with us. They obviously guessed we were the culpable creators of what was rather a neat little fire and didn't say anything to us. Instead they showed us their engine and said they enjoyed crawling under the bridge and putting out the fire. I guess we broke their boredom for the day, a simple event with no serious harm done. To be fair my mother could have put the fire out with a saucepan full of cold water. Later that day my brothers eagerly awaited our father's arrival so they could inform him of my illegal activity that afternoon. My dad called me a Haram-zada and kamina in a loud, stern voice, the kind that gives you a lump in the back of your throat as well as sending a cold shiver

down your spine. Surprisingly, to both my brothers' utter dismay, that was it. I do believe at that moment he thought of something much worse that he did as a child growing up in Delhi. This is a moment of great reflection as I call the period 1977 to 1981 the Golden era, since my other name beginning with P had vanished somewhat whilst in junior school. Maybe it was because we had moved to a slightly more affluent and suburban area – still it was a terraced house that we lived in, but we remained just above the breadline with little or no extra money – well not for a holiday anyway.

* * *

In 1998, almost five years after finishing medical school, I prepared myself to tackle the final fellowship examination. Once passed, I could call myself a surgeon, and change my title from 'Dr' back to 'Mr'. This is an historic tradition that dates to the Middle Ages when we were called Barbers, then Barber-Surgeons, and so consequently came to be recognised as the Company of Barber-Surgeons[1]. The company later split to become the Company of Barbers and the Company of Surgeons, with a Royal Charter bestowed upon the Company of Surgeons in 1800 to form the Royal College of Surgeons. Surgeons originally held the title 'Mr' as Barber-Surgeons, due to the path taken being of apprenticeship-style learning rather than a degree from medical school. So inevitably would-be surgeons decided to attend medical school first. After gaining full fellowship from the Royal College of Surgeons, successful candidates, who were already doctors, would revert to the historic title of 'Mr'. I found it a pity as I did like being called 'Doctor'. So a little bit of history for you all, which will especially help the citizens of non-Commonwealth countries reading this book, probably more so our friends and 'allies' from North America.

The examination was rigorous, testing your knowledge on various pathologies and refined diagnostic skills as I trust you will be pleased to know, because naturally you don't want just anyone operating on you or your loved ones. No surgical prowess, technical ability, dexterity or competencies that one would be expected to have as a skilled surgeon were under scrutiny. However, today, suturing and knot-tying figure in the test. We were assessed continually throughout our training on our surgical competencies and were expected to maintain a mandatory log of all our operations as trainees, which had to be signed off by our consultants as completed and competent – or not. Those not up to the job are sifted out, kindly asked to choose another specialty in the field of medicine.

I passed the main written exam with enough marks to be invited to the oral examination, which involved a long complex case where you had thirty minutes or so with one patient, then quick-fire short cases. If in the second part you ended up with only one patient, it generally meant that you were doing badly. Each candidate had four examiners, two for each section. The idea was that they were meant to 'trip' you up, or at least make you question yourself.

Disappointingly some of my contemporaries as well as older colleagues, remember my so-called friends, unequivocally informed me, "You will not pass first time, as you are an ethnic!" This fact was "always good to know", as I remarked with a placid reaction on this occasion. But when you've grown up in the 1970s and 80s and heard the P word almost every day at school, so much so that you eventually just learned to ignore it, such ethnic related comments were so commonplace by now that I generally ignored them too. This failing first time was a remark only and nothing in comparison to my earlier experiences, including my hovercraft journey as a student. To be honest if you ask yourself about my so-called friends, most had failed the exam on at least one occasion. They generally described how unfairly they were treated, how the examiners didn't allow them to answer the questions. They always felt they were up against it, also they were so heavily scrutinised even if they answered everything correctly during the examination. They were unequivocally of the opinion that they would have failed anyway. I personally believe they performed miserably on the day, so perhaps that's why they failed. But it wasn't their fault.

I was already a doctor working in busy hospitals, I was part of the generation that undertook long, long hours with no real time for rest all week. Some weeks we worked over eighty hours, but I enjoyed my job, a career that would keep me employed for as long as I wanted, with a half decent pay cheque at the end of the month.

The oral examination was at Hammersmith Hospital which meant I had to walk past Wormwood Scrubs prison in my nice new dark blue suit. It was a scary place for me as, in London in 1998, mugging was rife with my ethnicity making me a good target as we did not fight back. We tended to wear some gold (both men but more so women), and it was also agreed socially, that we could generally not run very fast! Yes, look at the last 100 years of line-ups for the 100m Olympic final!

I arrived at the hospital. It was a coldish day in spring, and the hospital foyer was as busy as expected. Once in the hospital, as exam candidates, the location of the examination was well sign-posted, so no issues. The Royal College of Surgeons has good finances, so this level of acute organisation was expected and well received.

For the examination, we were put in groups of six. An old colleague of mine that I recognised from a course a year ago was in my group. He was from Iran originally, very tall and had a good sense of humour. When we assembled in our predetermined groups, we were put together with four *Angrezi* candidates. The Iranian leaned over to me and whispered, "I guess we're both coming back in three to six months then?" I was and never am quite sure what they thought? Perhaps they felt that being examined alongside some ethnics actually made them feel more confident, so they would have a higher chance of making it through – well this is what the statistics say. This is nothing abnormal as one always sizes up the opposition, as not all of us will get through. My Iranian friend clearly envisaged that we could not fight this enormous white firepower especially as all the examiners were *Angrezi*, male as well as close to retirement or retired. Oh well, what can I say, just imagine being on the USS Star Ship Enterprise with your bright red uniform on, only to be called to the transporter room where Kirk, Spock and McCoy are waiting to beam down to a planet where little or nothing is known. Two things were certain, Kirk would get the girl and you almost certainly would be killed. According to Royal College tradition and my so-called friends, my fate was also predetermined like the unsuspecting, red-uniformed trekker beaming down with the *Enterprise* elite.

The examiners came into the room full of candidates in twos and would call out a name. They would be smartly dressed wearing their white coats and generally most, if not all, would be male. Once your name was called, that person would then walk up to you, shake your hand, and be led off to the wards. Everyone was nervous, eyeing each other up. There were mainly male candidates, with very few women. If you are already a fellow and the final fellowship exam is taking place in your hospital, you are allowed to watch the process, but merely observe, quietly. I am not sure if this still goes on, but again it didn't bother me as the career that I was about to go into was one where everyone would watch you, perhaps even scrutinise what was happening with your operation. You are expected to be confident, but not arrogant or a moron. I recall what my examiners looked like, they were very polite and shook my hand, introduced themselves and led me away to see the first patient. The recognised protocol is for them to take the candidate to the first patient with pleasant discussion down the hospital corridor. They then imparted a brief instruction to examine the patient's neck. I opened an exploratory discussion with the patient and started examining him while trying to answer the examiners' rapid-fire questions with the astuteness they deserved and that the examiners expected. As I started examining my first patient, trying to calm my nerves, I must have done something, good or bad, as when I turned around, they were suddenly gone! They'd left the room. I chased them down the corridor with the viva continuing in fifth gear.

In one case, they asked me to feel all the palpable blood vessels in the head and neck. I felt the carotid artery on both sides, facial artery then the superficial temporal on the side of the forehead. But the facial artery on the left I could not feel.

"Feel again," the examiner said. So I did.

"No, I cannot feel anything," I said, with an affirmative voice.

"Funny that," he went on to say, raising his eyebrows at his co-examiner followed by another sharp exit from the bay area. I was then asked to examine a patient with an enlarged thyroid gland (in the front of your neck). She was sitting in a chair with a glass of water next to her. I was to ask her to swallow this water, as the gland moved up when you swallow, with me, standing behind her feeling her neck. So in essence, there were some subtle clues and a giveaway of what I was expected to do. I do not recall this particular case as well; I asked her to take a gulp and swallow, as I felt the gland move up. As this case was going on, I do recall next to me another candidate was receiving a hard time from the examiners wanting more information on a patient whose hands he was examining. I could not help but notice the verbal exchanges, as they were quite loud, with the candidate feeling more than just pressure. The patient had Dupuytren's Contracture, where the last few digits of the hand become almost permanently flexed, tight in the palms so they cannot straighten their fingers. This can happen with age, as a result of trauma, from drinking too much alcohol or as a result of side effects from certain medications. My colleague didn't look happy and looked as though he was withering under the questioning. I was worried about him but covertly was glad it was not me. I managed to see at least six patients, which I felt must have been a good showing, but received no smile from either of the examiners, no pleasantries, and certainly no hint as to how I had performed. So you had no idea, with an invariable sense of having been exposed at a surreal event, which at times you had no control over, so inescapably you are just left with your neurons embedded with a convoluted thought of what you could have done better. After the clinical part of the 'test' I could not help speculating a most simple reaction, "What had just happened – now what?"

I met up with my co-examinee friend afterwards to head down to the college for the results but not before further sit-down oral examinations in the afternoon. I do not remember the exact details of the second part at the college, but I seemed to talk my way through their interrogations OK. The logbook part went particularly well, where they look at your signed diary to see what operations you have managed to assist in as well as carry out by yourself. They obviously could not tell who the pleasant neo-Nazi was whose appendix I had taken out – as any log contained only a patient number with no name or any other identifiable detail. The exam is very cleverly thought out as all the examiners from the hospital part in the morning are also there in the afternoon session, but you tend to be examined by the other ones now – so I guess they all get to mark you and if they all think you're bad then that is that. This way, you are less likely to suffer from any systematic bias. I asked my Iranian friend how the day had gone for him. He was totally clueless as to his outcome as well, and slowly we both began to think that we had failed. Before the results I visited the toilet at least eight times. My mouth had become grimly dry, and I was forming a slick layer of sweat. I still had a nice suit, though.

In the Royal College foyer there is a marble statue of John Hunter, a famous eighteenth-century Scottish surgeon who trained in London. The candidates had to stand there, while John Hunter looked on, and wait for the Senior College Examiner to come out in a splendid red gown accompanied by someone from the administration office. It was roughly 5 pm after what had been a draining and psychologically testing as well as brutal day for our adrenaline-soaked minds. The senior examiner gave a small speech about how we had all done well, but that only some had passed. He went on to advise us all not to be disheartened if we hadn't made it. He explained how he had failed this exam himself, many moons ago. As he prepared to call out the successful candidates by their examination numbers, one could not help thinking that John Hunter was looking down along with expectant stares by the surgeons in the oil paintings surrounding us. We were about to find out if we were to be honoured with the same fellowship as them, but until my number was called, I was still a 'Dr'. So the wait with bated breath continued. I had been advised by some of my so-called friends that I would fail with the prospect of still sitting this exam in my late thirties. While we desperately waited in the college foyer with our forlorn expressions, I started to reminisce as to why I was there, why I had put myself through such mental torture and why I held the dream of becoming a surgeon of some repute. Also what was it that drove me to want to wield a knife to salvage a human organ from disintegration, or see the beat of a battered heart restored. Yes this was a fantasy for me. But one that may still be achievable – a mark of success for me against my contemporaries and peers. However, I recall someone saying that you can be the victim of your own successes, especially in surgery.

The college administrator called out the numbers. If he skipped your number, it was unfortunately a definite fail. I cannot recall what my exact number was in the 400s, so let's say it was 434. As he called out the list of numbers of the successful candidates, we politely applauded. As the numbers were called out, those whose numbers had been missed left. My heart was beating rapidly and I was panicking. The numbers were approaching mine. The ripple of applause was slowly dying away as more and more unsuccessful candidates left. I was reliably informed by some of my again, so-called friends, that if they call the number immediately before mine, so 433, then they would not call my number, as they never call two consecutive numbers! Such comforting advice from my 'friends'! I wish I still knew them now, how nice they were, self-absorbed with their own illustrious careers, clearly the chosen ones or better still will one day bring balance to the force!

As the numbers were promptly called, my heart continued to

beat faster and faster, I was worried that I might need a defibrillator to shock me out of my supraventricular tachycardia. "431" he shouted, applause was barely audible now, as more and more unsuccessful candidates left, "432", two away from me, I hope he doesn't say the next number, because then I'm screwed! "433" well that's just utter nonsense isn't it, why me after all this effort? I have once again lost out to my tanned complexion, which in Brazil would get me a role in a popular film, no doubt. My wait continued; by looking around, I could see that the co-examinees from my group were all still there as well – "434!" whoops! that's me, I've passed!

Immediately a weight lifted off my shoulders, and a feeling descended upon me that I cannot truly describe. I walked over with a slight giddy step towards the chief examiner. After shaking hands with him, I joined a queue to a room where a formal but small ceremony took place where the examiners bowed to us to acknowledge that we had achieved what they had. We were surgeons together now. The lavish college room where we stood was decorated with oil paintings of former notable surgeons. In the moment, you can't help but imagine being up there one day too. My Iranian friend had also passed, the other four in our group had failed. We were under the impression that the two of us would be the unsuccessful candidates. Frankly, I must add that all this 'great and sound' advice as well as scepticism that I had received from my so-called friends was nothing short of nonsense and scaremongering. The moral here is that not everyone is your 'friend'. The stats were against us. However, the college examiners recognised that we were good enough to become Fellows that day. Despite the glow of success, in the pit of my stomach something burned as I realised that I was entering an intensely competitive field. You must hold on to moments like this for as long as you can. They don't come around often enough.

So this book is not all about doom and gloom about the maltreatment of persons of colour, but a realistic approach to life with its roller-coaster ride. The motto I would adopt at this point is a quote from Churchill – 'Failure is not fatal but the courage to continue is what matters.' The next few chapters do explore what can happen to any individual, but again, I will leave you to decide whether the colour of my skin played a part in the events as they panned out.

As for my Royal College, I will always stand up for this fine institution. I was examined by *Angrezis*, passed by *Angrezis* and trained by *Angrezis*. No place nor institution is perfect, but as a surgical body it is trying to make surgical training accessible to capable people from all walks of life. I make my contribution to the training of the future generation of surgeons and am pleased to say that some of my own trainees are now also consultant colleagues.

I dedicate this chapter to them.

Chapter Nine

− Registrar years − How to handle a sudden promotion.

When I neared the front of the queue, I saw that a few people were being led away. I wasn't sure where they were going but the US officials were evidently not happy with them. I twitched.

The immigration officer asked how I was. I replied that I was fine, then he took a look at my passport and said, "So let's see what we have here then?" with an awkward but self-gratifying grin on his face. Notably, most persons that I see in my workplace with such a grin are usually happy to go home, stay another day because they do not want to go home, realise they are about to receive pain killers, especially opiates or have just broken wind, which was probably much needed! He looked at my passport and back at the big screen in front of him. The bright light from the computer monitor was glowing on his rather rotund visage. He was clean shaven, and his skin radiated the reflected light in a dull bluish tinge. I'm not sure what he was looking at as he could have been studying with disdain or interest all the football scores as far as I'm aware. Whatever grabbed his attention, I believe it could have made absolutely no difference to the decision he was about to make. The shine exuding from his monitor was clearly a subtle 'professional' and above all credible distraction from his inevitable and deliberate action. So after wasting a millisecond on the pretext that he found the blueprints of a cunning espionage plan on his monitor, or possibly had orders from Interpol, without blinking his eyes or asking me any more questions, he proceeded to put my passport in a see-through plastic envelope with a red border and said, "Sir you need to go into that room right over there."

February 15th, 1999 – My first Northern Boss:
"Hi, I heard your father passed away?" he said to me in a telephone call direct to my room.
"Yes."
"I'm very sorry to hear that. I bet he'd be proud of you and where you are today."
I gave no answer.
After a pause, he gently added, "Listen, we'll be absolutely fine, we will manage, you go off and spend time with your family. My sincere condolences for your loss."
I caught a flight that very afternoon to London, where an old friend picked me up from the airport. Kindness and charity costs nothing.

★ ★ ★

Just before the end of the twentieth century I managed to secure a registrar rotation in the North of England. I had nurtured the ability to surgically remove a tumorous growth from a patient fighting for their life, to repair or amputate a severed limb, to make decisions that would affect the rest of another individual's life.

Although I trained in Scotland, I had worked entirely in London and the South East and was not really aware of the fabled North/ South divide. I arrived at the hospital after my journey up by car, using just a paper map whilst keeping one eye on the road, with plenty of road signs to rely on. It rained all the way past Watford. I was immediately treated with a bit more respect than I was used to. I was still only twenty-eight years old and looked a bit young, but as a registrar the title alone commanded an authority as you were one grade away from becoming a consultant. Out of the juniors, the registrars are the fewest in number at any grade. In most places, registrars are also fewer in number than consultants as, more often than not, they work for at least two. So, if a consultant is the Colonel or the General, perhaps a registrar is a Major or more realistically the Captain. But a straight jump to consultant level was not possible without one further examination towards the end after six years of intense surgical training to amass the experience to practise independently, although now we work more as a team with a subtle hierarchy of experience in place, a mark of respect more than anything.

In the doctors' accommodation, I had an upgrade from a standard room on the hospital site, with a lounge, separate dining area and the added privilege of only one other person to share with. I decided to be up early the next day as naturally a registrar carried a bit more responsibility. Despite the relative excitement, I was still considered young and I certainly lacked experience at this level. I felt that I needed to make a good impression, so I turned up much earlier than expected, and went straight to the consultant's office to introduce myself on my first day. He was what one may call a typical Northern man, genial, and down to earth. After a polite and cordial greeting, he asked me what I could do in terms of operations, as well as the cases that I needed help with. He also questioned me on where I had worked so far. He promptly noted after my replies that I was a fresh registrar, hot off the press after a successful conversion from 'Dr' to 'Mr'. Registrars took care of the patients while the boss was away, with other consultants there to help and supervise if needed. However, if you showed promise, you were, more often than not, expected not to bother anyone. But this is seldom the case today. Once he realised how green I was, there was not a sudden remark based on the thought that his work had just doubled, but instead the endearing remark that he would support me one hundred per cent, come in when required, especially when I was on call and so teach me the ropes. It felt good to be in such safe hands, training for the job that I'd coveted all of my life.

The Consultant asked me what part of the UK I came from and when I said London, he went on to comically remark, "Yes, a bit sunnier down there." I had just come from the South, where most of the registrars that I came across were white, very middle-class, some incredibly self-confident, possessed an infinite air of superiority with the habit of making juniors from other specialties feel like rubbish on occasion with belittling gestures at every conceivable opportunity. I wondered at that moment whether I should do the same. But this felt incorrect especially with my immigrant roots and past recollections as well as being educated at schools with persons of a humbler background. I had to demonstrate that I'm a registrar, I can do the job, and was also able to detect, as well as correct, erroneous decisions a few people may make. It didn't seem like the best way forward, but maybe it was what was expected of me. I didn't really expect there to be any problems as I have already showed that I could operate in other posts. I'm sure my operating ability, while fresh, would again come through. I felt I could manage with the six years ahead of me, after which time I would just need to pass the exit exam, publish some papers, possibly achieve a higher degree and maybe even some notice by my peers before consultant-hood.

The job got off to a slow start. Any new post relies on developing confidence in a different hospital, as well as with your boss. I was very happy. I spent more time seeing patients on the ward and in the emergency room than actually operating. You may think that this is not the best way to train a surgeon? But knowing what to clinically master before you operate, followed by the care required after surgery is unequivocally what makes a more learned surgeon. Most of the time whilst operating I now had the pleasure of being the first assistant. This enabled me to engage more in the procedure. I was still very green in terms of operating know-how, so couldn't undertake major large bowel cases by myself, for example. It takes time to learn to operate and understand new procedures, as well as there being much theory to study.

One thing I quickly realised was that most of my juniors, the senior house officers, were of South Asian origin. Nearly all had come from overseas to work in the UK. Interestingly they were all older than I was. I realised I was still only twenty-eight years old, but most of these doctors were thirty plus. I therefore made a calculated decision to not tell them how old I was. Yes, I actually told porky pies about how old I was. I didn't want to disrespect them; they were lovely young aspiring surgeons, most of whom are consultants in their own right nowadays. I could probably operate to the same level as them at the time, but I had a slightly more privileged job with a clear career path that led to consultant-hood. I cannot actually remember how old I said I was, but I do remember probably adding another four years on to make out I was at least thirty-two. This made the me feel a lot better as I think if I actually told them how old I was I would have appeared a little bit too self-indulgent, probably thought of as a little pretender, someone that they actually didn't want to work for or with, and then they would be less inclined to help me when I needed them.

So I did play a little polite game as I just wanted to get on, be their equal in every sense of the word – be their friend. One thing you need to know about surgeons is that we can be a funny bunch even when training. We just want to operate all day long. We find it exciting. It's why we decided upon this job, which carries great responsibility and requires utmost quiet confidence. But the competition is fierce. Some will happily push people out of the way to undertake operations they want to do. Overall, I tried to create a solid relationship with my juniors. Being a registrar perhaps creates an ever-present barrier between you and other junior doctors, which I tried to alleviate with kindness, patience and humility.

My underlying approach of humility towards my immediate junior doctors worked. I was called only the second day whilst there by one of them struggling to pass a catheter into a large vein into the neck, called the subclavian vein. Although I was able to do this procedure, I had only undertaken it about half a dozen times with varying success. Now that I was the registrar it was assumed that I would be the one to show how it's done if they failed. I immediately told him not to worry and that I would scrub up and help. I introduced myself to the patient made sure the equipment there was as per required, and I asked my junior colleague to grab the patient's right hand gently and pull it in a downward direction alongside his flat body. I popped the needle in first time under the right collar bone, and blood came flashing back quickly. I passed a wire into the vein using the Seldinger technique, and I completed the procedure. I was quite relieved to say the least because it was my first real test as a new registrar. Even the anaesthetic doctors were watching me knowing that this is the person that they're going to have to work with the next year or so in this hospital. At that point the new registrar's face was permanently inscribed on me.

After a month or so of undertaking ward rounds, seeing patients, examining, examining, examining, with some operating, my boss took me into his room and said we needed to have a little chat.

He had a relaxed look about him. He wasn't angry or upset. He then turned round and said:

"I only get complaints about my foreign-looking doctors. If you're African or Asian, particularly African, the patients often don't like you. Know that that's nothing to do with you, you're doing a good job, but you just need to be aware that there's a bit of racial bigotry in this area."

He went on to say,

"I'll protect you as much as I can, but maybe try to tone down a little bit of the arrogance. You know that Southern accent you have doesn't help up here. You're not in London now."

Being brown and being a Southerner were the two topics he addressed. Being brown, he couldn't care less about it, being a Southerner wasn't my fault either. I actually felt relieved. I felt pleased that this conversation had taken place only a month or so into my job and that I was working with a wonderful consultant whom I still remember and feel affection for to this day. I felt comforted that I didn't have to pretend to be someone I wasn't. I could relax, be more friendly, be more polite than some of my registrars of old. Finally, I thought that this non-conformist that I had become in mainstream society wasn't my fault at all – with the racial prejudice that followed me everywhere as a child then as a young adult, was not confined to every *Angrezi*, but some actually admitted that it was out there! Any arrogance from the South was slowly ebbing away from me. It has to a degree gone completely, but I remain confident of my ability with some modesty – OK come on, I'm not perfect! When I speak to someone, I do sound a little bit different from a Northerner, but I don't mind that, that's who I am, so most people can spot that I'm from down South originally. They never hold it against you, not up North anyway. The other way around I cannot say, but I reckon it's the same in the South as London is a true depiction of a worldly as well as a cosmopolitan society. To conclude I can't lose my accent, just alter it when needed.

This chapter in my life made me realise that the jump from junior doctor to registrar which is in effect the main middle-grade position, was fraught not only with intensity but uncertainty. There is to a degree some preparation for this moment, yet you are in fact the same person but have only just changed your job title. Call it a promotion, but it is at least three steps on a career ladder taken all at once, signifying to others that you can do more, much more. These days when I speak to some of my new registrars, I do ask them what level or grade they are at. This is important so I can gauge where they are up to in terms of their technical abilities and how often they will ask me for help and advice. To be honest, it does not matter how old or experienced you are as you always need advice, and the best doctors are the ones that realise this.

One of the lovely nurses at this time in my career asked me, "Do you know why we are so nice and friendly up North?"

"No, I don't."

"It's because we're nosey!"

As a consultant today, I also try to delve into other interests and traits of my trainees in terms of 'who they are'. If they have a foreign or non-British accent, I generally wait a little while to see what they are like as a person, try to get to know them, to see if they need my help, or not at all, irrespective of where their accent is from, and I never put them into an ethnic box. I find it fascinating to learn where they may have trained as doctors and how long they've been in this country, what their aspirations and dreams are. It was my first consultant as a registrar who taught me how to do this well. We all have to stop and learn, move on and make our own mark on society.

One of the biggest pleasures I had was taking my more junior surgical trainees through the operation I was once taught, the appendicectomy, a landmark operation to this day. However, the technique that I used to undertake in this procedure in the early to mid-nineties has evolved into a keyhole operation. No doubt it will change again, with robotics increasingly taking over. However, we still must learn to control the robot and keep up with the natural progression of the use of technology in the evolution of surgical practice. There are and will always be some cynics out there that believe that technology has gone as far as it can in surgery. But I imagine that in twenty years or so, eighty to ninety per cent of operations will be undertaken either by using robotic methods, or small instruments through even smaller incisions than we use today. I can say this for my own specialty and I'm sure other specialties are moving in the same direction. I'm proud to be part of that advancing process.

Chapter Ten

— Chicago — We are going to America!

The Atlanta airport immigration officer asked me to go into a room not far from the main immigration counter, my passport in a transparent plastic folder with a red border. I was dumbfounded and gave him a confused look.

"Excuse me?" I asked.

"You just need to go in there, Sir."

This was not a request but an order. I felt so insecure, almost guilty of committing an atrocious crime, of which I was clearly innocent. I was really quite worried.

He was very quick with me, his decision so resolute that it would be impossible to imagine that he spent time deliberating this verdict. It is also very difficult for me to describe him in words. He was, as I have already said, a bit chubby and had grey curly hair, but I also saw by his name that he was possibly of Italian descent. I couldn't really understand what his problem was. He did not fingerprint me as us Brits were exempt from this part of the vetting process at that time. He didn't say many words, just stared at my passport and then looked at his 'bright' screen. So, in retrospect, as I have said, any decision he had come to had already been made. He didn't even ask me why I was coming into the country; he didn't give a hoot as to who I was, he just saw my face, brown skin or was it my Muslim first name and decided that he didn't like one of those? He may have even used his small brain to try and work out my weird surname? I guess he probably thought, "I don't know what that's all about, but he looks weird, so we need to shake the bastard down!"

I approached the room, opened the door and walked inside. Immediately to the left there was a large counter with at least four immigration officers. There was a tray with transparent envelopes stacked up neatly on the desk, but these had yellow borders, whereas mine had a red one, which meant that it was promptly put onto a separate pile where only a few such envelopes were stacked; which seemed ominous to me. Why, I wondered, are the yellow ones so many and the red ones so few? After some mental readjustments, I began to realise that this 'red' pile must have been for the highly dangerous detainees. Yes, I use the word 'detainee' as this is what I and everyone in this room were. The yellow was a quick interrogation with red requiring a separate room with a more detailed debrief!

My first thought was that I clearly would not be carrying on with the rest of my journey. I would probably have to stay somewhere overnight while whatever issue it was achieved resolution, or worse still, they'd fly me back to the UK. I thought about how I would explain this to colleagues at the medical conference and the suspicion of no-smoke-without-fire that would haunt me professionally if I disclosed this situation. The reputational damage could be immense, especially for someone working on the frontline in healthcare with lives in their hands, and expecting the highest levels of due diligence and trust.

When I looked around the room, it was full of Arabs, Africans, people of East Indian origin and very few *Angrezis*. It was like a congregation of developing nations from the United Nations all turning up for handouts from the International Monetary Fund. I began to wonder if the abhorrent subjugations we read of in history such as slavery, as well as the Holocaust, must have felt like this, with a quick sieving of humans based on colour, race or religion. These two examples are the most devastating as well as horrifying ones that I can think of as I write this – gosh, I thought, we still have a long way to go as a species. As I sat down, I thought that perhaps I should text my wife to see if I would make my connecting flight. She replied and said that if I missed my intended one, I would have to wait until the next morning, meaning I would miss a large chunk of the conference schedule. Nevertheless, I thought, I'd better sit it out as there was nothing I could do or say. So I started reading my book on Thomas Cromwell set in Tudor times, a thoroughly corrupt moment in British history which I found riveting.

London 2001

"What was it like growing up in India, Dad, when you were a boy, do you remember?"

"It was Delhi in the 1930s. It was hot, and when it rained, we all danced in the street. When we saw Angrezi soldiers we used to follow them and try to touch their white skin as it glistened and stood out. We were told by our parents and grandparents that we could never look like that, never look so graceful, never look so pure, serene and wonderful. We knew our place, this is where we were." Ten years later the cries of *'Inqilab'* sent one million people to their graves, with the country divided into two, labelled as enemies forever.

★ ★ ★

In 2002, I was undertaking research in cancer studies at one of the finest cancer hospitals in the UK. I submitted the main results of my research to the American Society of Colon and Rectal Surgeons (ASCRS) as my work involved looking at using gene therapy to target a special protein marker of bowel cancer called Carcinoembryonic Antigen (better known as CEA). I was awarded an oral presentation, which meant that I had to be there in person to deliver my data to a learned international audience of surgeons.

Presenting your work at an international meeting was an accepted and coveted prize as not everyone managed this feat, but where the actual meeting itself takes place carries weight. There is a subtle hierarchy. Securing an oral presentation, especially at an American meeting, was high up on the academic ladder and regarded as a possible career-changing event, a larger-than-life box ticked, with the next turn of one's chapter turning three pages at once. It also had the potential to set you aside from your contemporaries by some margin.

It was June 2002, in the windy city of Chicago. The oral scientific presentation I was granted involved an earlier competitive vetting process. Being successful was a big deal. The flight across the Atlantic was easy enough, from Manchester direct to Chicago. As a Brit, at this time, I breezed through security, was welcomed by their immigration officers (yes, nice to see), not by music or a band, but I did sail into the US. Why wouldn't I, you could ask yourself? I am from across the 'pond' a citizen of the US's closest ally, I like to think a reasonable model citizen, with no criminal record, not even speeding points or any parking tickets at that time. As a surgeon (Americans call us physicians, which I actually prefer), a professional person the Americans hold in high regard, I faced no interrogation or suspicion. It was only the second time I was going to the states, but this was post 9-11. I didn't think of 9-11 at the time, or that it might cause me some difficulties in the US especially with a Muslim name. George W Bush was President and life in the US for me as a foreigner did not seem any different.

I arrived by airport shuttle at the hotel without undue hassle. I couldn't stay at the main conference hotel as it was, again, way too expensive for my junior doctor's allowance. The first day of the conference was fascinating, and I was learning a great deal already. That was followed by a big dinner, with a live band and lots of food from around the world. I was by myself, so I sat at a table alone but was swiftly joined by some Americans. They took one look at me, said hello in a congenial and familiar manner, sat alongside me and greeted me as Amit. It was only after they sat down, and heard me speak that they said, "Oh, you're not Amit? Our resident from India?" I saw the funny side of it and now I had some company to enjoy. Slowly more friends of Amit turned up, greeted me, one even patted me on the back and said, "Hiya big boy." Again, when they all sat down, they were shocked that it was not quite Amit at the table, just a lookalike. I never actually met the infamous Amit, who may actually have been sitting by himself somewhere, which is where perhaps I should have been? But if he truly was a big boy, I'm sure he would have found something or someone to be getting along with?

7th June was fast approaching, when I was due to give my talk in the afternoon. I had some time to spare in the morning and decided to watch the first half of England's football game in my hotel room. It was the world cup in Japan. The game was at the Sapporo Dome and it was against Argentina. It was just before halftime, with England winning a penalty kick. Beckham lined up and scored, straight down the middle. I screamed "YESSSS!" in my hotel room while watching Fox sports. The high spirits I was in really helped calm my own nerves about the looming presentation.

I caught a taxi over to the conference venue to take my seat in the large auditorium, hosting at least one thousand physicians. My talk was billed as second on the run order. Before me, a well-groomed young Korean surgeon was giving his presentation in broken English. He stumbled through his talk. He had obviously memorised by rote what he had to say for each slide. It was based on a large randomised controlled trial, which is the preferred type of research if you want your data to have any real credibility. The reach of his study alone meant that I was not surprised he was speaking. After his presentation, he was asked questions by the audience. This part mattered, as it tells the audience how well you have read around your subject. But answering questions was another game altogether.

"Was your study adequately powered to answer your hypothesis?" asked a learned member of the audience, undoubtedly an eminent American physician.

The chair of the session arduously repeated this question to him in pidgin English.

"Yes, it was randomised," he replied.

"Actually, I didn't ask that," the audience member chipped back in. There was a shuffling in seats and audible sighs as the chair of this session tried to help, while another member of the audience decided to interject with some sign language. Another completely different question was met with the same answer.

"Yes it was randomised." It made me realise what an advantage the Anglosphere has at such international meetings, ours being the lingua franca of the world, meaning we can fully relax, certain of our grasp of our native language.

My turn was next, and they called out my name. At American meetings, they call you 'Doctor' which I enjoyed. I hadn't heard the title for quite some time. I was sitting about halfway along the very large auditorium. I probably should have sat closer to the front knowing that I was going to speak, but this was my first big presentation and I had felt reticent about being too assertive or too conspicuous. The large audience waited in stilted silence as I walked to the stage, praying I would not fall up the steps, as no doubt the crowd would forget about your scientific presentation and all they'd remember is that last bloody step you took. I made it to the lectern where a microphone was angled in front of a screen you could glance at to see your own slides as they came up, which saves you turning around to look at the big screen behind. It was hot up there. Stifling. Vivid bright lights beamed down on the stage. I thanked the chair and the audience for the invitation to speak and sensed a ripple of relief when the audience noted a native English accent. One can only imagine, phew, they must have thought, someone they can understand easily – but to be fair, my Korean colleague had a very nice presentation, good data with nice slides, but he clearly had memorised what he was going to say for each slide in English, so that was about it for him as he could not predict the questions leaving him exposed with his rudimentary grasp of English horribly disclosed.

My talk was well-rehearsed. I had already presented it back in the UK at two sought-after conferences, but unfortunately, did not manage to make a shortlist for a prestigious medal called the Moynihan prize. This was a medal named after another famous British surgeon from the late nineteenth century. Some of the surgical instruments that we still use today also carry his name. Lord Moynihan is still highly thought of as a great surgical innovator of his time. My presentation went well, with the delivery as perfect as I could have hoped for. The bright light trained on my face ensured that I could not make eye contact with the sea of faces in the audience looking up at me. I probably should thank David Beckham for being so relaxed, so if he reads this book, I guess I can ask him to come over to my place for a nice cup of tea, bit of *gupshup* (light conversation), no social media, no tweets and I won't even offer him a hernia repair, which I would do for free anyway.

It was time for the audience cross-examination following my presentation. One question I recalled very well indeed – why had I not taken a tumour sample from the original bowel cancer rather than from its spread to the liver? I explained that the liver metastases sample was clean and uncontaminated, and so didn't need purification. Then I added I was more importantly working for a liver surgeon, so I had no choice. The answer spurred a pleasant chuckle from the now more attentive audience. I felt good, the chair looked to his right at me and smiled as I left the stage with haste to dash to the business centre of the hotel to find out what the final England score was on the internet. We had won 1-0 against Argentina. I finished up the day attending more talks before spending the evening in a jazz bar in downtown Chicago with a friend from Manchester as neither of us could afford to go to the black-tie congress dinner. You must be thinking that my budget for this meeting was based on a consumption of bread and water. To be fair, I could have been more extravagant, but a moral consciousnesses always sprung to my mind knowing that I did not want to seem profligate, especially as my clinical supervisor back home was so obliging.

The next morning when I woke up, I again weighed up whether to take a taxi to the conference or save my pennies by catching a bus. When I walked into the foyer of the conference centre, a few guests recognised me and called me over.

"Are you the British guy from Manchester?" I said yes. They informed me that I had won a prestigious scientific prize called the Durand Smith MD award for the best oral scientific presentation. I could not believe it. This was a major coup for me. A much sought-after international prize for research, and at an American meeting. A major boost for my growing surgical CV. If you have seen the film *Shawshank Redemption* or In *Pursuit of Happyness* then this was a moment of intoxicating delight similar to the end of those films. To win such an award, you need a bit of luck as well as making your own luck. The luck on my side was the energised state of mind having been uplifted by England leading against and then finally beating Argentina, as well as perhaps the speaker before me not being as conversant in the English language, leaving me an apt moment to talk the talk. My own luck was that I had completed a very scientific and purposeful project. The science in my thesis is used to help patients with bowel cancer and advanced ocular melanoma to this day. I had to pinch myself as this was an established international prize at an 'American' meeting which does carry weight.

I don't regret or begrudge the certitude that US meetings carry; the Americans are undertaking some of the best research that we have to date and they're incredibly forward thinking with arms reaching out galvanising advances in technology from every corner of our globe.

I received a large plaque in the post some months later, alongside a certificate with a $500 cheque. I cannot thank colleagues from the US enough for this award. The prize made me a marked man for much coveted jobs back home. My take-home from this conference was resoundingly that America is a great country, full of objectivity, intelligence and drive that rewarded hard work and effort, regardless of where you came from.

I end this chapter like the last with a feel-good moment. As I said before, these do not come around often, so when they do you must hold on to them for as long as you can. Yes, I did gloat when I got home with my so-called friends also showing extreme levels of ecstasy, so much so they disappeared completely from my life, albeit temporarily!

I guess like Andy Dufresne, I had already crawled through enough shit but this time came out clean at the end.

Chapter Eleven

– Surgical blood, bile and bowel contents – What size gloves would you like?

On watching the immigration officers, they were very relaxed. It was as if they knew that they were about to finish work soon and had a nice cold beer waiting for them. They also each wore a badge and held a gun, a bit like Steve Mcgarrett from *Hawaii 5-0* but without the quiff. I always wondered where those men canoeing at the end were actually going as it seemed a long way away, which is where I was right now, from home, in this room. One officer appeared to be scoping out everyone. It was bit like watching Arnold Schwarzenegger in *Terminator* just moving his head from side to side and generally taking readings to look for any imminent danger.

Maybe they had this magic eye which sent information back to Langley. I was on edge but kept trying to put my nerves out of my mind, as my perspiration increased. I kept telling myself this would be OK, but I didn't really know how the situation would unfold. Only time would tell, but I didn't have a huge amount of time on my hands, especially if I was going to make the all-important connecting flight. I felt uneasy at being detained. I looked across again at the immigration officers. They obviously had little say in who was brought in by their colleagues from the immigration desks outside, but there appeared to be a general theme of the type of person coming into this room. I've never actually worn South Asian regalia or Middle Eastern dress. I don't think it particularly suits me and I have no interest in it. But I was one of the few people of my ethnicity in Western clothes in this room. Surely as a powerful and rich world leading nation, the US should know who they are looking for on such screens? The immigration officer outside, however, had taken one look at me and immediately put my passport in an envelope. He didn't even ask me who I was, why I had come to the US or where I had been.

Summer, Empty London Car Park, 1980

My brothers and I often played cricket with some of our neighbours in an abandoned car park behind where we used to live. It was a great place to play any sport, as there were rarely any cars parked leaving a generous open space to knock a ball about in. That day, we had a new bat as our previous one had been stolen by a gang of boys. It didn't really matter who these boys were, they were just bad boys, and bad boys seem to have an innate sixth sense to pick on an easy target such as we were.

As we were playing, two police officers slowly started walking towards us, and then when they were very close, stopped and started watching. We carried on playing and then one of them, the shorter of the two, said, "We will field."

Excellent, I thought. Pity the bat-stealing thugs weren't here to see us play with the power of law enforcement. My brother asked if they would like to bowl and bat as well. One of us hit the ball with such vigour it traversed a perimeter fence into a building site next door. The policemen efficiently scoped the place to see if there was anyone in, as it was clearly locked. It was a Sunday and the sun's sudden movement to the horizon made us aware that it was getting late. One of them said, "I think I can jump over this wall," and did, salvaging our ball so we could continue playing. That day, we felt like Kings.

★ ★ ★

Have you ever wondered what it is like to train a surgeon? The notion that it is all pure, serene, with an artful display to repair the human body, is a misconception. I like to think that training to reach the high levels of an operating ability required to safely fix a sick individual carries such precision that it is like preparing a spacecraft. It takes time, resilience, confidence and ingenuity, years of work to hone precise technical skills. But with the subject of study being the human patient, it necessarily demands modesty and empathy, too. I was trained by many surgeons, to some of whom I owe a lot, and to some of whom I owe absolutely nothing. But it led me to believe something. Even with hundreds of hours of educational investment, surgeons are by nature different from most other medics. There is something inherent to the character of one who pursues such a profession that seems idiosyncratic to surgery, leading me to believe:

"Surgeons are born – not created"
Aali J Sheen 2021

Whilst training to be a surgeon, every six months or year, you have to move to a different hospital. One year I moved to a hospital and while visiting the HR Department, which is a normal and customary formality on the first day of any new placement, the young haphazardly dressed *Angrezi* medical staffing officer asked me for my visa and work permit. I was absolutely stunned.
"What makes you think I need a visa or work permit?"
"Well *you* do in order to work here."
"I've never been asked that question before in my entire life."
"Well now *you need a visa* and work permit to work here."
"Why do you think I need a visa?"
"Where you from?"
"I'm from London, originally though, Mancunian now though."
"Are you British?"
"Yes, but how many Londoners do you know that are not British?"
"Well, you don't need one then!"
"What makes you think I needed one in the first place?"
No answer was forthcoming. A mere momentary glare in my direction with an obviously uncomfortable silence that followed. Our surreal conversation ended with his indignant resignation that I did not have or now need a visa and work permit. When I came home, I informed my wife, and she was thoroughly appalled. She asked me to complain to the hospital, who *eventually* contacted me to tell me they had put it down purely to education. I actually went on to complain to the postgraduate dean, and now some nineteen years later I'm still waiting for her to reply!
What next you ask? Over the years, I have gone on to train many surgeons myself, all of differing backgrounds, ethnicities, gender and sexual orientation. None of these personal characteristics

make a blind bit of difference as to how good a surgeon is or will become. Some can operate, others can't. It is still possible though to guide the ones that 'struggle' to a level where they can improve and be safe to then be signed off as competent surgeons. They may not be the innovators who will try new operations or craft an ingenious technique with novel instrumentation. But so long as they are safe and competent, that is all that matters. There are some though that are beyond cure.

But it is those that think they're good when they're not that get themselves into trouble. You only have to glance at various newspaper articles or disciplinary proceedings to find them. I don't feel sorry for them but do believe many have been let down by a system that didn't allow them to have their faults ironed out or redirected them down a different career pathway in medicine. You don't have to be able to operate to be a great doctor. Most of my friends and associates are non-surgeons. They're absolutely brilliant doctors and excellent at what they do.

With each year of my own training, I became more accomplished, largely due to the accumulating experience I was gaining, and still am to this day, a learning process which will go on until the day I retire. I must add that I unashamedly admit, albeit proudly, to have learnt from my trainees as well as more junior consultants – this can only be good for both you and your patients. There is only one consultant more senior than I in my department and I do look to his experience when required, but also take counsel from all my colleagues. Your training as a surgeon yields experience, so once you have removed a piece of bowel, the next time it will be easier. In training, all surgeons undoubtedly at some point face difficulties, but this is where experience comes into play. All healthcare systems need to recognise that it is experience that matters.

After almost six years of training, one of my last nights on call was memorable, to say the least. I felt that I had actually achieved something significant that night. No one can describe to you the job satisfaction that you experience while working as a surgeon or any healthcare professional, but I can't take all the credit for myself for such nights like this – I give credit to my trainers and this chapter is dedicated to them.

It was a Friday night in a very large, busy hospital in the North of England. The weather had been unusually mild for the time of year, so I was expecting a busy night; when it pours with rain or in heavy snow it's customarily quieter. I was the registrar on call with little or no action until around 5 o'clock in the evening. Friday nights are notorious providers of inadvertent as well as unpredictable events in hospitals with this night on call being no different. Reading this you will not be surprised to know that of all the on call days, a Friday remains one of the most difficult times to swap for another day of the week. All that was lined up was an appendicectomy on a twenty-one-year-old female who was an aspiring dancer. She asked me about keyhole surgery. I said that in my hospital, at present, it was not practised, but I would see what I could arrange for her. I was very lucky to find, on entering the operating theatre, one of the nursing sisters with whom I had developed a good rapport. I explained to her the situation, to which she asked if I had ever used this technique before. I said yes, in a few other hospitals, but at this time, using keyhole surgery to remove the appendix was not fashionable or deployed by many surgeons, it was still early 2005. A decade later it would become normal practice. We discussed what I needed; a few small ports and a little bag with which we normally removed gallbladders via keyhole surgery. When I informed the patient that it was a go, she was delighted.

We got her up to the theatre quite quickly. But, while the patient was in the anaesthetic room, something happened. I received a call from the resus room, which is where ambulances bring critical patients to the accident and emergency department. I was told a major trauma was coming in. The patient had a flail chest – bad rib fractures – and was in breathing difficulties with a possible fractured pelvis too.

My brain started working overtime. I had to get the young female patient off the operating table quickly, but safely. As the registrar on call with only a relatively junior senior house officer, I needed to make haste. The young lady was wheeled in, we made all the necessary checks, she was painted and draped (the term we use to describe preparing the patient's skin with antiseptic, after which we apply sterile drapes to keep the operating area clean). I made a small hole in the belly button to put the first port in. With this, using a camera, I could reach the appendix to observe that it was a bit fat, clearly inflamed with pus, but without too much widespread contamination meaning that I could surgically remove it quickly without much fuss. The next two ports went in at lightning speed. I managed to lift the appendix up, snare it with a special loop or pre-tied stitch, took it off cleanly and popped it in the bag the way I had been taught, after which I zipped it out through the belly button wound. I then sucked out any pus and made sure everything was left tidy. All the wounds were sutured closed with lots of local anaesthetic to prevent the patient waking up in too much discomfort. Not all surgery for appendicitis goes as well as this, some can be very tricky; there may be lots of pus with an appendix stuck in the pelvis, with some requiring a much larger incision as performing a keyhole approach would not extricate the appendix safely enough. I was very grateful that this patient had a very nice keyhole operation in quick time, with small wounds, which would reduce the amount of pain killers she required. Her recovery was therefore quicker, but credit goes not to me but the scrub nurse. Without her support this would not have been possible. The patient could now re-train in her amazing chosen career as a dancer quicker than otherwise possible had I used a much larger incision.

I managed to complete the entire operation in less than twenty minutes. Excellent. Down we go to the AE department.

When I arrived, there was already one young man in, not breathing very well. He was strongly built, did not look too pale, was lying flat with a neck brace as per standard trauma protocol. He had an oxygen mask on, was demonstrating agonising breathing patterns and was clearly frightened as one would expect. I spoke to him, said hello, and introduced myself – I doubt he acknowledged me but I think, when patients hear the word surgeon and 'Mr' or 'Ms, Mrs, Miss', they may feel some comforting energy fall upon their bruised and painful bodies. I said that everything would be OK. This was an instinctive but clinical remark, perhaps brave to say at this moment, particularly as his entire bodily injuries were not known fully yet. However, from experience I judged him to be more than just salvageable. He had already undergone a chest X-ray, a simple and easy to interpret investigation that showed a complete whiteout on both sides. This is abnormal as air shows up as black on an X-ray, so a complete white-out means that there isn't much air in the lungs. The young doctor in casualty, whom I remember very well, was a white South African. Both of us examined the patient's chest and felt that he needed chest drains to remove fluid in both of his lungs, which was likely to be blood. Actually, the fluid wasn't in the lungs, but in what is called the pleural cavity, which is a balloon surrounding the lungs. This is why he was struggling with his breathing and the reason for the white-out on the chest X-ray. I asked the young doctor whether he could put it in a chest drain, assuming it was a stupid question really as medics from South Africa had likely seen their fair share of trauma. He said yes, so I asked him to put one in on one side while I put one in on the other. We took a side each, made slight incisions with lots of anaesthetic while administering morphine to the patient to help him to relax. He was also on some oxygen and we had an anaesthetist managing him at the top end. As I was making the incision, making my way down to the ribs, I looked across and noted the young South African doctor had already put his chest drain in. He was now setting up the underwater seal drain. There was lots of blood coming out, which was a good sign as it showed we had made the right decision. I was impressed by how quick he was, as he was also at least ten years my junior. This patient went off after his breathing had settled to have a CAT scan of his head and neck, chest, abdomen and pelvis, in order to see if there was any damage to his spine or any internal organs.

My immediate junior then called with an air of anxiety in her voice. This is always an alarm bell when you have an excellent junior doctor working with you. If they feel compelled to call you with concerns about a patient, it generally means that there's something seriously wrong. I asked what the matter was. She went on to say that there was a patient on the orthopaedic ward who had suffered a fractured hip which had been repaired only six days ago, but that today they were presenting with a very tender belly. I asked her what she thought might be going on. It was a case of a possible perforated bowel, she remarked, but a CAT scan had been undertaken. I was relieved that a scan had already been undertaken as this would save me time in making a diagnosis. I decided I had better go and see. The patient was a very tough, fit woman judging by her past history and normal daily activities, despite being about eight-five years old. She was very polite and a no-nonsense person who clearly had huge respect for our profession as well as being the stalwart person in her immediate family – a typical matriarch. Her family were anxiously congregated in the relatives' waiting room. Even her great grandchildren were there. Once I saw the patient, she appeared very fragile in places, with a mustard complexion but notably bellowing that her movement was limited by her abdominal pain with her very bad smelling breath called *foetor oris* medically – a sign that something is amiss, with a possible perforated viscus inside her belly or even crippling appendicitis. I examined the CAT scan images which were nicely tucked under her bed, thereby saving us at times an unnecessary and laborious task of searching for them in the bowels of the radiology department.

Once having carefully inspected these films, a mandatory conversation followed with the Consultant Radiologist on call. "Looks liked a perforated diverticular disease of a thickened segment of left sided colon, but a possible malignancy cannot be excluded as the bowel is so thickened," he went on to say. I made the decision that we needed to operate to remove the piece of bowel which had perforated. Faecal matter was building up internally, making her sick. Without an operation, she simply would not get better. I had a quick conversation with the consultant on call who gave clearance to go ahead, knowing that I was able to undertake the operation by myself. My anaesthetic colleagues raised concerns over whether the patient was maybe too frail to undergo the surgery, but I was confident she would be fine. The Anaesthetic Registrar, whom I'd known a long time, said to crack on as he made the same clinical call as me. At the age of eighty-five years with a good quality of life and fitness, it suggested that her physiological resilience would help her, with more than a slim chance of making it through – her family agreed, but were also made aware of all the risks including death or a stroke after surgery in view of her age. Making decisions like this back then, which were mostly based on clinical acumen, did allow experience to come into play. Now, almost fifteen years later, we have to jump through more and more hoops to get anything done.

In the meantime, I went to check on how the young patient with fluid on the lungs was faring in the CAT scan room. The investigation revealed he had a smashed-up spleen. While he was OK for now, if his blood pressure did not improve, I would need to take out his spleen too.

A certain amount of time had already elapsed and the patient was relatively stable, so I could wait an hour to assess how he was progressing. I once again spoke to my consultant who was at home. He instructed me to wait a few hours to see if his blood pressure dropped again especially while giving him intravenous fluids, as well as blood. If so, I was to remove the spleen. "I'll catch you later," he concluded before terminating the phone call.

Back upstairs we were almost ready to take out the perforated bowel of the elderly female patient. In such cases it is usually the left side of the colon that perforates. The operation usually requires bringing the loop of the bowel out into the abdominal wall, with the patient ending up with a colostomy bag or stoma for the rest of their lives. This is indeed what I found. In such an operation, the most important part is removing any contamination from the patient's abdominal cavity. The anaesthetist is trained to recognise a sudden drop in blood pressure brought on by septicaemia, poison in the blood taking over, causing the patient's heart rate to increase. Stabilising the blood pressure often requires powerful medication, which she was already on. You have to be quick to remove the toxins, then clamp the bowel followed by the careful extraction of the section that's perforated, which goes into a bucket and off to the pathology lab for someone to examine under a microscope to make sure, mainly, that there's no cancer in it. The clean end of the bowel is brought out to fashion into a stoma; again, the most important part here is to check its blood supply is intact as the last complication you need is for it to look black and near 'dead' only a few days later only for another operation to ensue. The procedure is completed with a drain (plastic hollow tube) left in the pelvis as this is where pus can collect. The operation was done.

Most of these patients do very well indeed if their bodies have been able to manage the sepsis in the bloodstream. After the operation, I went back to the relatives' waiting room. By now, the number of relatives had multiplied to about fourteen. It was approaching midnight, and they had stayed through the night. The congregated crowd looked very tired indeed but expressed gratitude for what I had been able to do. Her daughter hugged me. I actually don't mind a degree of tactility with relatives. A hug can actually help to bring adrenaline levels down, helping you to again feel human, which is, after all, what you are, regardless of what you have to face in the operating theatre.

The histology lab results a few weeks later showed that what I removed was actually a piece of bowel containing within it a cancer. This had perforated so the prognosis was poor, and she subsequently required some chemotherapy which she duly managed to have, despite her age. I lost touch with her after this as I was appointed Consultant, and so moved on to another hospital, where I am today. But a few years later she developed spread from the original bowel cancer to her liver, called a metastasis, and this was an area I now specialised in. Patients have a knack of finding you and cling onto you like glue especially if you have served them well and she promptly managed to get a referral to see me as a consultant with a small tumour (metastasis) in her liver. Interestingly, I only recalled her case after she reminded me. I am therefore relieved to report that at the grand old age of eighty-seven years, I managed to remove a small piece of her liver very safely by a new specialised keyhole technique, one that I have promoted since then. It is uncanny how this patient remembered me and forged a link as many do.

Time was pressing on. It was now about two o'clock in the morning and I still hadn't managed to get any sleep. The young man with the ruptured spleen was not faring very well. His blood pressure kept going down, so both the anaesthetist and I decided we had to see him and concluded that the spleen needed to be removed. Today, there are other various measures that we can undertake to try to prevent removing the spleen in a trauma situation. But this was the only option I had at this time, so back to the operating theatre I went. Removing the spleen is something that I had undertaken only a few times before. It is usually a last-resort operation to save a life from horrendous internal bleeding, commonly as a result of trauma to the abdomen. The trouble with this organ is that it is tucked quite high up in the left side of the tummy, under the rib cage. It can be especially difficult to access in a larger patient. As the surgeon, it is your responsibility to decide what incision you're going to use. You must take into account where the injury is, in this case the spleen, with the mindfulness of the possibility of damaging nearby organs such as the stomach as well as the pancreas, or the left kidney, which is not too far away either. I decided to use what's called a 'rooftop' incision, well not quite a full one, which is known as an extended left subcostal. Prior to this decision, another quick call to my boss was mandatory. The patient wasn't desperately small, so I needed all the room I could muster to get into this space. I managed to source all the surgical kit I required. This is where your scrub staff become your asset. I decided to wear a headlamp. This was unusual, especially among the surgeons I had been working for in this hospital. Such a headlamp was difficult to come by, but we managed. I moved the colon out of the way. There was lots of blood in the abdomen, which had to be removed first by packing large swabs into the area of damage to control the bleeding. I persisted before finally finding what I had been looking for, clamping the big blood vessels as I found them, before the spleen was ready to come out, albeit in a piecemeal fashion as it was smashed.

It's an amazing feeling when you finally accomplish this feat, as most, if not all, the bleeding automatically stops. There's a little bit of ooze, which you need to take time in controlling, but that's about it. I was indescribably relieved as, at one point, the bleeding was so much that I had started to worry about needing to call my boss at home to come in and rescue the situation. All the years of training, surgical experience, reading books, of sitting exam after exam, are designed to prepare you for this moment. If I had been in a desperate situation where the bleeding was *bad*, there were certain protocols to follow to basically stop the bleeding and save the patient's life, giving the surgeon the option of being able to come back and fight another day. Even now as a senior consultant, we must be prepared to ask for help. I will call a colleague to seek assistance at a drop of a hat. Patient safety is what matters, one's ego can take a hike.

The night did not end there. One can only fully relax at least a day after such a night on call. You do go home in the morning, but the adrenaline streaming through your circulation prevents you from sleeping for at least a few hours. I had to go and see a patient with quite an advanced cancer. My aim was to speak to both the patient and his family to pass on the traumatic news that they were going to die. This is one of the hardest aspects of the professional life of a doctor, facing the enemy: Death. There is nothing more you can do for the patient. They are already on morphine, the cancer has left few organs spared, they are in pain, most likely hallucinating, they may not have eaten at all for weeks or months and are less than half the size they once were despite artificial nutritional support. A macabre sense of fear can come over you – and still does to this day some twenty-eight years after I finished med school. But you must tell them that we would not call out the arrest team when their heart stops. I cannot imagine a more undignified end, with your body being pounded on the chest, while powerful drugs are being pushed into your body to try to kick start the heart. These are difficult decisions, but as doctors we have to make them. But we do not take them lightly or make them in isolation. At this moment I found my cadence of language, a learned style of empathy as well as professionalism towards a patient and a family about to enter the state of bereavement. We must make them all understand as best as possible using a layman's terms that their life is nearing the end. No quantity of drugs, chemotherapy or experimental treatment is going to save them, so we need to make sure that nature takes its course, with the utmost respect for their dying body as well as their final moments with their family. No matter how many times you say these words, your body loses its spark temporarily and any joy you feel in your work ebbs away. As a doctor, you have no choice but to distance yourself from any emotional attachments to a dying patient as much as possible – but this is near impossible and it always hurts.

I had experienced many similar on-calls during my training years, but this was an on call that I would never forget. I imagine that the present cohort of junior doctors and nurses still do well. The insurmountable dedication any doctor in training must try to assign to his or her chosen field is valued most when the knowledge gained will help save someone's life in the future. As a consultant you can become quite sheltered from the direct patient care and familial interaction aspect of the job. I always bear in mind that I must support my junior colleagues and other health professionals in such circumstances. However, it only takes a moment of brain activity to dig deep into our past training to fathom or decipher a remedy to aid our trainees. If I didn't have a team of people around helping me, none of the lifesaving or life-altering procedures I carry out would be possible. It is always a team effort.

At this juncture I will recount to you some lighter moments during my years as a junior surgical trainee. In 1995 as a casualty officer whilst working in a hospital in inner city London, I was observing that the delightful cleaning lady wearing rather splendidly her dismal green NHS cleaner's outfit, was working at a snail's pace whilst mopping the rather extensive floor. It was two o'clock in the morning, incredibly quiet, and I didn't have any patients to see – a comforting rarity that all doctors and other professionals enjoy – so I decided to put my stethoscope down, take the mop off her hands and get cracking. I have to say, I think I was managing quite well. I recall this moment quite well as I had frequented several Prince concerts. This often left me in high spirits during this stage of my career. A very short while later as I was cleaning this large creamy, vinyl-clad floor, a rather large, frankly obese Pakistani gentleman came in wearing his *Kurta Pyjama*. He nonchalantly walked past me giving all but a fleeting gaze. I noticed that he was a tad breathless as well as clutching his chest. All the same he did manage to walk to a bay area unaided. The nurse quickly triaged him and asked me to have a look at him as a patient with suspected chest pain having a possible heart attack.

I promptly asked him some very clinically orientated questions; I believe I clearly identified who I was, read his ECG (electrical heart tracing), took some blood tests after which I promptly sent him for a chest X-ray. I even examined his heart sounds with a stethoscope. I recall from memory that his heart was making all the right noises. When he came back from X-ray, briskly I might add, as they were quiet too, I went to speak to him.

"I don't think you're having a heart attack, but we may need to keep an eye on you for twenty-four hours or so."

"When is the doctor going to come and see me?"

"I am the doctor."

"I thought you were the cleaner??"

A few months later in 1995 while still working in this very busy casualty department, there was a young man who had come in complaining of back pain. All we knew was that he previously had taken intravenous drugs. As I drew the curtains back, I saw that his body up to his hips was at the end of the trolley and in between his legs was standing a young lady. She appeared to have head movements going up and down. At the moment I drew the curtains back and walked in her head movements suddenly stopped. She covered up her 'client's' legs with a blanket. Even to the untrained eye her actions were obvious. When I stealthily approached, she had just crossed her arms in front of her with this ever so slight bulge underneath the blanket. The patient with back pain seemed frustrated. I said to them both,

"Why don't I come back in about five to ten minutes? Then you can tell me all about your back pain." I thought I should maybe tell my senior registrar, he just looked at me and said,

"Do you think he climaxed?"

When I recount these tales, I don't recall anyone saying to me that they would rather see an *Angrezi* doctor. I don't recall anyone saying to the nurse that they didn't want a 'curry-smelling' carer or questioning whether I spoke English well enough as a foreigner. So why are doctors of colour more likely to receive complaints and find themselves in the dock, with an over representation at the GMC hearings? Is this a mark of societal problems and an area where we must try to dispel bigotry or wrongly held common beliefs displacing objective reasoning?

I have to ask myself whether doctors like me are statistically more likely to suffer prejudicial treatment under draconian measures designed to weed out professionals guilty of misconduct or misrepresentation to their patients. If we have made the effort in educating ourselves, have become thoroughly accomplished in our fields and have also continued to mentor future trainees like everyone else, then what is left to cast doubt on our virtuosity? A doctor's success is nurtured and measured by their knowledge and skill. Not by their reflection in the mirror.

All health care professionals are charged with the protection of the health and well-being of others, but why are BAMEs not provided with a caring and above all sympathetic civility with simply a 'benefit of doubt'?

To end this chapter, it would be a good idea to relate a very interesting event. In 2009 I was asked to be on an interview panel where we were to select suitable candidates for senior surgical training posts in England and Wales. I was paired up with a nice *Angrezi* colleague of mine. We also had a lay person with us to make sure we were fair. I think bringing in a non-medic created a more impartial approach to choosing our future surgeons. In between candidates, whilst talking to this layperson, I discovered that she was a retired teacher who now sat on GMC fitness-to-practise panels. For some unknown reason she relayed to us the fact that most of the doctors are 'Indian or Pakistani, but definitely foreign, they're atrocious'. She went on to use more unpalatable words with a conclusion that, "It's ridiculous what they're getting up to."

I was astonished that she put such remarks in this way. We later had a young Asian doctor; he was British born but he had a stutter. He was clearly nervous and when I asked him a question, he stuttered. It wasn't just a stutter, but more of a complete inability to articulate the simplest of words in one sentence. I leaned forward and made a sign with my hands to indicate 'let's slow down'.

"I'm going to ask you a few questions. We are going to take things real slow, so don't worry. And what I want you to say is 'yes' or 'no' as a reply to my first question, then we'll move on to the next question."

After I dispelled his nerves, he relaxed. The leading questions I asked seemed to have worked. The rest of the questioning showed that he had much promise and potential.

The lay person was promptly very impressed with the way we handled the situation

"You were both incredible, how did you manage to get him to say anything, you have thankfully scored him well for a post on the rotation."

I immediately turned to her and candidly replied,

"If this person was with a patient and they stuttered, he could be more likely to get a complaint against him, perhaps because he is an ethnic minority?" I went on to say, "Then the complaint would go further, and somehow the fact that he is actually a good doctor could even be ignored, he'd then end up in front the GMC?"

She had no reply, but merely listened.

Chapter Twelve

– India Visa – To the ancestral home

Back in the holding room, strangely a satellite convention centre for developing countries of the United Nations, waiting to learn of my fate, I started to think as to where I may have been recently that may trigger alarm. Iran, no. North Korea, no. China, no. Did I leave a package on the plane someone might think was suspicious? Did the air marshal make a call? Did I seem so much out of place to them, in a nice suit, being well-spoken, middle class and a surgeon from the UK, that it triggered alarm? I looked like nearly all of the people in the congested room in terms of skin hue, but was one of the few persons dressed like a European. There were no magazines or newspapers to read, although why would they grant us such pleasures? We were being detained there for a particular reason and certainly not to get our hair cut. I was feeling hungry, thirsty and anxious. It is possible in such a scenario that food deprivation and dehydration could actually lead to a state of mania, forcing people to behave in an irrational manner. Giving zero information to a confused crowd while containing them in discomfort is bound eventually to lead to the sort of behaviour that would see one's detention justified. I'm sure if I had asked for some food or drink nicely enough, I may have got something. But I wasn't about to stipulate a *halal* snack, worrying that it would send very much the wrong message.

March, 1978, London

The teacher turns to me as another teacher enters our classroom. She asks three children, whose families were new arrivals to the UK, to join her. She then looks at me, as well as two of my friends who were also of South Asian origin and asks us to join them too.

"You three go with the language teacher to the special lesson."

This extra class was meant for children that really could not speak any, or very little, English.

"Yes, Aali, now what part of the body am I pointing to?"

"That's the arm."

"Yes, well done, anything else."

"Well yes miss, there are the legs, and the face, and the head," I replied curiously.

"Well done. That was a very nice English accent, too."

The class was a ridiculous waste of time for the three of us additional students, clearly misjudged by our regular teacher. The other children there really were not that conversant in English, yet at the time, the three of us with English as a first language didn't twig that perhaps we were not supposed to be there, going simply on blind faith based on what the teacher had determined. Never mind, easy class and that's what you want when you're seven years old so we had some fun, c'est la vie!

★ ★ ★

In 2008 I was asked to go to Mumbai, India, for a conference, the International Liver and Pancreas Cancer meeting. Both my parents were born in what is India today, as well as all four of my grandparents and all eight of my great-grandparents. So this felt exciting, as it was hopefully to stir up some sense of genetic connection I had never experienced, as I had not been to my country of ethnic origin before. I had an almost mouth-watering anticipation, feeling this trip was long overdue. I was desperately looking forward to it.

I think I was chosen to speak as a potentially young and up-and-coming surgeon in the field, someone that could hopefully articulate well, with the added prospect of inviting one of their own back home for potential future enterprise, coupled with a heavy dose of sentimental nostalgia for my inherited traits.

I was going with colleagues and we all decided to apply for our visas together by completing a form and posting the application.

Some of my colleagues queued up for the day in Birmingham, which was the nearest Indian High Commission at this time. It was an all-day affair as the subcontinent countries had placed visa restrictions on all UK passport holders, most likely in retaliation for similar restrictions placed on Indians coming to the UK. I decided to await a response by post. I waited, and waited, and waited, quietly confident as I was going to my country of origin, where everyone looked like me, somewhere I would blend in quite easily, that is until I opened my mouth and labelled myself an *Angrezi*.

I received a number of phone calls asking me to clarify various points, mainly about where my parents were born. India, I said. Later I received another call asking me why my father's name was 'Sheen'. I thought this a rather bizarre question. Sheen was the name on all of my own documents, plus sadly he had passed away some years earlier, so further information was not possible. The wait continued and questions slowly started to creep in once again. Eventually they asked if my parents had visited, or lived, in Pakistan. I said yes, they went there as children after the partition of British India, so they became Pakistani.

The response to this was sudden shock, as this apparently makes a world of difference as to whether I would be granted a visa. I realised that I was incredibly naïve to think otherwise. The Berlin Wall has come down, the Cold War is over, the Iron Curtain is probably see-through now, but Indians and Pakistanis still haven't learnt to get along with each other. Surprisingly so, as phenotypically the same people, with the same food, same culture when it comes to parental hold and emotional blackmail (especially when it comes to marriage), the same interests, yet a bitter animosity remains. And not just over cricket.

I was advised to discontinue the application and complete another form, go to Birmingham or London, queue up, to try my luck at the Indian High Commission in person. I headed down with a close friend who had already secured her visa with no issues whatsoever as a native Anglo-Saxon. Based on my upbringing, who my parents' friends were and the fact that we did not suffer overt discrimination from people that looked like us, I thought prejudice was largely contained to differences in skin colour. It was January 2008, and the conference was at the end of February into early March. My wife was pregnant with our third child – due mid to late May, so I needed to get to India and back in one piece.

I decided to travel to London as I thought going to the High Commission in the capital was perhaps a safer bet – a city where I had one of my first jobs as a doctor, but also where I had grown up, so there was some partial familiarity? I arrived at the Commission after a very early start from Manchester at 04:00 to join the queue already forming for visas as early as 06:00. The queue was largely Indians, mainly expats who had given up their Indian passports as they could not have dual nationality, so consequently had to obtain a visa to go back home. This was technically a formality for them and I suppose should have been the case for me as well. As the queue grew longer, a *chai-wallah* (a tea man) turned up with a trolley to capitalise on the early morning congregation of South Asians in a queue that clearly was there every weekday and was often very long – meaning plenty of tea drinkers and entrepreneurial cash to be made. It was cold but the sun had come out to bestow upon us what I could describe as good skiing weather, frosty but pleasant. Everyone looked rather wearied and fed-up. Some I guessed were obviously tourists going to a country with vast history, cultures and monuments to be looked at in awe, a truly popular destination, where you come back with a suntan, nice memories and hopefully not Salmonella or E Coli gastroenteritis.

One queue became another queue once inside, where we were to take a delicatessen-style service ticket before finding a seat, drinking more chai and watching the flickering TV in the corner of the waiting room. I sat in the large room surveying the anguished faces and recalled the time when I first became a consultant in 2005, when I had to remove a large solid, long vegetable from an anal orifice. The patient had disclosed how he waited in the accident department in pain, desperate to see a doctor to have the offending item removed. He described that he dare not break wind during the long wait, shifting uncomfortably in fear that he may painfully deliver the rectal vegetable in full view of everybody. Normally we try to remove such objects back down through the anus while the patient is fully anaesthetised, and it is always important to deal with this situation on the same day as the accident has occurred, as you do not want the patient to be in pain or worse still, suffer a perforated rectum. Sitting in the High Commission, I was also waiting rather uncomfortably, worried about what may come to pass, but thankfully did not have a vegetable stuck in my anal orifice.

After a while, my number was called. There was a screened counter, like in a bank, where a staff member waited. I handed her my form, which she scanned intensely. All of a sudden she barked at me – "You – Pakistani?!"

I said, "No, I am not," very calmly.

"Your *pather* is Pakistani, so you are Pakistani too, no? You have to see Mr Topi." (Topi means hat in Hindi, sub-continent dwellers replace f with p and w with v in most spoken English sentences – hence *pather* and not father – my late father spoke like this so it was only what I was used to and to be honest preferred by my ear in some banal way.) I was wondering if she wanted to ask me any more probing questions, like why I was going to India. But the conversation didn't carry on. That was it. You are Pakistani and that was that. She then said that I had to sit back down in another waiting area, once again marked as a 'special case'. I was born and raised a Muslim, like most people of Pakistani origin, but it is worth pointing out here that there are interestingly far more Muslims in India than Pakistan. I guess I can't help where I was born, or what decision my grandparents made in 1947 as many persons in this situation did at the time – thirteen million to put a ballpark figure on it. Was this event in 1947 going to decide my visa application? My level of education and status as a Consultant Surgeon also did not matter anymore, it was a whiff of the fact that I had a Pakistani connection. Come to think of it, Cyril Radcliffe's ill-thought-out map of a newly divided India which caused one million deaths, led to a reward of a knighthood for him; however, its ramifications are still palpable to this day, with persons like me subject to a feverish cross-examination over seventy years later just to visit one's homeland. So it came to pass whilst joining another queue. It made no difference that I looked like them and could speak their lingo. I was under scrutiny once more. I wished at that point that I was an *Angrezi* – life would have been so much easier – no 4 am start, no queues, and a visa in the post.

I waited for about forty minutes with another chap I found out was called Abdul. By now it was around 11 am. Mr Topi called me in to see him, leering at me from under a mop of artificially dyed hair. In Asian culture having grey hair is a big no-no. My mum has been badgering me to dye my hair for some time now, but on some days of the week, especially weekends, if I skip the razor, I quickly sprout salt & pepper chin stubble which would raise the alarm bells at my seemingly jet-black hair. Also, I have found turning grey to have its dividends. The look of maturity helps people to trust that you can operate.

Mr Topi looked at me and sensed that I was one of his people. I have vegetarian legs and actually I think look like a Hindu over a Muslim, if you can say such a thing. Mr Topi asked me why I was going to India. I explained that I had been invited to speak at a conference. He went on to read all my accompanying invitation letters and asked me if I had ever had a Pakistani passport. I gave him a perplexed look and said, "I have never, but perhaps I could get one if you think it will help in my visa application?"

"No!" he replied. Then he looked at where my mother and father were born. He observed that my parents were born in British India, as it was before 1947, and not India, so he crossed off India from my application form and wrote British India instead. I was fine with this as he was technically correct. He then asked why I had put that my father was Indian and Pakistani. I explained that my father didn't migrate over until at least the end of 1948/49. I also had two aunts still living in India. I've always wondered about whether to call myself of Pakistani or Indian origin. Therefore, I have stuck with South Asian, as it's easier. The problem I had was my birth certificate said the place of birth for both of my parents was Delhi, India. This should have channelled me down an ethnic line of being perhaps recognised as Indian at school, probably even at university too, but until now I hadn't really thought about it, I certainly did not want to be disingenuous about what I thought was my ethnic origin.

The conversation continued

"*Vy* did your *pather* and *mudder* leave India?" He then gave me a look and shook his head slowly from side to side.

I looked up into the air wondering why he had asked me this. Was he not aware of his own country's history? Was he not aware that after colonial rule ended, divisions were created or formed, and the nation split with, I repeat, thirteen million people uprooted and one million dead? There was then a transference of power from one English-speaking elite to another. For persons of subcontinental origin, was it our self-instigated holocaust, or was it caused by the then colonial masters? I think the latter, obviously. Homo sapiens are truly crazy beasts with huge emotional and incomprehensible traits. It's legitimately considered hard work trying to understand such historical nuances designed to destroy as well as divide nations by our own species. I think I will just stick to treating them when their bodies fail.

"Forgive me," I said, "but have you heard of the Partition of India?" "OK, Partition," he waved his hand at me in agreement and shook his head from side to side again – implying he was happy with my answer. Head movements are more common in the South of India and Sri Lanka, while those from the North and Punjabi descent tend to gesticulate more. Although the gesticulation was sometimes my parents waving their hands at us with a clasped slipper, intimating that my brothers and I were cruising for a bruising.

After accepting that my parents and grandparents were from his great nation and perhaps realising that my lineage could be traced back to a Hindu ancestor, he very quickly turned his attention to me and gave me a two-month visa.

"Is a two-month *weeza* OK?"

"Yes, thank you."

I thought about adding in a line of, "Why the fuck have you brought me in here? If I was an *Angrezi*, I would have received my *weesa* by post, innit?"

But some or most such thoughts are best not said.

Mr Topi called me a few days later, as I had asked him to notify me when my visa was actually ready. He asked if I could write a letter to commend him to his seniors, which I did, as I thought, that for politically motivated reasons he was stuck between a rock and a hard place in this situation of interviewing someone like me for a *weesa*. I went to India a month later. At Heathrow airport, they checked my Anglo-Saxon colleague's visa status, but not mine – perhaps assuming that I was a native returning home for some *bhindi, daal, poppadoms* and mosquito bites.

As I was already married, I guess I wasn't at risk of entering, sometimes by force, into a marriage of convenience. Yep, this nonsense stills appears to be happening to this day. This is more of a problem for young girls in a sadly misogynistic culture. Post-pubescent girls are generally enticed to a holiday in the sub-continent, then trapped in a room and forced to come home with a strange man, who unbeknown to her is now her husband – frankly speaking, this is rape. God forbid they refuse to go on this lovely fake holiday or worse think of going to a university in another city away from their parents. Boys on the other hand can behave as they wish, as, whatever the religion that parents profess to follow preaches about equality, equal rights, etc, such sentiments have been bludgeoned from existence for centuries by an ancient conservative subcontinental culture that should by now be begging to be buried in an unmarked grave.

While boarding the plane, perhaps by not checking my visa, the airport staff were correct in their assumptions, that I was returning to what was once a homeland. Little did they know that it was my ethnicity and parental origins as well as decisions taken by my grandparents in 1947 that paradoxically made my life so difficult in getting a *weesa*.

In India itself, at the immigration desk upon arrival, the officer looked at me, examined my visa, saw that it was a conference visa, which lead him to promptly ask me what meeting I was attending. When I told him the nature of the academic meet, he asked whether I was a doctor. As I confirmed that I was, he shook his head from side to side quickly in approval and stamped me in. I started to feel like I was home away from home. I was able to converse with the locals fluently, which I thank my parents for, and received admiration for my social status and profession, a trait very common among South Asians. I didn't mind the March heat. The chaos was entertaining although my gastrointestinal tract with the normal British flora did loosen up a bit.

While in Mumbai, my colleagues and I decided to visit the Bollywood film studios. We had made some reliable and helpful local contacts who helped us plan the trip. I went with two *Angrezi* colleagues, both very grateful for the extra-curricular activity away from the conference. So off we went, able to take a taxi at local rates to take us to the studio. We were all somewhat afraid of the tuk-tuks though.

When we arrived, one of our guides came to me directly.

"Sahib?" he bowed, which means 'Sir' in Hindi. "Please come with me."

I followed him through to meet a large fat man sitting behind a big desk, who was conveniently flanked either side by his measurable subordinates as well as a flutter of even lesser considered individuals siting cross-legged on the floor.

"I need to know the names of all these *poreeners*," (foreigners) he asked me, so I gave him the names of the two *Angrezi* women and then I asked him, "What about me, do you want my name?"

"No!" he replied. "Just the *poreeners*."

I beamed, feeling like a long-lost cousin, the prodigal son, finally returning home, despite being warned back in Britain that I could not go to India because I was a Pakistani, a nationality that I have never had nor do to this day. I'm still trying to make sense of it all, so maybe I could ask the incumbent leaders for some advice? They possibly could help me, they seemed to be diplomatically aware of all the shenanigans! Best we leave it there – religious intolerance, we don't need it in society, we don't want it, best we got rid of it completely, let's see what the next chapter holds for us as all in the Indian sub-continent? Maybe in 10,000 years the landscape will certainly look different including all the borders, it most certainly did only 1,000 years ago. So why cling on to such fictionalised petty differences?

We witnessed a little filming, but what was most interesting to me were all the extras approaching my *Angrezi* colleagues to take photos with them. The actors wanted to engage in conversation with my *Angrezi* colleagues, but totally ignored me, making me smirk wondering whether if I offered to hold my colleague's bags, I might fit their expectations a bit more. I actually didn't mind being a *Kuli* for the day.

I will no doubt go to India again one day. I'd like to see the Taj Mahal. I long to see the big mosque in Delhi where my great-grandfather, grandfather and father prayed on a Friday, and the streets where my late father played, long before the lasting divisions between Pakistan and India were drawn up which haunt South Asians to this day. This remains a mere thought for now and unfortunately not a straightforward reality for me, I hope it will come true one day, as it will be nice to visit my former home if only to discover my origins?

Chapter Thirteen

– Egypt-gate

The stifling waiting room was slowly filling up with more and more people that looked like me. Another name was called out. Looking at the man summoned, I realised that he had actually been in before. I began to assume that he was in serious trouble, and I was being optimistic. He looked not right, well, to you and me, he might look fine, but he was wearing Middle Eastern clothes, had a nice, cleanly cut beard, and I sensed he could not speak English very well. I guess one should be able to dress how you wish in life, but, in reality, there are many styles that make one stand out in certain situations. It's like wearing a tux to a barn dance or a bikini to a ski resort or unfortunately my mother's *Shalwar Kameez* when dropping us off to school. She stood out, was different, and so suffered an egg-bashing because of it. I guess we are taught not to judge a book by its cover, which is good advice given by many but practised by few. I only had about one and a half hours to make my connecting flight, so a little panic started to set in. I decided to speak to one of the other officers about making my crucial second leg to San Francisco. So I tentatively approached the desk. Suddenly, an elderly English lady walked in and started making a huge fuss. She had a yellow envelope, but the same passport as I. A possible ally, I thought. A fellow Brit.

November 1985. School Speech day

I sat there waiting with all the other boys at the front, waiting to receive a prize. The awards were based on academic achievements from the previous year. I was about to receive the prize for the student who exhibited the most potential. I had achieved better than expected in my exams, so they awarded me this honour. Although my parents were invited, I hadn't told them. I just told my dad that there was a big meeting that he was happy to drive me to. Why only tell him half the truth and not that I was to receive a prize and invite him to attend? He always wore a suit and could speak English much better than my mum. I didn't tell my mum. She would insist on getting dressed up in her shalwar kameez and would speak to me in Urdu, even in front of my friends. And this was the sad reason I didn't tell her. I am sorry that she never got to feel that flush of parental pride on seeing her son receive a prize on stage to a round of applause. Quite simply, her son didn't want to be beaten up and called the P word the next day because his mum spoke to him in a strange language and wore a funny dress.

* * *

In 2009, for the February half term school holiday, we went with some friends to Egypt, to Sharm-El-Sheikh. My wife and I had good memories of Egypt. We had been to the pyramids at Giza in Cairo and the Valley of the Kings in Luxor on two separate trips before having children. This time we had our three young offspring with us. My son, the youngest, was only eight months old at the time. Egypt is a fantastic place to go on holiday. The food is always good, as is the climate, with warm and welcoming people with an easy sense of humour. We planned our second trip to Sharm-El-Sheikh, on the Red Sea, popular with divers and chock full of nice resorts. We boarded a Thomas Cook flight direct from Manchester. We did not need visas for Sharm, only for mainland Egypt. On arriving in Sharm, the queue for immigration was long but quick. The Egyptian immigration officers were working at lightning speed, barely even looking at the visitors, only the landing cards, which we had all completed on the plane.

As the officers stamped everyone's passports with a few incomprehensible words in Arabic, the queue of around three hundred people began to diminish within fifteen minutes. They were working at near escape velocity I thought, it was almost as if there was some free shisha available for the person that stamped the most passports; they were obviously not even looking at the passengers, they took the landing cards, which we had completed on the plane, put them in a pile, stamped the passports and off everyone went.

When it came to our turn, I had one of our daughters in my arms while my wife had our son and elder daughter at her side. The immigration officer took one look at us and immediately said, "India, Pakistan Visa?" He had our passports in his hand but chose to ignore our British cover entirely. He looked at us again.

"Visa, Visa, Visa, VISA!?"

Everyone that was in our queue waiting was now looking at us causing the hold-up. It would have been fairly obvious to all the persons behind whilst observing this action why the sudden cessation of movement came about.

"Sorry," I said, "we are British."

I momentarily thought about saying English, but he clearly was already confused at seeing non-white people coming off a plane from the UK. We looked more like him, with similar coloured skin, and were doubtless of the same religion (assuming he was Muslim as 80% of Egyptians are), but had been on the same flight as other *Angrezi* Brits.

I felt as though we were in a scene out of *Mississippi Burning*, where my wife and I as coloured folk had just walked into a whites-only coffee shop. The immigration officer asked again, "Where are you from? India or Pakistan?" He had though missed out Sri Lanka and Bangladesh. So perhaps he was familiarising himself with the sub-continent's geographical anatomy? He looked at us again, shouting, "Visa, visa!" His vocal cords were becoming louder. He really was struggling with the disparity between the way we looked and what our passports said.

"Where are you from?" he said again.

I should be entitled to a tiny royalty every time I hear this question. Ha ha!

I said that I was born in London and that I now live in Manchester.

"NO, NO, NO!" he said, then asked again, "Where are you from?"

I really didn't know what else to say. My wife was more pragmatic and immediately said Pakistan. He then crossed British off on her landing card and went on to write in Arabic 'Pakistani', after putting her boarding card to one side on a very distinct pile.

He then turned to me, he said again, "Where were you from before?"

"Before what?" I asked. Before the great migration from Africa about 200,000 years ago? Perhaps the Byzantine era? It would have been a long anthropological journey to trace.

My parents were both born in British India, so they were British at birth, but this fact would have confused him. So, with no capitulation from him in sight, I started to think harder, and we reached an impasse. Would a bribe help? I wondered, but this was impossible for me as a Brit not accustomed to such methods.

"I have never lived in, nor had any citizenship of another country," I said.

He once again frowned and repeated, "Visa, visa?"

I became horribly resigned to the fact that I was dealing with an imbecile. I was not white, which did not fit his expectations of someone with a British passport, and he did not like this. So for the first time in my life I said I was a 'Pakistani', a nationality I have never had. A country that I have only ever been to twice in my life. He promptly crossed off British on my landing card too, wrote Pakistani in Arabic and placed it along with my wife's in a very separate and distinct pile.

I wondered what would come of this isolated small pile of boarding cards. Where does it go, who reads it, is it sent to the Foreign Office in London? Maybe MI6 will be told that we're here in Egypt. I have no idea. Perhaps a drone was going to follow us our entire holiday? This would be nice so long as it didn't shoot at us, but just protected us from any unwelcome vagabonds that tried to fleece us while we were there or demanded too much *baksheesh*.

I took the humiliation rather worse than my wife. Why was he so intent on identifying us by the colour of our skin rather than our nationality by ignoring our birthplace? This was another painful example to me that I was different to my fellow Brits when travelling abroad. I was upset.

This was the last time that we went to Sharm-El-Sheikh, or Egypt. It was a sad end to our holidays in a country we had visited several times with great affection, with all the trips filled with many happy memories. I thought about complaining to the

Foreign Office when I returned home but chalked it up to being yet another in a long list of headaches and humiliations.

When you're constantly treated in this way you feel like you are 'a painted man'. I couldn't even begin to tell you what this feels like, but it keeps on happening. Back in 1995 a colleague of mine worked for an affable plastic surgeon who was also a medical officer at Silverstone motor racing track. We spent much time on weekends there as junior medical officers; we had our nice overalls which had 'Doctor' printed on the back, so that every time a car spun off you had the excitement of going and making sure the driver was OK. The entire team of medics, nurses and Marshalls had great camaraderie. The whole experience is still with me to this day and it's something that I would encourage all young doctors to do in some way or form to use their skills in another arena.

A Brazilian driver came into the medical centre where I was assigned for the day. His father had lost his contact lens up in his eye. It was a soft lens. He was pleasant, middle-aged and non-conversant in English. I couldn't speak any Portuguese but his son, being the driver, managed his English quite well. I suppose being on the international circuit as a racing car driver you ideally are encouraged to have some grasp of the English language. I looked into his eye and by using saline drops whilst making him blink, I found the contact lens and it was retrieved successfully. His son did ask if it was going to go back into his brain. I said no it wouldn't so don't worry. Actually, I could well have asked the same question myself had I not been medically trained.

The son kept staring at me and then asked me, "Where are you from?" I said, "I'm from London." He didn't really respond to that answer and then while I was treating his father, he asked again the same question, "Where are you from?" At the end of this relatively brief ordeal for his father, he passed on his thanks and said, "It was so good you were here in this country." I politely asked him as to what other country he would expect me to be in? He unfortunately, but unsurprisingly for me, didn't understand that what he was saying was purely and simply racist. I guess it was 1995, he was the young racing car driver from a country which is ironically very cosmopolitan in terms of race due to the mixture of people that have landed there over hundreds of years. I politely just ignored what he had to say and then had a joke about it with my colleague. I think he thought I was just some foreign doctor that just landed there with an English accent and was now treating his father. I'm not sure how the driver did but I guess he could drive fast, well faster than me anyway.

Chapter Fourteen

– European adventure, Brexit looming

As soon as the British lady walked in, she took one look at the number of people in the room, and ceremoniously made a very loud sobbing noise before proceeding to go utterly berserk. She went straight to an immigration officer and said this had happened to her a year ago because she had lived for some time in a Middle Eastern country, or she had been somewhere similar. To be honest I wasn't quite sure. One thing I was pretty sure of though was that it was not because of the way she looked. She fussed and fussed, becoming louder and louder, but she appeared to be getting away with it, because I suppose she could – she was white, an *Angrezi*. Her passport in a transparent sleeve with a yellow border was taken from her and not put at the bottom of this now large pile in front of the immigration officers. She was seen immediately, had her passport stamped, and thus left.

For the rest of us, it was an obvious display of disparity in the way you were treated simply for being an *Angrezi*. Nearly everyone in that room was African, Middle Eastern or Asian in origin. From the back of the queue, she had barked at the immigration officers and managed to get her passport stamped. Her total wait must have been about five minutes. If this was a courtroom and this was a stage and everyone saw what happened, it would be pretty obvious why. The *Angrezis* clearly had that enormous social control that was so close to divinity, their right of way was taken for granted with no lawful impediment in sight; would you hesitate to call this white privilege? My wait, on the other hand, continued. I wondered whether my native English accent would make such a difference at the desk as well as hers had. I therefore targeted the same immigration officer that let the other fellow Brit through. So I plucked up the courage to approach; now was my moment to dispel the mistaken tragedy of my being sent into this holding room.

"Excuse me, sir, I was wondering whether you can help me as I have a flight to catch to San Francisco and it leaves soon?" I used my most crystal-cut English accent. He looked at me and said nothing more than, "You just have to wait. The airline will put you on the next flight." I had the same accent, same nationality as the British passenger that made it through in front of us all in that detention room in record time, but I was perhaps the wrong colour. After what felt like an eternity of staring into space, an officer came out of a back office and called "Doctor Sheen". I bolted upright, gathered my things clumsily and walked towards him.

Scotland, Village GP Practice, 1993

When you're in your final year and placed in a GP practice, you're expected to undertake an audit. I had come up with the idea of looking at the number of patients that came in complaining of light-headedness to see if they were anaemic, over a two-month period. It should be a very simple audit, so I sat down in the medical records office in the practice.

"Achoo!" I sneezed. The receptionist gazed at me.

"Oh dear, you must be cold up here?" she said.

"Well, it's a bit chilly today but it's probably just my dust allergy," I replied, whilst leafing through lots of notes.

"No, I meant you must be cold here for someone like you?"

I didn't know what she meant by such a remark.

"What do you mean?"

"You're obviously Pakistani, and it's a lot colder here than in Pakistan," she smiled.

"Well, I guess so, but I've only been there once in my life and that was when I was a small child."

"When I see people like you, I just assume you are from back there?" she went on to say.

"Well, I've got news for you, I'm from London. Where are you from?"

When I honestly informed my GP supervisor of this conversation, he asked me not to tell the university, which I had never thought of doing anyway.

I travel through Europe a lot, but more recently have met difficulties. I'm not sure why, as Europe is a great place to live, with Germany and France both having larger populations of immigrants (mostly Muslim) than the UK. They have always welcomed the Brits regardless of how we look, and still largely do so to this day. In addition, I am a keen skier, so have skied in France, Germany, Italy as well as Norway. It is only the latter country where I am gazed upon, albeit rarely, by other skiers who appear aghast at this ethnic man sliding down the slopes without the accustomed foreigner's snowplough. Interestingly our Scandinavian friends are indeed very nice, welcoming people, with mainly Swedes and Danes actually working in the resort. I guess though a Norwegian owns the whole mountain.

Angela Merkel has led the way in Germany with her humanitarian gestures of looking after migrants from war-torn Syria; this act of kindness will put her in the record books of humanity I hope one day with a deserved Nobel peace prize. I often have to go to mainland Europe as I sit on various European boards and am warmly referred to as the 'English guy'. But three recent events in Hamburg, Amsterdam and Vienna stick in my mind. It was 2013 and I was invited as a guest of a large pharmaceutical company to attend a meeting in Hamburg to trial a new product. A well-polished and smartly dressed pharmaceutical representative originally from Bolton but of Pakistani heritage greeted me at Manchester airport. We then met with an old acquaintance who was actually from Pakistan originally. We chatted about lots of things. The Pakistani colleague had worked in many other countries, so it was interesting to hear about his experiences before coming to the UK. He'd been in Britain for over twenty years. We arrived in Hamburg intrigued by a new specialised technique of repairing an incisional hernia (a break in the abdominal wall) using keyhole methods. I was keen on understanding how this group in Germany at the institute we were visiting were approaching things differently, perhaps in a better way. Whatever I was to learn, I could probably make a difference to my patients back home, so I was looking forward to it.

Once off the plane we headed as usual to the immigration counters. At immigration, our other colleague from Bolton was up first, and was processed quickly. My naturalised Brit colleague was up next, and the officer looked at him, then put his passport on the scanner for some time. She then gazed at him again, decided to put it on another scanner, under a different light. If you're a *Star Trek* fan you could ask Spock what is beyond that green light, because he constantly looked down a scanner which was green like this one. He saw amazing things, he knew what was going on in the world as well as the galaxy, he probably even knew everyone's bowel habits, possibly even who was going to get screwed over next with an intelligent albeit scientific remark that the 'Klingons are approaching, Captain'. I reckon it was a prompt to help old Leonard Nimoy with his lines; after all, he was getting on so perhaps his memory was failing him? The immigration officer then picked up his passport and began flicking through all the pages violently. While this occurred, I loyally stood behind him, while others were not so patient and decided to join another queue. Yet another ethnic delay. Seasoned travellers should be mindful as to whom they stand behind at immigration! If you watch the film with George Clooney called *Up in the Air* one of the characters said you should never queue behind South Asian ethnics otherwise you could be stuck at the airport, especially when going through security. I will let you decide how true this might be. On this occasion she eventually let him through while, with my UK passport, I passed as quickly as the fellow Brit.

Once we had gone through immigration, we were swiftly approached before exiting the baggage hall by a German undercover police officer, or at least that's what I think she was. She headed straight to our Pakistani colleague. He was ever so slightly differently dressed from us, without a suit, and with a proper side parting in his hair aided by no wax, gel or mousse (possibly chambeli hair oil), a kind of hairstyle I associate with sub-continental dwellers. His trousers were large enough to allow at least two years' growth. He was also not clean shaven, with a moustache and a bit of a stubble. We both had little leather satchels hanging from our left shoulders while he clung to a Tesco's carrier bag. The officer asked where he was from with an aggressive demeanour. She had not even introduced herself and appeared to be stereotyping him as a possible asylum seeker. He replied that he was from Manchester in his Pakistani accent, so she asked to see his passport. While he was extricating this from deep within the inside pocket of his anorak, she finally flashed ID indicating who she actually was. This was good to know as Hamburg has an infamous and well-known red-light district and I didn't want to think it started from inside the airport. Once she was satisfied that he was legitimate, she informed him that he could go.

"Don't you want to see my passport as well?" I proffered, expecting to be similarly targeted. She said no.

I turned to the Pakistani colleague.

"I think it's best you shave that moustache off!"

He laughed and said, "Well I am used to it and it doesn't bother me." I suppose like my dad, he was pleased to be in Europe, able to provide his family with a decent and better quality of life. I, however, had struggled to feel equal in the country or even continent that I was actually born in.

Hamburg is a great city, cosmopolitan, chilled, relaxed, the people are nice, and no one stereotypes you or puts you into a specialised pot as a delicacy or merely leftovers! I've since been back for other meetings. I did enjoy my trip each time, so I will go again and hopefully one day soon. I learned a lot at the meeting, it made a slight difference to the way I approach patients with the type of problem I went to learn about. I think my colleague also learnt quite a lot too. We are very grateful to our hosts for inviting us. I found the biggest part of the unwelcomed entertainment was unfortunately the experience of my friend at Hamburg airport. You need to chill out if you read this and, if you are an immigration officer, calm down, don't put everyone into the same pot, look at each person as an individual; we may all look the same, but we certainly aren't what you may think we are!

It was June 2016, and I was invited to speak at the European Hernia Society (EHS) in Rotterdam. I have always enjoyed going to the Netherlands, as I had a Dutch uncle with cousins all born in Holland. I found the people nice, warm, friendly and of course very tall. I am still a big fan of their cheese, especially the Gouda with cumin seeds.

By this point I was well into my mid-forties, had operated on the rich and famous in the UK and managed to develop a good reputation in the medical world, and had been widely published in the surgical disciplines in which I practise. So what did the Dutch do all of a sudden to 'piss me off'? I don't think they really did upset me, but I will let you decide if what happened to me would have happened if I wasn't a man of colour? Yes, it's the same old broken record again.

When I was coming home, while travelling through Amsterdam airport, I was already checked in for my flight and eager to buy my favourite cheese after I had gone through security. The magnetic reader on my passport did not work in their machine, and so a large red exclamation mark lit up. I tried it again, and again, but it would not work. The passport was heading towards its final six months of service; however, I had used it on electronic readers successfully and very recently in Germany, Austria and Belgium as well as back home.

You will have noticed by now that I am a seasoned international but 'paranoid' traveller. I speak in many different countries, have continued to undertake research in important areas and regularly fly the flag for the UK in my field. But there has always remained a knot of trepidation in my gut especially when approaching an immigration desk.

It had been some years since I was first stopped and questioned purely because of my ethnicity. As a child it was the ignominy of the regular use of the P word that I was tagged with. Now as an adult, the prejudice had grown to be more subtle but just as deadly. You cannot get used to it. It always feels humiliating every time it happens. So, as time went on, the older and more experienced in life I became, I realised that as a British person who is law-abiding, hopefully nice enough too, I frankly should not need to tolerate such discriminatory treatment anymore. I decided that I had nothing to hide, so I should be able to defend my integrity as a fellow human being. Enough is enough.

All of a sudden, the gate opened, so I walked through. But as I did a young Dutch immigration officer came up to me and asked me to follow him.

"What for please?" I enquired.

"Your passport is not right," he went on to say.

"Well maybe your system is incorrect?" He steered me towards a female colleague waiting behind a desk. "Can I have your passport please?" she asked.

"No!" I responded, asking them to tell me what the problem was first. There was a momentary standoff. I flatly refused to give them my passport, but they would not let me go unless I showed it to them. You may think that I was behaving like a petulant child, but nevertheless I trust you understand that, by now, I was frankly fed up with being treated in this way almost every time I travelled. In some countries in the world, we are all witnessing the burning of buildings, attacks on police and vitriolic as well as lawless behaviour. So I guess I was never likely to behave in this way. But this had happened to me too many times by now and I was mature enough to have a reasoned discussion with someone, obtain an answer as to why they felt I needed to be singled out. There was nothing wrong with my passport; I knew that, they probably knew that as well and I doubt very much that persons other than those of my hue were being pulled aside like this. I noticed African people also tended to be pulled aside especially if there's something going on in the media or the world. I do think the media has a lot to answer for, as irresponsible reporting is what messes people like me up by placing us into a certain category where even MI6 dare not go.

"Why don't you just tell me what you want to know, and I will tell you – or are you just profiling me?" Boy, was I rude? A nightmare for any immigration officer. Confident and frankly a pain in the backside. They both were much younger than I was and remained quite calm. He apologetically said, "Very sorry, sir, but it didn't work on the reader, that was all, and we just need to make sure it was valid."

I handed the female officer my passport, and she made a call, reading out my name, before waiting a moment and handing my passport back, letting me go. I suspected what they said was absolute rubbish. Why would it require making a call if it is just a passport reading issue?

"Just put it on your reader and see that it's a genuine passport," I said. "You don't need to make a call if it is a passport reading issue." They had no answer.

You may read this and decide that I have developed rather a chip on my shoulder. I simply ask any of you to imagine whether you would be able to remain tolerant of this sort of scenario recurring time after time. I will then ask you to explain after reading all the above events what the common denominator was in terms of the rationale for my being confronted and/or held each time. If someone has an identical place of birth and passport as me but is a 'white person' with an Anglo-Saxon or Celtic name, would they have had the same sort of treatment over all those years? I'm sure you would agree they were unlikely to have been subjected to this type of 'profiling'.

In May 2017 I attended the annual European Hernia Society meeting in Vienna. I was travelling back with two female colleagues, both of 'native' English stock. This was my inaugural meeting where I attended as a professor. I had been fortunate to receive an honorary chair from a university in Manchester for my research with their science faculty. This was a proud moment: a pat on the back for my achievements to date. To be honoured with the title of 'Professor' signifies that you are both well-published and an educator in your field where trainees under your supervision have been enrolled into a PhD or other higher university programmes. I had also innovated some keyhole operations that received international recognition. However, I must also confess that the true head of a university department at medical school, e.g., Professor of Surgery or Medicine etc will hold the higher echelon of any professorial rank and file.

At Vienna airport, my two colleagues passed through security with ease. They were both tall and very blond. Their passports underwent a very brief look, and off they both went. When it came to me, the immigration officer took my passport, looked at me, then put it on the customary scanner. He then looked at the screen as a man possessed. The look on his face became both inquisitive and disgusted at the same time. He spent some time, after which he proceeded to punch some keys on his computer. This captivating screen somehow manages to talk to immigration officers, perhaps in a silent code language us mortals cannot comprehend. The information will clearly take stock of all our existence to date, it may even have a passage on there from the air marshal on the Atlanta flight saga?

I was wondering what this Austrian immigration officer would do if he was sick, in pain, in hospital, needing an operation and I took one look at him and said, well actually there was an infamous German Chancellor who was an Austrian painter before he changed profession. He caused a lot of havoc, killed six million people and so perhaps he would have to wait while I contemplated the reasons for operating and justifications for helping, because he was an Austrian too? Now you can see that when I put it like this that his actions seemed a little bit odd, stupid and clearly racist, frankly illegal! As a doctor I would absolutely never judge any patient based on what they looked like, or where they're from; remember we all cut and bleed the same. As an immigration officer he should have been a little bit more objective, treated me equally like my two co-travelling colleagues, let me through the same way he let them through – after all we have the same nationality and passport – but no.

When he had finished scanning, I asked him politely, as he handed me my passport, what he had been looking for. He looked at me and another officer standing behind him who also had a worried look on her face. I asked him again.

"What were you looking for?"

He then waved his hands at me to say move on.

"Don't wave your hands at me and please answer my question. What were you looking for?"

He said nothing.

"You need to answer my question. My passport is the same as my colleagues, you didn't check theirs, so why check mine?" I knew the answer already. If you have three persons that are clearly travelling together, two English, Anglo-Saxon, and one of South Asian origin and you only check the last person's passport then this can readily be interpreted as a clear example of racial discrimination. You may not believe this, but it affects persons like me in an adverse way as psychologically you end up wishing that you were white.

Despite my level of education, my surgical expertise attracting patients from around the world who come to see me in the UK, and the fact that I was also now a professor, I was still made to feel like an outcast. I had been invited by Austrian surgeons to speak at a very prestigious meeting, opened by one of their political leaders. I was invited for my expertise, for my interest in a vital field, for the fact that whatever I had learned I could pass on for the betterment of many patients in Europe and possibly the world.

When I eventually got through, my two colleagues asked me what took so long. Where do I begin?

I made some noise when I got back home. My host in Vienna is a very influential surgeon; he knows me well, so he told me that he would speak to a local politician whom he knows. He explained to me that he hadn't heard of any such treatment in Vienna before. To be fair to him, he did raise the issue, but I do not think he has many non-white acquaintances, so this sort of feedback about airport discrimination was no doubt rare amongst persons he knew. Vienna is a beautiful city full of art, culture and fine classical music. I have been there on various surgical orientated trips, but this was the first time that I had suffered such blatant as well as racist treatment. So I like to think and hope it was a one-off.

In terms of Europe and now, as I am completing this book in 2021, as a former European national or citizen of the EU (Brexit sucks), I must have been to at least ten different European countries. I am always treated very well and my children have all learned to ski on the mountains of Europe. I will continue to hold my European neighbours in high regard. Europe will continue to be strong as well as provide a careful balanced assessment on world issues. It has a large Muslim population, which it treats very well; it allows them to practise their religion, but is not restrictive in many ways, with the United Nations building in Vienna located on a street named after a famous, originally Austrian, Muslim cleric, and called Muhammad Asad Platz. I am sure some persons will disagree with what I say, but I do think, and have witnessed first-hand, that Europe is more open to other cultures than some countries around the world. However, I am not naive and know that they have learnt from their tarnished past and are continually trying to move on to a better place. I have operated in Sweden, Holland, Greece and Turkey to date. Each time it was a pleasure – my hosts treated me with great respect as well as the patients, who were very grateful.

In Britain we are fortunate to speak the lingua franca of the world. Perhaps this is why we have been more embracing of our immigrant population than some of our European neighbours. Let me provide you with another example. I was invited about five years ago to a huge meeting in Berlin, a coveted conference of about eight-hundred German surgeons. All of the live surgical operations I watched were narrated in German, but it didn't matter, as surgery is surgery. I understood absolutely everything during the operations. I had an opportunity to speak and present my research and it was well received. I had translated into German, with some help, every single presentation slide of mine. This was my testament to the respect that I had already received from my German hosts, as the German medics all spoke very good English.

I walked into the huge auditorium, but as I was approaching the front to sit down, one of my colleagues from the South of England stood up and waved at me to catch my attention. I noted him almost immediately, sporting an English college tie, waving conspicuously as though he was about to help land a plane. I walked over to him, shook his hand, then sat down next to him. I made myself comfortable with a small grin spreading across my face.

"How did you know I was here?" He and I looked at each other and laughed.

As we speak English, we attract the able surgeons from less developed countries, with many likely to come to our shores to practise. If they excel, they are certainly promoted and deservedly so. But this is not always the case with other countries. I'm yet to meet a non-white consultant from Italy, Spain or Germany. I would be very happy to be proven wrong. If you're a hardworking, able doctor from South Asia for example, you are unlikely to speak Italian or Spanish and so you would be less likely to practise medicine in those countries as an alternative to your own. We are in need of doctors, with the majority of our overseas doctors trained in the English language in their respective home countries. So it's evident why we should have more imported doctors in the UK than anywhere else in Europe.

It is easy for me to conclude in this chapter that in Britain we are less colour prejudiced than our European counterparts. I don't believe this to be the case entirely, but I did experience challenging treatment very recently in the twenty-first century in three separate European countries. Maybe the adverse media attention that people with Muslim-sounding names or ethnicity are receiving may have a part to play in the indifferent sieving through I have been subjected to. I'd like to think that Brexit may at least bring our country closer together although I remain sceptical about the whole situation, as well as our wider influence in the world.

I said before that I reside on a few European boards. I do enjoy spending time in Europe. I feel the change in culture and language such a short distance away is endearing in itself and I thoroughly enjoy the company of my European surgical colleagues. I do hope us Brits find some place in a mighty Europe politically, but surgically or as clinicians I can guarantee you that we already have. We share common ideas, surgical techniques, patterns of working in medicine which can be traced back to centuries of collaboration. Doctors all over Europe carry responsibility for their actions especially if they fall short of what is an expected standard.

Chapter Fifteen

– Cultural nuances and rituals experienced in health care

London, School of Anatomy 1995

Prior to that famous spring ligament moment, I managed to obtain a place on a prestigious course where we had tuition to prepare us for an incredibly demanding exam called the primary fellowship, which is literally a pole vault into surgery. This examination was designed to test us in the basic sciences of the human body with anatomy being the main topic. It was necessary to show a complete understanding of every muscle, organ, ligament, bone and blood vessel in the human body. To have a surgeon operate on you, it is comforting to know that the exams are very difficult, it's like swimming an Atlantic Ocean made from glue and those survivors at the end will be given the privilege and honour to operate on you. So why shouldn't it be demanding?

I recall a very important anatomy lesson where we were standing around a cadaver specimen. We were analysing the gastrointestinal tract, the part of the body where our food enters a digestive maze. The gregarious anatomy lecturer was discussing how much volume the stomach could hold, but when incorrect answers to his questions followed, he quickly turned to me and said to the room full of trainees, "I bet if I asked this young man how much curry he can hold in his stomach it would be a lot – possibly 3L or more."

I just had to take it on the chin. I had paid for this course and wanted to pass the exam. I should have asked him where the 'spring ligament' was, then sprung my foot into action on his rear end.

★ ★ ★

At this point in the book, I think I'll break away from my normal themes and look at some more of my experiences as a doctor in the NHS. I have also not continued my Atlanta diary as I will savour concluding this chapter of my life later. I've discussed, as well as laid out to you, the reader, the differing treatment which I have experienced based on my race and ethnicity. I've seen patients from various cultural backgrounds and ethnicities over the years, hence it is inevitable that I have observed certain traits. Some of my colleagues will agree with me, some may disagree, but I don't think I'm being prejudiced or racist in anyway. God knows I've suffered racism, so therefore, I'm going to be very careful in what I say by placing a real-life perspective on the events I relate to you – please accept that we are all individuals so in no way should any part of what I say be treated as a sweeping generalisation. As this book relates to an unforgettable trip to the United States, let's start with a patient, believe it or not, that I have managed, who was originally from there.

Our closest allies

I've always had fondness for our friends from the US. I recall one American patient when I was a very young consultant who had a condition where his gallbladder was inflamed due to a stone in the gallbladder itself, called a gallstone, which had impacted at its neck. This made fluid within the gallbladder fill up with what is called bile, which, when mixed with mucus, becomes poisonous as bacteria colonises it quite quickly. The patient had developed a condition called acute cholecystitis. The only way to really treat this is to either pop a drain into the gallbladder for temporary relief, or a keyhole operation to remove the gallbladder altogether, called a laparoscopic cholecystectomy. This is one of the signature operations that I carry out more than the average in number for a surgeon of my training and specialism. As I conversed with him, I noted his American accent. I asked him if he was here on holiday. He said he had lived in the UK for over thirty years. I asked him what the best part of living in the UK was.

"I guess it's that you aren't going to get a bill when you get sick!"

I then asked him why he had not lost his very American accent. I had been thinking about how common accent loss is. I know many people of South Asian descent who, when they travel to America for work as doctors, end up having an unusual hybrid accent that's half Hindi with some Americanisms thrown in. My dad had lived in the UK for over thirty-five years before he passed away, and maintained his South Asian accent throughout. He was very proud of it. The American patient explained that as a businessman, when he attended a meeting and spoke with his American accent, immediately everyone quietened down, almost stood to attention and listened very carefully to what he had to say. I commented that when my father came to the country in 1964, he had a Pakistani accent which he never lost, so when he walked into a room and spoke, it often had totally the opposite effect.

I remember operating on him. I fixed him, he was very grateful. So he went on his way, without a blimp on his bank account, hallmarking the benefits of a free healthcare system. I'm not sure what he's up to nowadays, but he was a nice chap. It was a very interesting story he told me. So I think whatever accent you're born with, be proud of it. I definitely have a Southern English accent, you could say I'm still a little bit of a cockney. I'm very proud of where I came from, the area I grew up in and I still use certain colloquialisms such as when something goes well. 'Dealt with', as we say in South London.

The other memorable American patient I saw as a junior doctor working in plastic surgery had fallen and hurt his finger. It was a very easy fix. All we had to do was put a ring block in, which was a local anaesthetic placed by injection at the base of the affected finger, a tight tourniquet, which allowed us to operate on his finger with him experiencing no pain, and with little or no blood loss. Once his entire finger was numbed, I could pull the bone back into place and stitch up the skin break. He thankfully did not need a plate for the small fracture. He could fly home to the United States where medics there could then tend to the injury. He was very loud, and his girlfriend was always with him. She usually used to lie on the bed with him. I actually felt like saying to them one day that if they decided to have sex or whatever they were contemplating, they had to make sure it was not too loud and to please draw the curtains around them, although I reckon the other patients probably wanted to watch! Generally speaking, lying on the patient's bed, having your legs sandwiched between theirs, isn't really a good idea.

A week or so later one of my colleagues asked whether we had charged him:

"Why would I charge him?"

My colleague explained that as an American, he must have been insured, meaning the hospital could recoup money from him. It was the first time I'd really come across anyone approaching me about charging a patient, as it's not a concept that we readily think about in the UK. I believe we are extremely fortunate to keep money out of the equation through having a National Health Service. We are able to triage patients, deal with them and do what is absolutely necessary without the temptation to over investigate and with no direct fee levied to the patient. Over-investigating means added costs, increased billing, and although a higher revenue for the institution and certainly the doctor involved, can lead to unnecessary treatment. As a consultant I undertake private practice too. But I do so with the same amount of respect and decency that I would in the NHS. I avoid over-investigation, although ordering a diagnostic test in the private sector is far easier than through the NHS, as well as getting another colleague to co-assess.

If you have a valid visa for the UK, you are allowed urgent or emergency medical treatment. If you come in sick and we diagnose a cancer, which requires further treatment or long-term care such as chemotherapy, we repatriate the patient for care, but only after any acute debilitating problem such as bleeding is dealt with. If their cancer is causing a bowel obstruction, such as a colon cancer, we operate to provide the emergent care and then repatriate the patient back to their home country once they are fit to travel. This is respectful of human beings, as anyone can find themselves through no fault of their own in a medical emergency abroad, and so we help them. I'm proud that the NHS does this. But I have also observed people travelling over here on the pretext of a family visit but are instead on a medical holiday. We try to sift these cases, duly investigate them and send them on their way. While as a doctor your instinct is to treat, but you have to be mindful too of your duty to protect the taxpayer's National Health Service.

South Asians

I have seen literally hundreds of patients of South Asian origin, and I hate to admit it, but there are certain traits that are all too familiar. First of all, most people of South Asian origin don't readily accept anything you say to them the first time and always question. It is more of an interrogation as panic sets in amidst the fear of the unknown. Culturally, we are quite emotional. We rarely are taught to use logic over emotion, engendering an everlasting battle that we seem to be fighting and losing. You can actually see the cogs in our brains turn around as we fret. The thought of logic may come into our minds albeit temporarily, No blow that, let's cry and worry some more. It's never going to happen. Emotion will always win I am sorry to say, but at least the family support is there.

When an elderly South Asian patient attends our out-patient clinic, it is likely that their entire family comes with them. Often, they don't want their grandparents or parents to know what the actual diagnosis is, and have to be made to understand that is not possible as it is their body. Without them knowing what the problem is, I cannot offer them surgery or any other treatment. What's important as a fellow South Asian is that the family do mostly feel a little bit gratified that I'm looking after their loved one, as I can speak the lingo. I will also empathise with a careful perspicacious judgment of Asian family norms. We often must endeavour to find and use an interpreter to speak to those that struggle with English and can't use their family, as at times relatives refuse to tell their loved ones what's wrong with them. I remember one such dialogue.

"Tell your mother that she has unfortunately developed cancer."

The relatives turn to the elderly patient. "Are you hungry?"

"Please tell her that with this diagnosis she will most likely need an operation."

"They have a special *halal* menu for you with *karahi* chicken on it."

"Tell your mother that we're going to try and fit her in, hopefully over the next two weeks or so for her operation."

"I wouldn't order the *saag* as it gives you diarrhoea."

"Please now ask her if she has any questions for me?"

"Everything is absolutely fine; we're going to go home now and tomorrow morning you're going to wake up and I'll give you a nice *paratha* with *halva* for breakfast, *teek hey*?"

This clearly isn't going to work; it's going to be complicated, problematic, so in some or many ways, we're not going to get very far.

I've actually said to a lot of family members in the past that they must not forget that just because their relative is older, it doesn't mean that they are incapable of making any decisions for themselves. They know what's happening to them, they know their body isn't right. And they are entitled to feel however they want. I try and remind them that their parents, grandparents, their loved ones, their aunties and uncles are actually stronger than they think. This first generation immigrated from a hot country thousands of miles away to a country where the culture was completely alien to them, survived, worked hard, paid the rent, brought you/us lot up, so we need to give them some credit and know that they can manage – they'll be fine. There is plenty of support in the NHS. You will see that they will never be left alone, and we are also mindful of certain cultural extras that they may need.

All my past, present and future patients of South Asian origin, like every one of my patients, are precious to me. I think realising that we, as doctors and nurses, at times have to approach things differently is reasonable, and we all accept this. Such patients do not intend to be troublesome. They are just culturally estranged from Western norms.

Pain control and mobilisation are other issues that I find South Asians struggle with. They tend to feel more pain and can show great reluctance in mobilising after surgery. When asked to walk after an operation, it is met with an inordinate degree of reluctance. They always insist on at least half a dozen nurses gathering around them and moving each limb in turn. It's almost robotic to a degree. Trying to get a newly created machine to undertake its first step sometimes you need to give it a little nudge. I wonder whether it is the often-augmented emotional side, as well as a pampering culture at home, that underlines this observed trend. Remember, hundreds upon thousands of South Asians died in both world wars fighting for the British Empire. These soldiers were not soft, but much tougher than you think.

My greatest memory, which I can easily recall when addressing cultural norms and practices, was when I undertook the same operation on two individuals at the same time, of course one after the other. Both keyhole in nature, uncomplicated and only requiring an overnight stay. One patient was a twenty-seven-year-old girl whose parents were South Asian immigrants and an *Angrezi* woman in her late seventies. Guess which patient went home first, by four days!

Anyway, this chapter is about my experiences as a surgeon. Hopefully any fellow doctors that read this will empathise and enjoy the humour.

The natives

I like to think I'm a native of the British Isles, but the people I'm referring to are what one may call the native Brits, Celts and Anglo-Saxons, or to me, the *Angrezis*. I find British patients suffer less with anxiety and depression when they get ill. They tend to take things on the chin, and while they have close family networks, they play more of a supportive role rather than one where you can feel emotionally drained by your relatives. Post-surgery, they don't appear to experience much pain. The *Angrezis* come across as more physically and emotionally robust than we South Asians.

I can imagine undertaking an open-heart bypass operation on a fifty-six-year-old man from Swansea. All of a sudden, he will wake up halfway through and say, "Oh what's that you've got there, boyo?" "We're just finishing off, so why don't you be a good lad and go back to sleep so by morning you'll be just right!" Then he would close his eyes to have a nap and we'd wake him up when we're done! Perhaps it was that, thousands of years ago, they came to a cold and relatively uninhabitable island with little hope of surviving: they then stayed. Could this have made the difference? So only the truly hardened survived. If my ancestors came, they would have almost certainly perished and/or decided to go back to a hotter climate where someone else would do all the farming and cooking for them.

I once treated a gregarious and incredibly articulate eighty-four year-old man, who, with his wife, also in her eighties, had travelled about three hundred miles for me to fix a persistent problem that he had. Two of my colleagues from other regions had already attempted to repair the problem unsuccessfully, so there was a certain amount of pressure to get this right. He had searched on the internet and had chosen me. I felt honoured when he came to see me in the clinic. He was so unassuming in his approach that it dawned on me how stoical his personality was. I took a good look at him and got him ready for the operation, which I am proud to say was a success. He had a son and a daughter who were both consultants working in the NHS, both in their fifties with their respective partners also medics. I had never met any of them to that day, which is normal. However, if this were a South Asian family, they would have likely been tracking my every move with serious intensity, phoning me left, right and centre as well as sending a plethora of emails, demanding all the blood results, ECG traces and other information I could pass on to them. They'd be emotionally distraught, possibly camping outside the hospital or arriving each day with provisions like freshly cooked basmati rice. They could well be under the cultural impression that their parents were incapable of making any decisions for themselves. But not this patient. Knowing these facts about his children, I decided one morning while reviewing him to ask:

"Do you know, I have not actually met any of your children?" He was sitting up in bed, looking at me and said, "What on earth for?"

He was right. Why did I need to meet them? I was managing a highly intelligent man, who still had his five senses working. Perhaps he found it insulting that I assumed he needed his offspring around him, overseeing the treatment.

"Yes, you are right. No reason."

Europeans

While I see patients from countries such as Poland, Lithuania and the Czech Republic, they are few and far between. It may be due to the fact that a lot of European nationals working in the UK are of a younger demographic than the first- and second-generation immigrants from former British colonies. Or perhaps they just don't get ill! I undertook a ward round recently while there were some visiting German medical students joining us. At the end of a very long ward round of over forty patients, I asked my colleagues how many patients were on our ward from Europe or other European countries. They obviously ask questions about Brexit and all the business that was going on associated with this bizarre end to our Europeanness. They thought a little while, then replied, "None." Yes none, so despite the pro-Brexit party claiming that we're inundated with immigrants, and they need to go back home as they are draining our NHS as well as other such resources, we rarely have any of these so-called blood-sucking Europeans on our wards. Without the immigrant population, whether first, second or third generation, the NHS would certainly struggle with human resources, and no one would be looked after to the highest levels that they are now, mainly by virtue of the fact we have just lost thirty to forty per cent of our workforce. Like the Brits, most of the European patients I see are unbelievably tough. They need very few painkillers, don't stay in hospital very long and are determined to get better as quickly as possible.

I had a young British girl who needed an operation to remove her appendix at exactly the same time as an overweight Polish builder. On the morning ward round the following morning, I said to the Polish patient that he could go home but would not be able to work for about three weeks. He looked devastated, put both his hands to his face and then muttered that he needed a sick note to prove that he could not work. I agreed.

Then I went to see the young British girl. The first thing she said to me was, "I need my sick note!" She went on to say, "I'm not going back to work, and I want you to give me at least a month off." I kept quiet, but finally agreed. I wonder whether sometimes in the NHS we are afraid to do our clinical duty over what the patient wants, especially if what they are asking for goes against good medical practice. Why did I agree, when I knew that if for any reason, she needed more time off than the necessary couple of weeks as a young fit, healthy person, the extra week or two would be readily given to her by her general practitioner, if she wasn't progressing? There was the risk that I could receive a grievance letter. Each complaint can cost the NHS up to £4000 to deal with. It would involve sacrificing my time with other patients to sit instead in my office going through the notes, to justify my decision. Even then it is often easier to resolve such cases through offering a profound apology, rather than an evidence-based rebuttal.

The NHS is embroiled with complaints and litigation costing us over £1 billion per year. I think what we need is to improve the image of the NHS. You'll see from my prologue, though, that during the pandemic the NHS gained much-needed respect as well as recognition as a fine example of social medicine. We would only need to start charging patients for a month for you to see your doctor and undergo treatment for everyone to realise how much the NHS actually costs us. Most people are actually very grateful for the National Health Service, they treat it as well as its staff with respect, but, unfortunately, I feel there is a long way to go to improve our image. And I hope our health service will last forever and not be broken down into a private healthcare set-up. Who will suffer if it does disappear? It will be the poor and the elderly, the most vulnerable in society that endure the painful agony of no healthcare. It will be just like any major catastrophe that occurs in the world that you see to this day such as the futility of war – leaving forlorn women, children and the socially deprived without support.

Chapter Sixteen

– Au Revoir, Atlanta or Bienvenu Guantanamo

Summer Memories

London, Summer, August 1984

I'm in the newsagents where I would work for pizza and free drinks. Mr Patel asked me if I had enjoyed the Olympic games in LA.

"Yes, they were fab! The Americans were my favourite team, with Carl Lewis the best-ever by a long-shot with four gold medals!"

I always envied the Americans for what they were achieving around the globe, yet at the same time admired them. Their landing on the moon, advancing science, famous universities, and baseball meant that my dream of going to America was endless, to progress as an equal in a country full of immigrants.

★ ★ ★

London, Summer 1976

My mother and I took the bus to Guy's Hospital to see my aunt who was a general surgeon working in Saudi Arabia. She was my aunt or Cha-Chi as she was married to my father's younger brother who himself was a paediatrician. They both worked in Saudi together in the same hospital, Al-quatif if I recall. My uncle reliably informed me many years later that she managed to obtain a post in Saudi first as she was female, Muslim and a surgeon. But she bartered a place for him as well or she would not go. This left the hospital administrators with the decision to reluctantly give my uncle, Cha-Cha, a place too, but with only a spot on the paediatric program. He loved this post, loved children and managed to head the department many years later, which was rare in those days as a non-Saudi. With his tolerance of rowdy children, he also became a handy babysitter.

My Cha-Chi was being treated for breast cancer. She seemed poorly. Her colour was like a yellowy mustard, with her sunken eyes and hair suffering from alopecia. She spent all her time lying in bed, could hardly move. To engage with us she merely rested her head on two pillows whilst turning slightly towards us both. She seemed tired. I was not sure at the time as I was so young, but on reflection, I believe she was having chemotherapy. Both she and her husband could afford the private care they were receiving, thanks to their well-paid jobs in Saudi. I recall her face, she touched me on the head in an affectionate way and called me betta (son). After our customary salutations, my mother discussed all the comings and goings in our household, while I was mainly preoccupied with the antiseptic smell in the hospital's nightingale ward and watching the doctors parade around magnanimously in their white coats. They looked graceful, with the nurses there at hand to assist when required. All the nurses wore hats. They were lined up from top to bottom of the ward. There appeared to be no shortages at this time.

My Cha-cha later imparted some candid information to me that I was not party to.

"I am the first doctor in our family, maybe you could be the second or third." I think he guessed that at least one of his children, who were all older than me, would follow in his footsteps and indeed one did follow suit. She is now a psychiatrist in the States. Guess I should have been the third but ended up the fourth as another older cousin took that spot.

A week later my Cha-Chi passed away. I knew then that I wanted to do this job more than ever. I am not saying that I thought I could have helped her, no doubt I would meet death and have done since with some patients. But I wanted to try to make a difference if I could.

★ ★ ★

When you're invited to speak in a country which is renowned for its esteemed values of human life, freedoms, and the rule of law it is always a great honour. Particularly when I had won an award there in 2002, a mere nine years earlier. Little did I know at the time that an act in a riveting spy thriller would appear to unfold! The experience I had with my young family in Dallas in early 2008, was becoming a distant memory, a one-off, during the

Bush administration, and after 9-11, so it perhaps all made sense. This trip was set during an administration with a very different and progressive president. A man of colour, a man who defied all the odds and made it to the highest office in the land to become the Commander in Chief. He didn't arise from a political family, nor is he descended from someone who came to America on the *Mayflower*. He came technically from a broken home, but was intelligent, articulate and above all reached out to people. With this premise and with such leadership at the top, I would have expected a different journey rather than the drama that unfolded with my arrival at Atlanta airport. I've never called this event *'kismet'* but just plain old bad luck. I was called over to the desk for Americans as there was a bit of a queue for foreigners. This immigration officer was obviously pleased just to wave on through citizens of his country all day, which you would expect. So, when I was ushered over, he had to make a split decision with the first foreigner he had probably seen that day.

He took one look at me and didn't like what was in front of him or just the way I looked. His mind had already been made up, knowing that the American public would gasp if he were to let me through without interrogation. Therefore, a knee-jerk reaction of *'protocolled'* was inevitable.

Having waited for what felt like an eternity in the detention room at Atlanta airport, I was finally called into a room at the back. My passport was still in its red-marked envelope. Perhaps I had been categorised as highly dangerous. In my turmoil I could only think that maybe I needed some skin-lightening cream so that in the future I could travel unchallenged, without the FBI tracking me.

The immigration officer in this room was a young man, my junior by at least ten years I reckoned, tall and thin, with dark curly hair. I was sweating heavily as I followed him into the room. I realised that there was nothing I could do. I could only wait and see what was going to happen and take it from there. But I had a sinking feeling that I was possibly going to be detained for a long time, missing my connecting flight. This was demeaning enough and would have left me feeling humiliated that day or any other day. I had no idea how the rest of this journey was going to unfold. I felt that there was possibly light at the end of the tunnel so I could then carry on with the rest of my journey. Although I did actually feel sorry for that person whom I would be sitting next to on the flight to San Francisco, as I was sweating so heavily now. He could quite rightly have asked to move to a slightly more salubrious smelling part of the plane.

The room I was led into was very red, with red carpet, and red walls like the red on the passport's envelope, and a large desk with two doors behind. I guess one was possibly a toilet and one led into a room where there was a one-way mirror with conceivably the FBI there watching as well as recording everything. If it was candid camera, then at least I would have gained a temporary moment of fame! I actually had no idea; could it have been that Mother had sent this man in especially on a covert operation to make me confess to making a hole in her precious carpet many moons ago? I could not help thinking that this room I was detained in had a furtive air of a court room for the guilty as charged. I felt that I was being persecuted. Jesus Christ was tortured for his religion and ethnicity; clearly nothing has changed two thousand years later. I was wondering whether the air marshal from my flight was somewhere nearby, standing next to the FBI. Perhaps they thought that I may confess to being an agent committing espionage or to renounce God. Yes, the scepticism of religion occasionally creeps in. My brain had started to spin into overdrive.

The officer was very polite and asked me why I was coming to the United States. I explained that I was a physician, knowing that this usually goes down well, and that I was invited to speak at a meeting in San Francisco. Hopefully he would then realise that I could miss my connecting flight and hence speed up proceedings.

"Are you a doctor, sir?"

"Yes, I am."

"What type of doctor, sir?"

"I am a surgeon specialising in hepatopancreatobiliary, or HPB, which covers diseases of the liver and pancreas."

As he was writing everything down, I realised that he needed some help to spell the medical words I had used.

"He-pa-t-o-pan-c-r--e-ato-bil- – i-ar-y."

He crossed it out and wrote it out again, actually a few times. He then scratched his head.

"I am also an expert in abdominal wall reconstruction and that's why I have been invited to speak in your country." The clock was ticking. Maybe I should have not added that extra bit. When you're in this situation and innocent, you funnily enough don't know what to say and how to say it. I hoped he was thinking 'what on earth is he doing in here with me?' In the highly dangerous queue; well, for this I could only thank his colleague outside.

I imagined my flight to San Fran being filled with aviation fuel and completing the final engineering checks prior to boarding the passengers. He then checked through my passport, noted that I hadn't been to any of the 'Axis of Evil' countries, and scratched his head again. The only thing I could do was stare at him as well as perspire heavily with a tachycardia (very fast heart rate). I reckon he was at least college educated and he seemed like a reasonable bloke. He looked over at my book on Thomas Cromwell and asked if it was a good read. I said, 'Yes,' as it showed how corrupt sixteenth-century England was at the time. I was pleased that he didn't take this remark in any other way than it was meant to be.

He stood up and went away to consult with another colleague. Interpol perhaps or even a quick call to MI6, who knows, what if it was the air marshal? I guess I would find out soon enough if I was catching my connecting flight to San Francisco or Guantanamo!

I could and perhaps should have ruminated on divine inspiration at that moment. My parents always believed wholly in the idea that saying the word 'Inshallah' at the end of every sentence meant that, 'Allah would grant their prayers.' But I know that it meant, 'If it should please Allah.' Unfortunately, uttering this very word meant I was to have a more protracted stay over a departure to freedom.

Before the immigration officer came back into the room, I had started to feel mounting alarm as to why he had needed to leave. I knew that the ink in his pen had not run out, as bless him, he was using a Bic biro if I recall, cheap but effective. Perhaps before he left, I could have shared my altogether familiar experiences with using such a pen over the years. Easy to write with, painless to find in most shops, even the ones that sell stuff you don't need. I reckon you could probably find them in a pound store. So why did he leave, maybe his bladder was painfully full and knowing that I did not have a license to practise in the US I could not catheterise him if needed. I also knew that back home MI6 were probably asleep or between shifts. Maybe worse still, they were measuring me up for an orange suit – a proper onesie!

It's at times like this that one can ruminate over all sorts of potential scenarios. I often find myself doing it about patients long after I've come home. Have all the blood results come back normal? Has so and so passed water yet? Have they been able to move their bowels? Did that operation go as well as it could have done? What am I doing tomorrow? I had better check with my secretary! Even homely chores are brought into question, hmmm, have I forgotten something? Did I put the keys where they should belong, did I leave the iron on, has the washing machine been fully emptied (yes, I do think about it), was the dishwasher ready to be started, oh and yes, as I'm going abroad have I remembered my passport?

I kept on thinking that I will be treated like a US decorated surgeon from the UK, which was technically correct. I may even be receiving an invite to the White House, although it was short notice, so I hadn't probably packed enough shirts or ties. I was a bit tired but knew that I also had to board another flight to San Fran.

The United States is the self-appointed number one country in the world. Well look at their international dialling code for starters – 01. Then what do they do? They procure talent from around the world, whether scientists, sports champions, doctors, engineers, writers, artists etc then endow a subtle gift – to fulfil their potential in an unadulterated 'free' manner. So if you get the best out of everyone, then society will benefit from their various accomplishments, which is a good recipe for continued success. I guess most persons in the waiting room outside wanted to just get that entry part over, have their passports stamped so they could move on most likely to Florida or LA. After all, Atlanta is a hub. I guess many wished to enjoy the sunny beaches, ice creams, possibly even visit an outlet store to get cheap Tommy Hilfiger jeans – yes this is a trendier brand in Europe than the US.

Have you ever wondered if anyone of your friends and colleagues have been treated in this way, irrespective of where they are from or which country they are visiting? I think probably this may be a phenomenon which exists all over our precious and unevenly divided world. But you may observantly note that it actually does, more so than ever; racial inequality exists throughout society and in every corner of the world. When are we going to live in a world that looks past the way you look and start judging you by the quality of your mind? I think there will always be a group of individuals that will have a serial mistrust of another group of individuals. This human trait is called overt tribalism. Our innate nature to bond more closely with our fellow tribesmen remains to this day, and probably still defines homo sapiens. Human emotions, combined with aligned political ideas creates another dimensional tribe, helps forge further ties with each other which may govern our actions. Maybe we rely too much in this so-called modern time on definitions of humankind and so we do need to change, otherwise anger as well as hatred will continue even once petty differences are identified.

I thought about another friend of mine that had also been stopped some months ago, just before my trip to San Francisco. He was actually born in Pakistan, but his family came to the UK when he was two years old. He informed me that they had asked him why his parents came to the UK and how often he goes to a mosque. I, of course, was born in the UK, so didn't feel that I would be asked this question, but what about the mosque? I had enough time to think about it, so I was going to say, "I am not exactly the most regular mosque attender, but if I did go, I would know what to do there."

This seemed reasonable, to the point and above all, the truth. Reflecting on it, I thought to myself that the regular mosque attender is likely more pious, God-fearing, peaceful, and self-reflective. Actually, the majority of regular mosque-attenders are, from my experience, pensioners, except on a Friday when all ages and denominations flood the floors to attend the largest communal ritual of the week. In my personal experience, Islam isn't actually a dictatorial religion. You have to make your own decisions and are encouraged to read for yourself. Like any religion it is peaceful, tolerant and demands respect for human life.

The ordeal had already cost me a nice layover meal in a restaurant, some duty-free shopping for my three children and much-needed downtime after my mental joust with the air marshal on the first flight. It had also left me with considerably sweaty armpits, a naggingly full bladder, and my irritable bowel about to kick in.

In my mind I had created a list of American colleagues that I could call upon if needed. I'm sure one of them knew a few senators that they could summon with one phone call and express some concern over the treatment of a British friend. I wasn't quite sure how to go about this as while I knew most of their emails, I only had one or two of their phone numbers. Thinking about it, I actually didn't really want to call them and embarrass myself by admitting to being held in a detention centre by their immigration officers. I was panicked that I would have sounded like someone clutching at straws, really desperate, encouraging them to conclude that there's no smoke without fire.

My perspiration was increasing and the fear inside me was rising too. Not knowing was worse than knowing something, for at least you would know where you stood and be able to assess what you could do. I've never actually been put in this situation before, but if you think about it, probably thousands of people in the world are put into such a position of worry, uncertainty with perhaps even death as a feasible outcome through no fault of their own. Maybe because they were born somewhere poor, are the wrong caste, colour or creed, sexual orientation or conceivably they decided to follow the wrong God from the viewpoint of the majority or even have no religion, which in some places is considered worse than sacrilege itself. That of course is not true everywhere; we can live together peacefully and realise there are some bad people in the world whom we need to sift out. But overall, if you think about it, most people are good.

I remembered reading that the famous Indian actor, Shahrukh Khan, was held in a similar manner. He's a contemporary and truly famous Bollywood star, a bit like Tom Cruise in the States. He was fortunate enough to have phoned the Indian Prime Minister, who negotiated his release without too much of a diplomatic incident occurring. But could you imagine old Tom being detained in India? I also recall a similar incident being reported of members of the UK parliament, so was the 'holding ethnics treatment' perhaps contagious? They were like me, of Pakistani in origin, but born in the UK, and were also detained by the US immigration officials while visiting. I recall one of them quoted in a newspaper article as saying very politely, "I think it's reasonable to afford the same kind of courtesy and respect to a Member of Parliament visiting the United States as we would to a senator or congressman visiting the UK."

Time to reflect, I thought at this moment. I'm almost out of Atlanta airport, I don't think there's any reason for them to keep me and perhaps I will make my onward flight. But I don't think I can manage any duty-free shopping; the kids will just have to wait or go without. This will be a story that I will tell my grandchildren, but you may as well read about it now and then you can decide whether it should have happened or not. I was anxiously wishing for this ordeal to be over. At this point, however, I was still unsure of the outcome. I could just take it on the chin and move on with the rest of my life; in fact that is exactly what I have been trying to do, despite repeatedly facing this mental persecution. But we all must remember the basic truth, that when you're humiliated because of the colour of your skin, it is difficult as well as a testing experience for any person, irrespective of how psychologically strong they are, or think they are.

I wasn't sure how much longer I could hold on without a proper bowel evacuation – the kind we all look forward to but would never admit to. I didn't want to soil my trousers, although the likelihood was getting closer the longer he stayed away and the more time I was detained. Yes, these are the kind of colonic rumblings and explosive motions that I get when I'm a little bit stressed. I am never sure when it eventually will settle down, sometimes I have one or two episodes then it all just sort of crashes out and I go back to normal. I didn't really want to do anything; I clearly now also didn't even have time to dose myself in the latest cologne in duty free. Yes, you're all thinking out loud that I'm some sort of freeloader, but I suppose we all have our subtle habitual nuances. One meanders through duty free, splashes on a few colognes; actually I reckon if you undertook a controlled experiment there may be a few colognes that you could mix and it would give you quite a decent aroma, possibly even get you laid or you may even help you to join the Mile High Club. I haven't quite got that far yet, so cannot recommend what fragrant mixtures would give you that favourable smell, but I'm working on it.

Maybe that's where he went, he realised he had an opportunity to go quickly to duty free and buy some nice expensive Cologne the kind that I was looking forward to buying or at least trying on, well actually 'just' trying on. I didn't want to buy anything other than some presents for my kids. I wonder if he had any children, I wonder if he had bought anything for them or was going to buy something? Actually I was wondering if he was allowed to shop in duty free? Remember, he was a US immigration official. Maybe this was something they couldn't do. So many questions with so many answers that I needed.

It's at times like this you actually recall any religious upbringing that you may have had. I just really wanted to get on with the rest of my life. I hadn't even drunk enough, but I felt reasonably inebriated, which is not good as I'd rather have had a shot or something or even a smoke! I was unsure whether to start reading my book again, reasoning that getting out my laptop or phone might look suspicious if I was being watched. I was already expecting a sizeable mobile phone bill as I had sent my wife a number of text messages. So this unplanned as well as inordinate delay was costing me in more ways than one. There were no doubt a few hidden cameras in the room, as well as what looked as though it might have been a one-way mirror. I continued to remain very calm on the outside, but I could not help but feel a bit jittery on the inside as there was nothing I could do. The actual time I had waited overall was probably not too long I believe, but at times like this, minutes seem like hours.

At that moment the door was flung open, and he walked in with another two men either side of him. One was recording the entire episode, so I incorrectly assumed this was candid camera. They looked like they had ninja outfits on but possessed big automatic machine guns strapped to their chests. The shorter of the two then threw a large orange suit onto the desk in front of me.

"Sir, you are being detained!"

I had no reply, just a shocked look, felt ill and was about to vomit. Didn't wet myself though.

"Please do not move, we are about to frisk you, please place your hands in the air and walk towards us."

What had I done? I knew I should not have had that beer, or maybe the air marshal said I left the toilet in a mess – if I did it was certainly his fault. Perhaps my Muslim meal was my undoing? I should have ordered the regular meal, it would have tasted the same as all the others, no doubt, and I didn't feel so Halal anymore. What on earth was I supposed to do? I was in deep trouble, more than just a bit of a pickle. At such a moment it is almost as though a trance has fallen upon you, you have a sweeping array of electrical activity in your mind, with countless possibilities going through your mind. At forty-one years of age, all the training in life that I had had along with a sense of duty as a father and husband with a medical career moulded to care for the sick just flew past.

I decided that as a mature man and US-well-recognised overseas surgeon, they HAD to listen to me. I had at least paid my taxes back home.

"What have I done wrong, I am old enough to drink?" Then I panicked and went on to say something much worse: "You won't get anything out of me, I have been trained by the best, FBI, CIA, MI6 and my neighbour, I am not the Haram-zada you think I am, mate."

They were literally stunned by my audacity, they must have thought my neighbour was some 'bad' dude who was an expert in guerrilla warfare in at least two continents – with Antarctica being one of them…wait – they are about to counter my outburst as I awaited a scream of 'arrest him!' Guess my Halal days were now certainly ending with good old Shaitann finally getting the better of my brief life.

I then stood up and started slowly making my way to the door. I didn't raise my hands, thought better of it; I decided that I was going to make a run for it – it would be reasonable to assume that I had enough time to devise such an exit strategy with my window of opportunity open, but time was against me as I was about to discover with this 'window' about to be closed.

"Stop. Right. There. Sir!" – the senior officer screamed at me. I could see that his other colleagues had their taser guns locked onto me and set to stun – I just hoped that I wouldn't become impotent after this looming electric blast to my torso!

"We have reason to believe that on and after the flight you phoned a non-combatant."

Shit, they really did know everything; yes, I called my wife who was a non-combatant, well most of the time anyway, unless I did something wrong! All that was left was for my mum to walk in behind them and remind me to tell my wife that I prefer Chapatti to rice, and the desserts must have extra sugar in them to ensure that I would become diabetic by the age of fifty-five! This was sardonically met with a 'I told you so' rendition by an ex-girlfriend or even one of my so-called friends reminding me that I should have become a back-street abortionist as they predicted at med school. Guess I was met by Lee Majors, but it was as the 'Fall Guy', or Colt Seavers with no special powers like Steve Austin with the bounty being on my head.

I could not muster any intellectual reply so blustered out:

"I want to speak to President Obama." I tried to sound awfully convincing, so I suppose for a split second, I was like an American Hero – Lee Majors – our 70-80s Hollywood legend.

"Sir, please turn around and brace yourself!" "You have the right to remain silent…"

I could not make out the rest of what they were saying, it was like turning the TV off after a film had ended with no regard for all those hard-working film crew, the names of which as the credits roll no one reads other than themselves. My time had come to surrender my fate at the hands of the US authorities. I had little knowledge of why my phone battery was low with no respite in sight.

I couldn't think of what else to do, I knew I wasn't going to get away lightly here, they'd cornered me. After some quick mental calculations, I decided to make a run for it. The door was electronically bolted closed. I turned round sharply and took off my left shoe as I knew I could run with just one right shoe on. I threw it in the air and whilst it made a mesmerising circular motion in the air, little did they know that this shoe was a weaponized tranquilliser. My shoe landed on the desk with only a momentary pungent odour from a nine-hour flight escaping into the room's atmosphere. The tranquillising effect had passed. Pity I thought. This act of audacity was not going to go unnoticed...................

Paranoia and momentary lapses into hallucinations can create a melee of scenarios such as this. For heaven's sake, I thought while still sitting there for what seemed like an eternity, I operate on people for a living, save lives and this is what I have come to. So I continued my slow but steady incongruous stare at the walls of this, my room, without a view, with both my shoes still firmly on...and as yet, no orange suit!

★ ★ ★

The officer did eventually come back, perhaps only a few minutes later. It did, though, seem that time had stood still with only dreams and my vivid imagination to keep me company.

His hands looked partially dry, so I had guessed correctly; he had been for a toilet break. I had already mentally prepared myself for some further interrogation. The names of all my brothers would be easy, as well as the present whereabouts of any of my family. The family question was a possibility though.

In late 2007, my pregnant wife and almost two-year-old daughter visited family in Texas. This trip was my first encounter with the detention room. At this time the number of persons being called in also appeared to me to be fewer. At Dallas airport, the immigration officer asked only me and not my wife, "Are the rest of your family in the UK?"

My wife and I looked at each other and she replied, "They all are, aren't they?"

"Yes, they all are," I replied, slightly bemused.

I then went on to ask, "I am not sure where else they should be, please?"

She did not reply and promptly stamped my wife's and daughter's passports.

"You need to be checked out before you come into our country."

Before I could ask why or say anything, we were swiftly taken into a small room and asked to wait. I was protocolled (taken in as someone fitting a protocol driven suspicious look), for the first but unfortunately not the last time.

The line of questioning by this officer was clearly aimed at my ethnicity. If I were an Angrezi, then I could correctly assume that I would not have been asked this question about my family. Once in this rather smaller detention centre, I didn't wait long with my five-months-pregnant wife and two infant daughters. Common sense dictates someone of interest would rarely travel in such a manner. From behind a glass window, the more senior officer asked me the purpose of my visit and then for any other form of ID.

I presented my NHS ID card.

"Are you a doctor, sir?"

"Yes, I am a cancer surgeon."

"Sorry to have kept you, sir."

He stamped my passport and that was it. I did ask him why I was stopped; he politely ignored the question and I left with my family.

Back in Atlanta, I was prepared for this family question. It was another disparity with an *Angrezi* that I once again failed to understand. He asked me when I was going back to the UK. I said in four days' time. I guess he wasn't in the Secret Service so he couldn't hold his right hand to his ear, press a button, have a quick chat, get a response and then carry on. The person, if any such person was watching him probably wanted to know what was going on and to make sure everything was secure. I suppose at some point he did need to move on to the next detained and protocolled passenger.

I was immediately worried that he would start thinking what this man could possibly do in four days in San Francisco and LA. I immediately regretted disclosing other travel plans and decided to just limit my answers to the minimum, not wanting to further confuse or complicate the matter.

He was in a pleasant mood, hopefully feeling that his time had been wasted with me. To my indescribable relief, he proceeded to quickly stamp my passport and said that I was free to go. *That was it.* No lasting damage, but horribly unnecessary and unashamedly so. The fact that I was not white and bore a Muslim name was my crime.

I turned to him as I was leaving and asked him one simple question:

"I have reached almost the pinnacle of my profession; I have tirelessly worked hard all of my life to better myself so that I can help others. I am an eminent decorated surgeon by the United States, so why have I been taken in for questioning, please?"

I had gone from hero to villain in the country that I had yearned to live in the most, since a child. He paused and looked at me.

"There is nothing I can do about that, sir."

This comment I guess didn't explain the past two hours, but the fact that he said I could go on my way was conceivably what it was like to smoke weed. I needed to get out of there pretty damn quickly, say goodbye to Atlanta and make this plane to San Fran, hungry, sweaty with a look of anguish painted on my face.

Mental cruelty and anxiety are hot topics around the world these days. This episode in my life to date was the worst in terms of being sidelined for being 'different', unconventional, a polite man with a British accent, but not an *Angrezi*.

It was still dawning on me that it could have been much worse. I could have been with Kunta Kinte, born free in West Africa and then inexplicably taken in chains to a foreign land in the mid-eighteenth century. What must have been going through their minds, a fate worse than death, enslavement and a life of immiseration with legally enshrined inferiority for you and generations to follow. Or what about Anne Frank and her family, stuck in a makeshift house behind a book closet, realising each day that this might be your last if you were caught? Having to walk stealthily in your house, unable to play, laugh or even sob at your immense displeasure of being in a world where your differences are a crime rather than a point of celebration. Just imagine your mind being filled with thoughts of desolation as well as a perceived inferiority based on a physical or cultural difference. This moment in my life had given me this thought – and it remains to this day.

The UK continues to invite American leading surgeons to come and speak at many auspicious British academic surgical meetings. Just imagine if our immigration officers decide to take in a leading American physician for questioning for a few hours. Why, God knows, but they end up being detained for some time before being allowed in; maybe they had an Irish surname, and we were still holding on to some notion that 'all' Irish are anti-British. Wouldn't that make us look a bit stupid? Wouldn't that be embarrassing or constitute inhumane treatment? This may have happened, but I have not read any sensational press on this ever occurring. Rather, I have heard about our welcoming attitude.

I had much to thank the US for, especially from earlier in my career. I had also, I felt, much to gain by attending meetings in the US, so I expected to come again. We do value their medical ingenuity as well as forward-thinking approach to clinical practice. We have common values, share ideas, collaborate in research regularly, as well as respect each other's medical training and expertise. Our actual schooling and medical infrastructure are both similar in many ways, especially the way we approach patients. But the greatest thing we have in common is language.

The American constitution prides itself on its laws, adherence to jurisprudence and its 'Bill of Rights' gives all persons an unequivocal right to freedom, civil liberties and of course right to religion, to name just some of its conditions. I honestly believe this should be 'true' to this day as well as taught in school to all Americans. The US constitution is formidable and prides itself on the protection of the sanctity of human life, bestowing freedoms that all persons deserve. So there is light at the end of the tunnel, but does it depend on who is in that tunnel with you? Almost every time I have been across to the States, I have been treated very well, welcomed with open arms, never been asked if I was anything else other than a Brit as my accent as well as mannerism are those of a native of our isles. Perhaps the immigration officers in Atlanta and Dallas were just following instructions from higher up. Surely a country such as the US has more access to intelligence than any other country notwithstanding the fact that I am from their closest friend and ally, the United Kingdom? But that mattered little.

As I left the interrogation room in Atlanta, I looked at all the faces of the remaining detainees. They looked worn out. Some had been there a long time, perhaps several hours, and most were in the 'yellow' queue, so it meant that they had to wait longer as there were more yellows than red. They were nearly all dark-skinned individuals, some entire families, women wearing the hijab and men in Arab dress. I felt some pain and anguish as I looked at them all; they looked the same as me, only I had 'Western' clothes on – I was an *Angrezi* on the outside, but brown on the inside – but what were children doing there? Why were they not let through? The moment I was about to exit through the glass door, a woman of South Asian origin caught my eye. She was wearing a pleasant sari with her three very young sons around her, fidgeting away as any small children would do left in a room with only seats and no toys. My mind exhausted and saturated by frustration was suddenly permeated by a vivid memory of seeing them mirroring a picture of my mother and her three boys. To complete my recollection, her middle child gazed and smiled at me as I walked past, which struck me as poignant as I am the middle child too; my heart broke and I worried that visceral prejudice will linger on for some time like the stench of smoke in the air. Children can be affected by such experiences from an early age, as I know from experience. Most will take it in their stride, leaving a reduced but memorable impact on their future.

But it will be naïve of the world to think that this will be the case for many others who are so young. Children just want to live a life filled with happiness, laughter and above all safety, which is what the United States is all about – a land of immigrants, built by them and by later immigrants over the past five hundred years. Repeated instances like this in a person's life can mould the future terrorist unless society has a way of dampening down any negative effect by creating a positive, loving and more tolerant environment for all individuals. If society hates you, then human nature dictates that you will end up resenting what life events have been dished out to you. It's a no brainer. So let's not sow the seeds of an angry and misrepresented society wherever you are in the world.

If I were let out and they were all detained or worse still if they were all to be put on a train in shackles only to head to an unknown destination, I would inescapably feel the absolute desire to ditch my *Angrezi* attire and join them – what else could I do? It was a natural calling for me as it would be for anyone; otherwise, I would be letting myself down. I knew though that this would never happen.

The red or 'highly dangerous' category that I was put in

was much smaller, so I made it out a bit more swiftly (about an hour and a half, I reckon, is quick). But in this category I was interviewed in a separate room, which I suppose could have been a bad thing with a worse outcome. For once I was grateful that I was in a highly dangerous queue, as there were less of us, however, it meant I was treated like a possible but serious threat to the US. There is an article I had read recently which described how Muslims with European passports were the most dangerous suspected terrorists in the world. Perhaps this is the reason why I was detained. I was for a while under the impression that my baffling detention was designed by a capricious immigration officer; analogous to a schoolteacher subjecting an entire class to an after-school punishment rather than just the guilty one or two?

I ran out and hurtled to the baggage area, where my bag was easy to find as it had been taken off the carousel and conveniently parked near the San Francisco conveyor belt. I quickly asked the baggage handler whether my luggage would make the flight.

"Yes, sir."

I noted that the flight was due to leave in thirty minutes, but the gate was a fair distance away in this huge hub of an airport, requiring a shuttle train through to the appropriate terminal. So I headed towards the shuttle, passed the duty-free cologne, passed the food hall, with all the delights of the airport transit lounge forgotten courtesy of US immigration. This shuttle was an excellent and relatively pleasant journey.

Thankfully we did not have to stand too close to each other as I guessed that as a man, I may not have had the best aroma exuding from me, especially as I probably had over-perspired during the most nerve-wracking experience of my life, and with no timely access to duty free cologne. I managed to get there in good time to board the flight. I tried not to run, managed to empty my bladder, good job too as my prostate was only just over forty years of age, so doubly made sure no one suspected me as a 'nutter' with dark skin running through an American airport!

That was close, I thought. Too close. I had missed my newfound primary boarding time as a front-of-the-plane passenger, only to join a large queue heading for the gate. I texted my wife to let her know I had made the plane, and she was relieved to say the least. She had already worked out a contingency strategy to get me to San Francisco the next day. Flying to San Fran I could not shake the thought that I had paid the price with an unscheduled delay purely based on the colour of my skin or my Muslim name, I am still none the wiser as to which it was. Not knowing meant that I might have to endure this fate yet again on my next trip to the US or elsewhere.

I normally speak to the passenger sitting next to me on the plane, and this is usually much easier in the States where people are culturally more open and talkative than in Britain. My neighbouring passenger was an American businessman and was not intent on speaking to anyone, but rather got absolutely hammered. He must have had an entire bottle of wine before we even took off. I was tired. I had missed the opportunity to eat. I couldn't sit down comfortably or relax, covered in perspiration and with a tight knot still in my stomach. But I was on the flight to San Fran and not Guantanamo. Was this to be my destiny from now on when travelling, a statutory stop and search? Despite my respectable occupation back home with its ability to affect people's lives with the decisions I make, I would need to hit a dizzier height in life, somehow, not to be stereotyped as a possible threat to any country I visit. I am still trying to fathom out a meaning of this confusion in life that I felt, created by the hand of fate I had been dealt.

The meeting was a huge success, with my trainee at the time winning a poster presentation prize. San Francisco is a lovely city. I liked the trams, although I took none and managed with taxis everywhere, saw the Golden Gate bridge, went to Alcatraz (as my Indian colleagues were intent on making the most of their trip in terms of a financial recoup). I even celebrated St Patrick's Day. The colleagues that I met at this meeting remain my very close American friends to this day. I still contemplate working in the US and think I would fit in well, be respected for my professional qualifications, expertise and have ample opportunity to conduct extensive research, which is where my real passion lies.

To be fair, in the UK, I have not been impeded in any obvious way; making consultant at thirty-five and an honorary professor at forty-six years of age is surely a testament to the opportunities that are afforded to me in my country, especially if you work hard and you're good enough? I could feasibly argue that any hostile treatment I have suffered has been balanced or even superseded by the kindness and humanity I have experienced at home, allowing me to progress in a competitive field. However, my perplexing and woefully unnecessary encounter and undignified treatment at the hands of the US immigration officials still overshadows the memorable congress and has undermined long-held dreams of relocating to the US. I never mentioned to anyone what had happened to me before the meeting, I was just pleased that I made it. I was worried that any loose comment could seep through the cracks of the conference halls, creating potential problems for the two further plane journeys I had yet to endure.

For anyone that is singled out in a queue because of the way they look, I would not hesitate to recommend to the person triaging the queue that they should always reflect on why they are making any decisions. Humility is important for all persons to share and, when faced with prejudicial treatment based on your skin colour, one can only sympathise with the lack of understanding there is still in the world today. Disparagingly, some may not care as the power they wield in this scenario maybe all they have in this world. If true, it is but the reality of a world that we all are culpable of designing.

I wouldn't describe the immigration officer's actions as idiosyncratic as I honestly believe he was probably just following orders. What this 'order' or sanctioned protocol may actually entail; or even the rationale behind it, will remain a mystery to me.

"Let us not ill-judge those that merely look like the perpetrators of heinous crimes as this failed judgement will not only fail you, but humanity itself."

Aali J Sheen, 2021

Chapter Seventeen

– Things past cannot be recalled

London. Summer 1976

Boy, it was hot this summer. I can recall even aged five or six years old that we spent most of our time on our small balcony or in the park wearing our shorts with sandals (with socks I might add) and eating ice cream. My mother often used to take us to the local corner shop near where I grew up on the council estate, around the corner from our school and the infamous egg attack. The shop sold mostly everyday items, such as bread, milk, eggs, candles for the power cuts and newspapers, as well as possessing a very nice and well-stocked confectionery counter. While my mum shopped in this and in any shop she frequented, my brothers and I would argue over the futile things in life such as who was stronger and would win a fight – if for instance it was Superman against Batman. Needless to say, each of us three had a favourite, my older brother's was Superman, mine was Batman, and my younger brother's was Spiderman, although he liked the Hulk too. It was easy shopping with my mother as she rarely scolded us, and spoke to us only in Urdu, meaning when a telling-off was met with laughter and further childish play, onlookers would consider us with endearment rather than disdain. 'Look,' they would sometimes say, 'how lovely they are.' We weren't always pleasant, I can assure you of that. The only discipline we knew was from our father, and we knew how to stay out of trouble at school. I guess my father's reluctance to give us sweets and allow no sugar in our bottle feeds when very young was one of the reasons why as South Asian kids we still had all our milk teeth!

At the checkout my mother would usually buy us something from the ever-glittering array of sweets. Smarties were my favourite as you could shake the tube like a maraca. The shop owner and her husband were both Angrezi, a rarity these days as most corner shops now have immigrant owners.

She smiled at me.

"You will see all of those Smarties on the shop floor in a moment."

Lo and behold she was correct, as with a sudden pop, the lid flew off with all the coloured little chocolate sweets now decorating the floor. A few must have escaped under the long shelves as well as under the counter, no doubt, a nice supper for the in-store resident mice.

"Oh dear," she said, "I told you!"

*She was very nice about it and even gave my mother another Smarties tube for free. Life was not all bad. If it wasn't for people like the shop owner with her kindness, I would have said to my parents why live in a place that does not want you? Let's go to where we will feel some love as well as be appreciated for our contribution to society. My father left for UK shores to start a new life in a rich, powerful and supposedly more civilised country with more opportunities; although he was 'invited' to apply as 'they' needed persons like him. Little did he know that he would enter into an apparent war zone with race the defining reason for everyday conflicts, that not only **he** would witness the discord through no fault of his own making, but his children would experience the alienation in more ways than one, perhaps even for the rest of their lives.*

★ ★ ★

Growing up in London, I learnt at a tender age that the apparent hostility that I was often subjected to was not bullying or hate crime, but a depiction of what racism actually looked like. Most young children do not know what racism is, an example of the innocence of the very young. But all too often I experienced a sudden deviance from this purity by someone creating a discriminatory racial bias, possibly as a result of a contrived form of brainwashing. But by whom? An individual, society or is it an inherited trait? From a small child playing in infant school, when I believed that I was not any different, unaware of any immigrant blood running through my little veins, I was under the impression that all my playmates, including my *Angrezi* friends, went home and spoke a different language from the one we spoke at school. This plainly was an example of the innocence of children, which is best left untouched and unbroken? But all of a sudden, this innocent life I was living as a child came to a premature end! I came to realise, through no fault of my own, that I was being subjected to unfair and unkind treatment, leaving a mind, like a river, polluted with bad memories, which has resulted in a person with delicate sensitivities due to the flashbacks of childhood racist slurs and other such misdemeanours. I was subjected to racial taunts from as early as I can remember. If I were to guess, I reckon I was about four or five years old when it consciously started to influence me. Ever since then, each day of my life, my inner voice has told me that I am a coloured, and therefore an inferior person in my world.

They say that you cannot help where you are born, and this is true irrespective of what divinity you hold dear. I guess I was 'lucky' not to have being born in the US before civil rights were established. I could have been born as a Christian in Roman times, a coloured man in the Deep South in the 1930s, a Jewish person in Germany in 1937 or even recently as a Rohingya Muslim in Burma, to name just a few examples. My life to me, like yours to you, is dear, and the examples above show it could have been so much worse had I been born in a different time or place. I sometimes ask myself whether I have ever truly been happy, with no bitter, empty feeling inside or the fear that another moment of discriminatory forms of behaviour is just around the corner. I honestly can answer and say, 'No.' And this feeling I will perhaps miserably take to my grave.

History has shown that humans have controlled the ecosystem by claiming their superiority over animals. This can be found in all religions even as far back as ancient times. Even in my own country's history, one 'tribe' has always dominated, be it the Anglo-Saxons, Romans, or Vikings, before the concept of one nation was developed. Conversely, where my parents came from, the Indian Subcontinent, tribe and caste still matter with a one-nation concept still unable to surface.

However, maybe now over the last four to five hundred years there is a feeling that some ethnicities or tribes will always overshadow or will be superior to others? Yes – the concept of 'racial superiority' as we understand it only began to surface in the Early Modern Period. This is the thought that goes through my mind a number of times as I feel that an unwarranted hostility has followed me in an almost orchestrated manner. I naively presumed at one time that as an adult I had weathered the racial storm in my life in the 1970s and 80s. But no, it keeps happening, forcing me to question whether these man-made and at times baseless differences become irreconcilable. I hope they do not.

So one has to consider the reasons why I experienced such human hatred and denigratory perceptions – can I logically assume that we all have inborn animosity to persons that do not look like us in terms of our hue or complexion? I must ponder this question, 'Is there a genetic allele that can be identified?' which will then scientifically provide an explanation for me. To me, logically, this cannot be so, as so many *Angrezis* have convincingly as well as unashamedly helped me. Was it because I was lucky enough to be born in a country where there are no laws to bring about such racial crimes? Nor Members of Parliament enticing racial tension and banning the erection of new religious buildings other than those for Christianity? As described above, in our past many were not so lucky, as their laws once upon a time allowed vilification and persecution based on race. So can I conclude no, because I expect as homo sapiens this is not 'in-built' in us? It can be readily argued that the human subconscious has somehow finally prevailed and rejected their antiquated poisonous beliefs, as well as the so-called ingrained traditional concepts which have insisted on divisions as well as segregation leading to the subjugation of one tribe or another. I believe that I was lucky enough to be born in a tolerant country that has learnt from its past, with unfortunately many still around the world yet to follow suit.

Nonetheless, despite this lack of hostility, with the force of jurisprudence on my side, these episodes of racial intolerance that I have chronicled throughout have, regrettably, kept on going in an unrelenting manner and are now *flooding* into my adult life, with my chin literally just above water. So all I need now is for someone or society to just pull the plug so I can stop treading water and feel no more the need for a subconscious level of pain, hurt and uncertainty as to whether I will be singled out again. I somehow reached the profession I coveted; I have hit obstacles all the way, but the ability to jump hurdles and not be derailed has been an achievement. I do wonder how I have managed so far so well.

Looking back on my childhood, one must ask, if it's not in our DNA, where did 'they', the other children, learn these phrases and subsequently discriminate? Parents, I guess, or someone older is where I would first lay the culpability, in other words a traditional belief, where any belief can bring about an end to reason. Or was it from television? We had programs such as *Love thy Neighbour* and *Mind your Language*, which my parents as well as us kids actually loved to watch, more so as ethnics were on the TV.

Now due to a belated sense of political correctness they are gone. But were they responsible for people's behaviour, or was it just that particular time where differences were made more apparent, so much so that their very recognition meant that we could be used as a malicious target, as well as a source for comedy? But this was all simply accepted in society at the time and unfortunately tolerated as the norm.

Surely an egalitarian society is what everybody wants? But this remains an incendiary idea almost certain to be catapulted at first sight into a forgotten land, with an occasional guest appearance at an apt moment of deep thought and moral consciousness. Will there always be a self-perpetuating belief that one ethnicity is better than another amongst a few persons, antediluvian though it may seem? It is a reality for an unfortunate few. If this is so, then we would need to find a genetic link to confirm this; possibly differences in thinking ability, ageing process with even the know-how for asexual reproduction, who knows?

Has the power of inbuilt hatred now reached its apogee or are we only preparing ourselves for more prejudice and irrationality? I can only trust that this is not the case and that any hatred based on the way we look is ephemeral.

Yet, with education now being what it is today, in addition to the profoundly obvious fact that we have all co-existed in this great multicultural society for some time now, I think we have a greater understanding of each other. What is the denominator for prejudice? Poorly understood differences. I guess if you go back in time even recently in my country, the Jewish diaspora suffered, over one hundred years earlier, what the Bangladeshi community are now experiencing in East London – a difference was found, unnecessary separation was forged. I see now from the 1970s to the early twenty-first century that in many areas, integration and racial awareness, as well as equality, have improved. Laws have changed, attitudes have been moulded by the impact of at first the Race Relations Act in the UK passed in 1965[4], which more recently has been replaced by the Equality Act in 2010[5], correctly covering all the protected characteristics including gender and disability to name a few, but disappointingly not caste. So prejudice cannot be attributed to inherited traits, but must have come from our community beliefs at the time?

If society is like a restaurant, you could even give it a Michelin star in some parts of the world. But in this restaurant, instead of having a set menu whereby there is no other choice, no social mixing, rich don't meet poor, signs saying 'coloureds only' or even 'no Irish, no Blacks, no Dogs', mixing of persons of a different hue are now thankfully more likely. We now see a buffet-style menu whereby you can choose whatever you wish, and you can decide who your friends are. It doesn't matter what your plate of food looks like so long as you're happy.

Overall, I think equality-driven policies and laws have led to swifter changes in attitudes, as life events and real-time history is taking too long to wait for a solution to forging alliances between races, where instead we are continuing to witness alienation based on petty physical differences.

I am a second-generation immigrant; my father was unequivocally told that he was not an equal. His education to qualify as a lawyer in Pakistan was undervalued and so in effect he was barred from ever being promoted. You will have read that despite having been born in a country, nourished by Thames water, to then grow up speaking and sounding like a native of the British Isles let alone over the phone, but in person – I still have not been measured as an equal at home and definitely not when travelling abroad. I am proud to be British and a European with an affinity for values such as liberalism, the rule of law, equality and tolerance. Despite the fact that I reject misogyny, anti-Semitism, islamophobia, racism of any kind and homophobia – I am still unequal in certain eyes. Now my children are third generation immigrants, they are monolingual and as English/ British as they come. What will the future hold for them? I must ask myself how many more generations we must go through before we are accepted, having lived in our family's home since 1964?

One thing that goes through my mind is that we as a nation are changing. This is evident as the pendulum has certainly swung in a direction that I could only imagine when I was a child, away from a racist ideology. My children haven't suffered what I had as a child; they are growing up in a more tolerant and equal society. Only time will tell when they're adults and whether they are able to achieve what they set out to do. Whether one of them (or someone like them) could become prime minister of our great nation is a test that will signify our country's intent of creating a more pluralistic society.

The templates that were categorising us all are, thankfully, changing. But it is not haemorrhaging away with the speed that one would hope and expect; perhaps this book has demonstrated this very fact aptly enough to even those determined to deny the existence of racism, whose persistent cognitive biases will taint any of their objective decision making.

There was no let-up in the P word when I was growing up and it has dissipated to a degree but, as I have already said, not vanished though from some sections of society. I have seen on social media some Asian MPs and celebrities have been insulted with racist slurs for all to read. Disappointingly no criminal actions have ensued as a result. In addition, I feel that the P word is used in a much more indirect manner these days. I hear it in my mind especially when I sense injustice has befallen me; call it paranoia, but I cannot help the fact that society has made me this way. So if I ever hear patronising remarks by *Angrezis* against any Asian and Afro-Caribbean friends or colleagues, I think about the last time someone threw eggs at them because they looked different, especially as a small child. Both my parents had made a decision to emigrate to a cold, wet and completely different country halfway round the world for a better life, away from the corruption and needless constant injustices that they felt Pakistan was afflicted by. Remember their respective families had already been uprooted once in 1947. There was no trust in their government and whilst working in chambers in Karachi, my father realised this after he was reliably advised to offer a 'bribe' to the magistrate to win his case. If he didn't win cases, then fewer people would come to him. If fewer people came to him, he could not earn a decent living and so the cycle would go on, as it would anywhere else in the world. This predicament is not unique in time and place but left my father an indignant resignation that if he could not beat the system, he would need to be part of it merely to survive; it was the same old proverb, 'If you can't beat them, join them!' He would have had to play this game, but he was an idealist and not a realist.

I must give him credit for the journey he made, the treatment he must have endured and taking a low-paid job in the UK with no hope of promotion or a hint of a pay rise. He never complained, despite the fact that in the mid-1980s, two of his colleagues from his chambers in Karachi went on to be appointed to the Supreme Court of Pakistan as Chief Justices. One of them was also appointed Governor of a province called Sind. I asked him once why he didn't stay. We probably would have had a better standard of living, or at least more respect, than we had in the UK where we were subjected to a covert racial divide through no fault of our own. I recall his reply to me being simply, "When I write a letter to anyone here in the UK, I receive a courteous, civilised reply. There is also no corruption, so I do not need to bribe anyone."

This was enough for him, he was happy to hear the occasional P word, but he was still grateful to be a guest in a country which had given him an opportunity to change his life, was clean with ready access to fresh water by merely turning on the tap in his kitchen. He could also trust what he ate in a restaurant without worrying about contracting salmonella. I could not disagree with him, and I think about his sacrifices that allowed me to be born in a great country, which has already given my family and me much. Needless to say, he was happy with less than equal treatment at work. He never assumed he would be afforded the same privileges as a native. Perhaps this was the reason he held onto his past by keeping abreast of regular updates about Pakistani politics. But should the same thing be true of us second and now third generations?

Much has been said and analysed in this account of my life events, especially of my visits to the United States. I actually still go to the US a lot, enjoy it every time, have relatives there, admire their enormous work ethic as well as belief in always trying to move forward in a positive direction, which is what is culturally imbedded in them. Remember that most if not almost all of the people that are in the United States are of immigrant stock. The actual native population is very small so the proverbial question that some may ask others such as "Where are you from?" is a non-starter for ten with only the true native Americans claiming land rights dating back over a thousand years. This drive that the newcomers, 'Americans', have whether they have been there for just a few generations or many, is not surprising when you recognise that they decided to leave their homeland in search of a new and better place to live. Their founding fathers affirmed this notion in a new land. Once you arrive there comes a pretext for a fresh beginning. You will naturally work harder than most, try to make your lives better, which in turn will have a knock-on effect on the adopted country. You will then inevitably reap the rewards of your hard work. This 'Get up and go' mentality can be passed down through the generations, whether they are first, second or sixteenth, so maybe that is why perhaps they are so successful as a nation. If you have a high concentration of high achievers in one place with that sanctuary of entrepreneurial thought multiplying generation after generation, controlling the world's economy will be inevitable.

I accept that some can be left behind, but this is true of any part of the world. However, there is a caveat as some of the population say that they were not there of their own free will and are unfortunately reminded of this every day with over four hundred years of incommensurate treatment. The BLM movement again has galvanised itself in 2020, for hopefully one final time to forge equality, which has traditionally been confined to the colour you are born. It remains irrefutable to a degree that if you have an African ancestor in the States, they survived what can only be regarded as a horrific journey across the Atlantic over four hundred years ago . This fact gives much high regard to their progeny, who undoubtedly have huge potential. It may be a prudent place in my text to remind our American allies and friends that it was at this time the first Muslims arrived in their country. It has been said by many that they've only been there for a snippet of America's immigrant history, but history dictates that this would be incorrect. Plenty has also been said of their incumbent President in 2020, a self-made billionaire businessman who is putting America first. Well, let's just think about that, shall we? Why not put the persons in your own country first, everyone else does? Why not allow people into your country that actually are coming to learn, teach or provide an invaluable service, why not let persons into your country that will respect your laws of tolerance, equality as well as the inherent and documented freedoms? So I do not disagree with this stance, it is not disingenuous, but what I, like anyone else would object to, is a 'blanket' stereotyping of persons based on their colour or religion.

What of assimilation? One can change one's name, but why

change a name that your parents gave you with all that love and affection? This is something that I mulled over many a time to the point of actually choosing a backup name, Aadam, meaning First Man in Arabic, with that spelling. Regardless, I cannot change the colour of my skin – well I could, but I think skin-lightening tablets are scary and I guess I'd need a lot with the additional risk of developing skin cancer!

You'll be interested to know that I have been stopped by immigration officers in the States during both the Bush and Obama administrations. Since being decorated in the US in 2002, then questioned as a suspected terrorist in 2011, I have been back to attend conferences since President Trump came into power and have seemingly waltzed in. I bet that surprises you!? I have actually asked my children, when they're the right age of course, that it would make inordinate sense that they might wish to consider a good university across the pond. Going abroad opens your horizons and influences your outlook on life more creatively. I think this is good. If you look around the world as I've already mentioned there are many places that basically will just look at you and your inherited DNA, then shout out various incomprehensible words resembling an elephant trumping a warning to their herd when a lion is close – hey India! Worse still is the treatment of African students in India, ridiculed as they walk through the streets – because in India a darker complexion is less revered.

I have many colleagues from the US so I am regularly invited to speak there, but I will never forget that as a young man who came to one of their largest meetings in 2002, whose presence on stage was possibly a refreshing attraction for the audience with his vernacular, as well as a language they understood, only to leave with their most coveted prize as the best scientific researcher. This American Surgical Society ignored the way I looked and my Muslim-born half-name did not matter to them. But what carried weight was that I was better than the rest at that meeting, on that day, at that time and moment, so much so that they recognised me with a much-desired reward – so thank you, America.

I have always felt a deep sense of loyalty to my country, the UK. Both my wife and I have ensured that our children are patriotic, too. Despite certain trials and tribulations that I have faced throughout life, I still regard the UK as one of the most free, fair and forward-looking nations on earth. I therefore take issue with those from immigrant backgrounds, especially those lucky enough to be born in the UK, who frown upon our way of life, our tolerance, religious freedoms, social responsibility and liberal views. They always have the choice to leave and settle elsewhere, just as their forefathers emigrated because they were not happy where they were living. They, of course, have an inalienable right to protest along with everybody else, as well as disagree, but if the objection is that our culture is reprehensible, there are plenty of countries in the world that reject our liberal values, so why not live amongst those who share the same mindset? While I uphold that every global citizen has a right to criticise their own country, if you are not a native *Angrezi*, such criticism is likely to be taken the wrong way, with remarks such as 'Go back to where you came from' ensuing. Non-natives and new arrivals should embrace the expectation that they should aim to grow into their adoptive society, while the host country should equally provide space and freedom that allows people to not have to reject outright and forget their own heritage and identity. The *Angrezis* tried in India and failed; they conquered, subjugated the natives and left under a cloud. So giving all communities room and respect for each other you may think is a modern idea, but even I know that the mixing of cultures in history has or must have worked otherwise we would not have survived this long. Unfortunately, *Angrezis* are more likely to be classed as racists, but I have shown how it can be overt as well as just as profound when people of the same colour are themselves discriminatory towards each other, hence my experience in Egypt.

Whilst my history has been peppered with perceived prejudice, I struggle to think of incidents where I have experienced overt racism from patients. If you are sick, unwell, cannot move, need help, and feel incredibly vulnerable, you don't tend to mind who looks after you or treats you, as you want to get better. Arguably it has aided the reputation of people of South Asian origin in the UK to have a proportionally greater representation in the NHS than in other jobs in mainstream society. About 35% of NHS doctors are classed as BAME and so provide a sizeable part of the workforce. Considering that the actual percentage of doctors that are of South Asian origin is 23% when we make up only 4% of the entire population, this demonstrates an inherent drive to succeed and climb the social ladder as well as perhaps our cultural inclination towards the status that comes with white collar work.

Yet if you look at the number of complaints and GMC (General Medical Council)[6] proceedings and disciplinary actions, medics of colour are very much over-represented and are twice or sometimes three times more likely to face such challenges. This can be true of any person irrespective of their parental background, i.e., whether they were born in the UK or not. It appears that an *Angrezi* doctor is more likely to be given the benefit of doubt by an unhappy patient.

One thing is for sure. Everything that you read in this book is tethered to an ever-evolving generational perspective. My parents were first-generation immigrants with a very different viewpoint of the world. I am second generation and my children third, and I am pleased to say that they have not experienced anything remotely similar to the events I've described above, especially at school age. This means as a society we are surely progressing in the right direction, moving positively forward, but unfortunately this cannot be said of too many parts of the world where religious hatred, misogyny, discrimination and overt tribalism still thrive. We must ensure we do not import these cultural flaws and allow them to take root here too.

You may think this is easy – changing not our attitudes but those of others that come from countries that are not evolving in the same way on race and discrimination as we are.

So here is an example of a kind of visceral racial profiling or box-ticking that does not need to happen but does, albeit innocently. I invariably order an Uber when I travel. The Uber will naturally come to my house to pick me up; generally speaking, without wishing to stereotype, most of the drivers are of South Asian origin, nice chaps, good drivers who can get through traffic like a rat up a drainpipe. When I sit down, I invariably notice that they look at me in the rear-view mirror inquisitively. Reading my surname, then looking at me, reading my name again, then looking at me sends a signal of mismatch into their minds. They may even double/triple/quadruple check my name on their Uber monitor to confirm that it is correct? But I can't help feeling that it still sends them into utter confusion!

Uber – "Sheen?"

Me – "Yes, that's my name and thank you for picking me up, can you take me to the airport please?"

After a prolonged repetitive stare at me through their rear-view mirror, they go on to say:

Uber – "So basically where from you?" which in layman's terms means what is your ethnic background?

Me – "Well you just picked me up from my house, that's where I'm from. I'm from here!" Somehow, I gather that this route of conversation that I have chosen isn't going to work.

Uber – "No, where from you?" I am asked again. And so,

Me – "What do you mean exactly?" They then reply:

Uber – "NO, basically where from you?"

Me – "Errrr, not sure what you mean, can't you tell by my accent?" I guess I am referring to my ever so *Angrezi* accent.

Uber – "Where are from parents? Mudder, Pather, you look Indian, yes?"

Me – "OK, where are my parents from? Right, well I was born in London."

There's no let-up with this answer as it usually can make matters worse!! I also realise that I am in a taxi, so I don't want him to crash!

Uber – "No you don't look from the London!"

Hell, I should have done a Brummie accent! He clearly was not happy:

Me – "I'm from the London alright, fine," so then I quite cleverly say:

"Well yes, I see that you have got my accent all wrong, I was actually raised in South London but born in North London, hence a slight confused disparity in my London tone, but I'm clearly not a native Northerner, they generally speak differently. Well done, you should work for MI5!"

The driver at this point gets really baffled, bemused frankly, is taking me to the airport, the mileage is clocking up, I've realised roughly how much I'm going to pay and that's about it for me but they don't really let it go...!

Uber – "No, not the London, where from parents, India, Pakistan? So I guess Sri Lanka and Bangladesh are once more excluded, but this is not unnatural, more a pleasant exclusion. I must though apologise to my friends and colleagues from either Bangladesh or Sri Lanka, there is really no offence intended, but perhaps a nuclear arsenal may help, only then they may achieve enough international recognition and notoriety in the world.

"Right, OK, you wanna know where my parents are from, not where I'm from?"

Let's look at this objectively again, shall we? Ideally, they shouldn't really be looking at me for the colour of my skin or my name in order to try to automatically assume they know where I'm from. It shouldn't really matter. But knowing the nuances of South Asian culture, they are from countries where you're defined by your caste, religion, colour (the darker you are, the less people will think of you), where you are living, whether rich or poor and so on. We are though, in the UK, living in a more pluralistic society. So I do forgive them as they are not the lawmakers in their country. I also generally understand that they're trying to relate to me. So, most of the time, I say OK, fine I'm a Pakistani man or possibly an Indian. I go with whatever the taxi driver is. I assume is if he looks Pakistani or I think he is, mainly because he's got a Muslim name, I then say I'm Pakistani and if it's Indian I say I'm Indian. I reckon the closer I forge a familiar inherited trait with the driver, the more likely I will just get an easier and hopefully less political ride. Some of them go on to berate the other countries, but I'm just grateful that they're not going to crash.

I'm generally just messing with them, but I'm also trying to teach them in my own little way not to judge a book by its cover. I usually go on to create an ethnic bond and when I leave their taxi, I say thank you as well as speak with them in fluent Urdu. This way they can feel satisfied that I am one of them.

On a final note, to conclude my taxi extravaganza, I do admit though when I pop into a taxi and the driver is Eastern European possibly Ukrainian or Polish, they never actually ask me where I'm from. I guess the hint of my accent possibly gives it away. So I guess this could come down to a difference between continents in terms of perception and human description with the bare fact that in some places we still have to categorise people. Some countries I guess are still using this all too familiar grouping process, where humans are subdivided, which I might add is likely responsible for some conflicts as well as wars around the globe? Thankfully, though, most countries have stopped. So where does that leave us, you ask? You could say that being unmanaged or poorly tolerated in those countries/ communities creates misunderstanding which in turn leads to frustration and probably anger. Anger then creates hatred, then hatred will create conflict, conflict creates further denigration as well as dehumanisation, which will eventually lead to an unnecessary and futile battle resulting in deaths. So who will suffer in the end, the poor, women, and children?

As I approach the completion of my fiftieth year, I cannot bemoan what I have achieved so far as a Senior Consultant Surgeon in our beloved National Health Service. I am grateful to all my bosses who have helped and supported me, from all backgrounds. I cannot change the way I look but I have managed to gain an international reputation for my skills and research as a surgeon, have been awarded a chair with a university giving me the title 'Professor'. I have received global board positions and prestigious council appointments to some leading surgical societies. Patients travel from far and wide to see me including from abroad from such places as the US, Middle East and of course, Europe, with their respective problems in my area of expertise. I try my best to help, as any good doctor would. To quote Hippocrates, *'Wherever the art of medicine is loved there is also a love of humanity.'*[7]

I have kept on going despite the 'pot shots' life has taken at me largely because I am descended from immigrants. I wish that my past experiences, especially whilst travelling abroad were different and I cannot see what will assuage the anguish I feel each time I approach an immigration desk in any country. I believe that this missile aimed in my direction, more commonly known as racial stereotyping, will continue for some time, but importantly my children already see a different, more tolerant Britain than I did as a child, which is excellent. However, time will tell if this equal treatment remains when they venture into adulthood. I am not bullet-proof though, so one day the pot shots I encounter will hurt more than ever. I will then bleed. When that day arises, I will most likely take on a much lower profile, perhaps not travel as much, even consider becoming a total recluse, or worse quit my job as one can only take being called a P so many times. I could try and change perceptions in the world, but for this I would ask that the media attempt some responsible reporting. This will help persons like me especially by the avoidance of words like 'Islamist', I am yet to meet a 'Christianist', though I have met Christians (but I have certainly met a Buddhist).

Personally, I am now partially immune to many racial taunts, although you are never completely insusceptible. The word 'Paki' will always bring back awful spine-chilling memories. But this is now a part of me and defines who I am, as those are my life experiences. Notwithstanding my past, I will never become complacent or reticent especially when it comes to witnessing overt discrimination against any person for their race, religion, gender, marital status, disability, pregnancy, sexual orientation, size, hair colour, dress sense, nationality or age.

Perhaps education did help me get out of poverty, it most certainly did provide me with a better quality of life, a little more respect in society but unfortunately did *not* overcome racial stereotyping as well as prejudice.

Have you ever thought that your life may be on trial and one day you could be asked to defend your actions or inactions?

Mock Courtroom

Barrister – "Professor, I assume this is your correct title?" (Guess Sir or Lord may never have arrived.)

"Yes, that is correct."

Barrister – "Do you feel you were unfairly discriminated against in life both as a child and adult – if so why?"

"Yes I must confess this is true, from as early as I can remember; I guess it was mainly due to the colour of my skin more than anything. When a child it was physical with obvious accompanying bile and vitriol spewed in my direction for all to hear as a description of who I was. And, if you let me finish – as an adult a more surreal encounter occurred with an impenetrable barrier erected before me at an immigration desk."

Barrister – "Has it stopped you achieving your goals? Has it prevented you from earning the title Professor? Did it stop you from undertaking the job you so coveted to do since you were young?"

"No, although maybe I may have achieved what I have sooner or more easily."

Barrister – "So what is your problem, Professor, don't you think you're taking things a little bit too far, don't you think maybe you have a chip on your shoulder, don't you think maybe you should just brush it to one side as there are much worse things that could have happened to you in life?"

*"Yes, **you're right**, at least I'm alive, I'm physically intact, I still have my health and I don't have anything growing inside me that could upset my normal life and end it prematurely. I'm still working. I've been afforded a title and respect, but have you heard of mental cruelty, have you heard of mental anxiety and depression? Have you heard of the desecration of your brain cells to such an extent that you are prone to respond with fear and anguish each time you are confronted because of your race, defined by your colour rather than your persona and not by just Angrezis, even those that look like you with an air of resentment? Do you know what it is like never to be given the benefit of the doubt? This is where I am today and will be until I go six feet under."*

Barrister – "So have you failed to accept your colour, your race and your perceived inferiority or is it just that you have a sensitive persona which society shouldn't be blamed for?"

"I think society has made me what I am today – the mental battering and at times physical bruising I've experienced has created this individual before you. Culpability must rest with our environment, but it is now

time for our human community to change and thankfully, it is altering,
perhaps not everywhere in the world, but in the place I call home."
   My case rests...

I was born while my parents were living in a single room in
Kilburn, after which I spent my early childhood growing up on
a council estate, so I understand what it means to be white and
working class as my childhood was spent in this social circle. I
also understand what it's like to be educated, middle or upper
middle class in 'multi-cultural' Britain as this is where I found
myself working and still do to this day. These past experiences
of mixing across the social divide helped ensure that I can relate
to any individual patient that comes to my clinic in more ways
than one. Understanding and empathy are traits I hold dear as
they are powerful weapons that can be used to quash any ignorant
hostility one may face due to visible differences.

Do I lament my entire past? Certainly not, as I do have many
happy memories whilst growing up. But am I disappointed by
what has happened to me on too many occasions now, through
no fault of my own? Yes indeed – you can hopefully see why I do
feel pain when I see such treatment and foul play still happening
today in the world, with the effect more profound especially when
it happens just around the corner, at work, whilst travelling or
directly to myself? You will understandably also now realise why
I will always stand up for the weak and disadvantaged, encourage
all and promote those that are worthy, irrespective of where they
are from ethnically or in the social ladder. So if you are white,
Anglo-Saxon, *Angrezi* who went to public school, are good at what
you do – then you deserve success just as much as the next person
in an equal manner. To this end with my life experience across
the classes and racial groups, I have maintained my loyalty to my
country. The irony is that, despite the racial taunts I have been
subjected to all my life, I do defend my country's overall record
on race relations in the modern era. After all I have travelled the
world and witnessed both subtle as well as overt differences on the
way you are treated due to the content of the melanin in your skin.

For years I have only thought about what has already happened
in my life, the ceaseless speculation of what if...what if I said
something, what if I had chosen to strike back and what if my
mother and father were not immigrants. But choosing not to say

what I thought was the correct decision at the time, I dealt with all the dilemmas and human chaos around me with silence. This book has finally broken my silence, which until now has been my true friend, with my pen now becoming rightfully my 'voice', but not to yield pain or revenge, instead to appease my anger and frustration at being labelled and treated differently.

Remember, I have already suggested and refuted the answer of an inherited predisposition to hatred based on race, so the denouement of my fate merely rested with a speculation of what is bad or good, what is *haram* or *halal*, what is inferior over superior – my colour and lineage. So once we think in terms of nature versus nurture, all I can conclude is that nature made me look the way I do, but nurture has made me what I am today – a persona non grata, with a daily memory as well as reminder of my supposed weakness. I trust you have found that there is a fundamentally flawed existence with my own persona, a dual existence, with a cause and effect and no end in sight. Disappointingly, to date only a small number of *Angrezis* has actually understood this fact.

For me to think that the world or importantly my 'troubles' will change before I leave this earth would be counter-intuitive. Life and our thinking about what is right and wrong no doubt will continue to evolve. Look at one example, that of women voting. That there was even a notion that this was not possible is hard to believe in this day and age.

I have spent much of this book being critical of persons in the way that I've been treated in life through no fault of my own. I do not intend to paint a rosy picture of myself. I may be self-deprecating with a modest assessment of my own abilities; I, like most humans, will sometimes incorrectly label someone, with an overriding guilt of distress and shame if I do. I remain, though, mindful every morning or night with a bag packed full of overnight needs, that when I need to travel somewhere, I endure persistent thoughts, until I arrive safely at my destination, of whether I'm going to be treated with indifference or not, or with an intransigent marking, stereotyping or being protocolled. So only time will tell if people read this book and wonder how this could have happened. But it did indeed happen and may still happen in whatever time you find yourself in.

All I can say again is that nature made me look the way I do, but nurture has made me what I am today.

From the painted boy, I became the painted medical student and, for now.

'The Painted Surgeon'

If you ask me, "Where from you," I simply say, "London."

Epilogue

Old Delhi, British India 1932

My grandfather and father used to walk everywhere together, which was not uncommon at this time, as there was some public transport but generally no one in my family had their own car. My father was more than a trifle insistent as a child, he informed me of this annoying trait of his youth, a time that I remain mostly unfamiliar with, and so he used to make uncalled for as well as unexpected demands when my grandfather was least expecting it.

"Can I have some sweets from here?"

My grandfather knew that the area he was in was not 'their' neighbourhood.

"Why not wait until we are near our home?" my grandfather replied.

"No, I want some now, look that shop there has some!" My father described this moment as an example of his *ziddi* (fussy) nature.

"OK, let's try this shop then," and with a semi-reluctant gait he would walk over, eager not to disappoint his son. As he walked to the front door, the shopkeeper hollered out to him, "Stop right there, we do not need the likes of you infesting my shop, whatever you need, send your son."

My grandfather was upset, quite angry and I believe in Urdu we would say his blood was boiling. Realising that he had let his guard down by venturing into a Hindu neighbourhood shop, he nevertheless tolerated the situation he found himself in and duly sent my father to procure what they came for.

My grandfather wore standard Indian attire, but his style of *topi*, as well as an obvious beard, identified the religion that he followed as Islam.

My father told me this story a few years before he died, when I asked him why India, a country that had existed for many hundreds of years, was split into two in 1947. He remarked how there was a subtle air of religious discrimination, which you could sense but not overtly see or experience most of the time. There was a noted sectarianism especially when it came to choices of schools, shops and sometimes bazaars, between Muslims and Hindus. This did, though, stop at hospitals or your local doctor. But there was a separation nonetheless, for example inter-marriage between Hindu and Muslims was very rare indeed, the Sikhs were so few in number no one really cared what they did. But the most important facet of all of these cultural nuances to note, which were largely hidden undercover, was that it only needed a small spark to convert two groups living relatively peacefully side by side into frenzied mobs trying to kill each other. The partition of India did just that.

By telling me this story I don't think my father was trying to put me off any other religious denominations from South Asia. To be honest, I don't think he really minded whom I associated myself with. I knew he had no animosity towards Hindus as most of our social friends in London whilst I was growing up were of this religious persuasion. As mentioned, we had a colour perspective that aligned us all as one group in the 60s, 70s and probably beyond. We were reared to be very respectful of each other, and my brothers and I since childhood had to hold our hands together saying *namaste* or *sat shri akaal* when we walked into our Hindu or Sikh friends' households respectively. This may well be regarded as a political linking that gave us a black British identity.

This conversation dated from when I was reading much at the time about Indian history and I came across the partition of India and the formation of Pakistan. My father explained this one story about when he was a child and politely explained there was a quiet, albeit hidden, lingering air of animosity which was palpable in the atmosphere. This would have continued for many years unless there was some give. How accurate this story was is not entirely clear in my mind, as I was not there. I imagine that a Hindu would give a similar description the other way around, which would be reasonable. Tolerance was debated, but when a civilisation for thousands of years is based on a system of categorisation, with no mingling and defined barriers to integration, and educational rights are afforded to some groups rather than others. This air of volatility was capitalised on, and partition was the eventual give. It did indeed receive a very determined push, kindly provided by the British rulers at the time.

When 1947 came, my grandfather decided to remain in Delhi for a while as he had a small shop fixing watches, and was a religious teacher during the night. This shop of his was eventually burnt to the ground. My father who was almost twenty made the journey by train to Karachi. Karachi was the new capital of Pakistan, and this was the first step in a further chain of immigration to follow for my family. He did though witness first-hand the raising of the Indian flag on August 15th, 1947, along with his friends. He described this day as momentous, with almost an armistice and no killing of migrants who were still deciding which of the newly formed independent countries they were to live in.

My father said it took time for their adopted country to settle down. They were classed as refugees. They were given simple, meagre accommodation, and of course high schools and universities were all closed. Eventually once a system started to gather momentum and universities opened, my father's quest of becoming a doctor slowly vanished, through costs mainly. Although to be honest, this idea was shunned by a few of the local *Maulvis* as they reliably informed my grandfather that all Yahya would be doing if he became a doctor would be smelling other people's urine. Such fallacies about Western education were rife throughout the Muslim community, spread possibly by an ultra-conservative right. As my father was good at Urdu and English, he sought to change his subjects and eventually qualified as a barrister in 1958 with a BA degree followed by an LLB. Truthfully, he probably lost about five years of his education through British India's decision to split.

Immigration has its effects on people as I noted from reading the translation of a family tree fortuitously in our possession, which dates back to about 1750. Our family is generally North Indian Punjabi from the cities of Lahore, Jaipur and Delhi. Now all of a sudden, we set roots in Karachi. This is a city in the Sindh province and, although we're not ethnically Sindhi, without warning we had to adjust to a new life in a strange city in a newly formed country, one that we never thought we'd actually end up living in. My mum's family ended up in Rawalpindi mainly because her father was an Air Force officer, and this is where the armed forces were based in Pakistan. It wasn't too much of a disruption for them because ethnically being Punjabi and ending up in the Punjab itself was a lot more of a straightforward transition. It will be important to recognise that many Hindus and Sikhs that lived in the northern areas of the newfound Pakistan, such as Lahore and other parts of the Punjab had also to uproot, ending up in Amritsar, Jalandhar, and Delhi through no fault of their own and would have faced a similar upheaval. Chaos!

I think back to this time with my father; having already experienced the partition of India and being an immigrant, this transition of his continued, but to a much more foreign land. It was colder, a new language, a completely alien culture. However, you may think it was altogether foreign until you look at a railway station in India and then look at one in England, for they are identical in architecture. In the legal system there were no major differences that my father could readily see or notice and working in the civil service was generally quite straightforward. He tried his best to become a fully-fledged lawyer but there was too much resistance from the legal hierarchy for someone like him to earn the rights of audience in an English court, so this quest was abandoned. I'm sure it could have happened but at the time it didn't for my father. As I've already explained he was happy with his decision. Maybe the fact that he'd immigrated once before gave him some know-how or strength to undertake the large journey, brave it out, spot cul-de-sacs, not consider any potential failures as such and bring up three boys in a foreign land. A land that actually wasn't adopted for his children, but they were made to feel it was foreign as they grew up in it. It must have dawned on him and his wife that their children were not entirely happy. But the thought of going back never crossed his mind. I think he thought that time would help and heal the indifference felt. He hoped that his children would one day see why he had made this decision. In addition, he may have hoped that somehow society would allow them to adjust and be considered equal in the eyes of the law. I think he was correct.

Up until the death of my grandfather in 1977, I remember that my father received an aerogramme from him at least once a month. It was quite nice just to see the Urdu writing, although it was incomprehensible to my brothers and me. Sadly this script will remain, unfortunately just pretty writing to us even to this day.

The effects of uprooting and moving has been a theme for my family for generations, mainly as a result of work. In 1947 it was in the subcontinent where they came across to a land occupied by their own indigenous population. There were no differences in their hue or the way they looked, language and customs were non-conflicting, with any religious differences noted with a muted patronage or mild discrepancy. The partition of India caused millions of Muslim refugees from what was becoming India to arrive in Pakistan, with my forbears being included in this group. The sudden transition was not met with immediate huge hostility, and it was not until many years later that rival factions were created with the migratory community and the local populous especially in Karachi. Political factions were forged with some violence, all in all defying the very reason for the creation of a country. So again, there was unnecessary carnage as a consequence of a lack of tolerance. So any form of immigration has its potential failures, or would one consider them as complications?

The next phase of immigration for my family crossed continents. Here one subtle disadvantage my father suffered is that he and his fellow South Asian immigrants to Britain did not look the same as the indigenous population in the UK. Their differences in language, religion and culture were so marked, almost alien, that it created fear, possibly amongst the indigenous *Angrezi* population. I can only imagine that this is the reason why my brothers and I faced such hostility all our childhood lives and now beyond. The memories of the contemptible behaviour we experienced will remain with us, it is difficult to wipe them away so all I can do is carry on and do the best I can in what I consider to be my country and my society. But time is the best healer; my children haven't suffered what I did. They have an advantage in that their parents speak like the indigenous population, they were educated in the same manner and understand the cultural norms and practices of the Western world. In summary, I must ask myself when a time will come when I am not treated like a foreigner in my own country? I think that time is near, you can see from examples that we have in politics with our Chancellor of Exchequer and Home Secretary to name a few people in high office of South Asian descent. It shows much progress has been made. However, the top job seems out of reach for now.

I recall at this point a dinner at a surgical meeting. I was sitting opposite a retired surgeon along with his wife. She was a very pleasant lady and somehow the trajectory of our conversation ended up by me saying,

"One day I can imagine seeing a Black or Asian Prime Minister of our country."

This comment fell on deaf ears. Either she failed to acknowledge it, or she chose to ignore it, but there was absolutely no reply. She really did look as if I had said something so obscene it was positively rude, uncalled-for, and perhaps should be reported as a misdemeanour to the society. One will undoubtedly meet people with this attitude throughout one's life. Wherever you are in the world. I wouldn't call them right-wing; I would just say they are insular and not worldly, incapable of comprehending anything that disturbs their world view. This is where I think the Internet is a great asset in many ways as it has made us reach out to people halfway across the world, but it also is fraught with many caveats and dangers.

Positions of influence should be awarded on merit and not as tokens. In America, 'Affirmative Action' tried to address a balance where there was a shortage of Latinos and African Americans gaining places in higher education, particularly medical and law schools. I think everyone deserves a chance in life. However, if you have been brought up in a poor part of your country, you are less likely to have experienced certain educational advantages, so having a policy where such persons need slightly lesser grades to gain a place at a good university, probably, is a progressive idea. This will help break the cycle of social hardship equalling a poverty-stricken education.

In the United Kingdom, from my subjective observations, I think we need to see more examples especially in the judiciary, barristers' chambers and the publishing world where there is a lack of representation of non-white persons. I'm not sure why this has happened, but perhaps there is covert discrimination in these fields. I think there are plenty of talented writers, lawyers from the Black and Asian (BAME) communities and I'm sure it's only a matter of time before we notice differences especially in the higher courts. However, what better than to look at examples in a country considered to be still developing? Where my parents came from in Pakistan, I have some first-hand knowledge of the Supreme Court as two of my father's friends were appointed there. In the Supreme Court archives, you will find the appointment of a Parsi, Christian and a Hindu to the highest bench of a country which is largely a Muslim diaspora. A country paradoxically actually created for Muslims of India. This could be regarded as a testament to their understanding of tolerance, equality and diversity. It is a well-regarded principle that when you seek to change opinions, it is best done from the top downwards. When you hear of examples like this you realise that there are both good examples as well as evidence of pitfalls of human relationships throughout the world, where perceived differences are hopefully becoming vanquished to the confines of history.

After reading this book, I can honestly tell you I've never actually asked for anything in life. I've never sought special treatment. I've never asked for privileges. Everything I have achieved, I have fought for, I have done so with hard work and effort. But I am not the only example in the world or my country of such efforts. I managed to become a doctor against the odds and now am fulfilling further dreams with some gentle acceleration towards hopefully more than just being a competent surgeon. I am now, in 2021, the President of the British Hernia Society, the first person of colour to head this organisation. It is a great privilege and I have asked people to not only mention this fact, but also that it is something that should be celebrated as an example of tolerance and equality as well as what can be achieved. I do wonder what life would have been like if I were an *Angrezi*. I do not begrudge the fact that my parents were immigrants, moreover this fact is giving me another dimension or community to relate to. However, it has left me open to strangers judging me by my physical appearance rather than the reality of who I am. I'm very proud of my country, of what Great Britain stands for, what it is achieving in the world, although the latest episode of Brexit has caused me much more anxiety than I would have liked, as I'm sure this feeling did and still does resonate with at least half the country. Being a citizen of the UK as well as the EU, albeit temporarily, remains an honour.

My last words will further reiterate to you in fact that I don't think that I will be completely relaxed when approaching an immigration desk at home or abroad. I will be categorised whichever way the immigration officer wishes to do so. Most of the times it will be just welcoming me home to the UK or as a British visitor abroad to a friendly nation. But unfortunately, despite my glass-half-full attitude in life, it may be something completely alien to both me and my passport?

Acknowledgements

I could not have written this book without the support from my family especially as I spent time away from them by sitting in front of my laptop. I have many people to thank and obviously I've dedicated this to my wife, but I must also thank my three children for just being there when I need them the most, just seeing them every day, healthy and happy is more than any parent can ask for.

In terms of helping me with this book I'd like to thank Alex Phillips from GB News for her initial editorial review. This was not only excellent but weeded out all unwanted as well as waffly material and for this I am very grateful. Of course, the book's final script was prepared by Dr Jackie Moore from somewhere in Cheshire, whom I am also very grateful to. She undertook a final polish with editing and re-structuring of the book. Moreover, she provided great encouragement and was especially keen to see this book published particularly with the story it tells. Also a special thanks to Anirudha Dhanawade for his help with proof-reading.

I would also like to thank 'The Literary Consultancy' https:// literaryconsultancy.co.uk/ for their initial read and advice. It was at a time when a much-needed appraisal was required with a complete overhaul and help in the structure of the chapters of the book. Special mention goes to Karl French and Nelima Begum.

From my work perspective I would like to thank my dear colleagues Mr Saurabh Jamdar and Mr Christian Macutkiewicz for their more than just optimistic support in this project, in addition to a genuine excitement. They are both not only very close personal friends of mine and expert surgeons in their own right, but I had the pleasure of training them both for a while during their earlier careers. This was easy as they both were so dedicated to learning the art of surgery.

I also would like to thank one literary agent in particular, Mr Greg Morton from WGM Atlantic who has now moved into the music world, but he deserves a special mention as he provided me with credit for pursuing this literary piece of work as well as the encouragement to continue despite numerous setbacks.

Publishing the book, I did so very carefully as it took me over two years. I did search for a literary agent but unfortunately, I couldn't find anyone that really understood what I was trying to say. Importantly, there are apparently scarce literary agents from my own ethnicity. I could not stimulate any positive vision in the few I found.

Those agents that took the time to reply to me I'd like to thank you very much.

The book cover was designed by Ken Powell from Blackbox Ecom https://www.blackboxecom.com/about.

It is not easy to write a book but if you sit down and give it time what you 'create' is your *own* creation. I am of this firm belief.

What I have written is my own creation from its inception to conclusion, and that is it in a nutshell. So, if you ask me whatever you decide to write, if you're writing for others to read, then make it a topic of interest, the more controversial the better and each person reading it must be able to turn a page.

Finally, I must thank all my patients, past, present and future. I will continue to do my utmost and treat them to the best of my abilities. On reflection, I've chosen the correct career for myself and if you eliminate all the professional envy and politics that unfortunately rears its head more than one would care to choose, especially if you are successful, medicine does remain a thoroughly enjoyable career to be in. One thing I can say is that I will always try my best for every single patient whose care I am involved in, and I'll be the first to admit that unfortunately not every single patient will be happy with one's efforts, but please feel rest assured I have and will always try my best for you.

References for some points of history and interest:
1. Barber-Surgeons and their history. Loudon I. Why are (male) surgeons still addressed as Mr? *BMJ*. 2000;321(7276):1589-1591. doi:10.1136/bmj.321.7276.1589
2. Life of George Floyd https://en.wikipedia.org/wiki/George_Floyd

3. Life of Emmett Till. https://en.wikipedia.org/wiki/Emmett_Till
4. Race Relations Act 1965. https://www.parliament.uk/about/living-heritage/transformingsociety/private-lives/relationships/collections1/race-relations-act-1965/race-relations-act-1965/
5. Equality Act 2010. https://www.gov.uk/guidance/equality-act-2010-guidance
6. https://www.gmc-uk.org/news/news-archive/gmc-targets-elimination-of-disproportionate-complaints-and-training-inequalities
7. Stone L, Gordon J. A is for aphorism – 'Wherever the art of medicine is loved there is also a love of humanity'. *Aust Fam Physician*. 2013 Nov;42(11):824-5. PMID: 24217108.

Summary of events

August 1970 – *Born in London to immigrant parents*

1993 – *Qualified as a Doctor*
1998 – *Qualified as a Surgeon*
June 2002 – *Decorated by a US institution for cancer research*
Dec 2005 – *Appointed a Consultant in NHS*
March 2008 – *Taken in for questioning at Dallas Fort Worth Airport whilst on a family holiday*
March 2011 – *Taken in for questioning at Atlanta airport*
June 2016 – *Accosted at Amsterdam Airport*
Nov 2016 – *Appointed Professor by Manchester Metropolitan University*
June 2017 – *Scanner quizzed at Vienna Airport*
25th May 2020 – *Death of George Floyd in Minneapolis[2]*
June 2021 – *Awarded Honorary Clinical Chair in Surgery, by University of Manchester*
The future – *When will I be treated as a Human Being first when travelling? – I have some hope and will keep the faith, will you join me…*